On the Art of Singing

On the Art of Singing

RICHARD MILLER

New York   Oxford
OXFORD UNIVERSITY PRESS
1996

Oxford University Press

Oxford   New York
Athens   Auckland   Bangkok   Bombay
Calcutta   Cape Town   Dar es Salaam   Delhi
Florence   Hong Kong   Istanbul   Karachi
Kuala Lumpur   Madras   Madrid   Melbourne
Mexico City   Nairobi   Paris   Singapore
Taipei   Tokyo   Toronto

and associated companies in
Berlin   Ibadan

Copyright © 1996 by Oxford University Press, Inc.

Published by Oxford University Press, Inc.,
198 Madison Avenue, New York, New York 10016

Oxford is a registered trademark of Oxford University Press

Library of Congress Cataloging-in-Publication Data
Miller, Richard, 1926–
On the art of singing / Richard Miller.
p.   cm.
Previously published essays, in part revised.
Includes index.
ISBN 0-19-509825-0
1. Singing—Instruction and study.   2. Singing—Interpretation
(Phrasing, dynamics, etc.)   3. Singing—Vocational guidance.
4. Voice.   I. Title.
MT820.M599   1996   95-30176
783—dc20

7 9 8 6

Printed in the United States of America
on acid-free paper

To the Memory of Luigi Ricci

Acknowledgments

For permission to reprint previously published material, much of which has been revised, thanks are expressed to:

The NATS Journal, for permission to reprint the following essays: 1, 3, 4, 6, 7, 8, 9, 10, 11, 12, 13, 15, 16, 18, 20, 21, 22, 23, 24, 25, 26, 27, 30, 31, 33, 34, 39, 40, 41, 44, 45, 46, 49, 51, 52, 53, 54, 55, 56, 57, 59, 60, 61, 63, 64, 66, 68, 69, 71, 72, 73, 74, 76, 77, 78, 80, 81, 82, 83, 84, 85, 86, 87, 88, 89, 90, 92, 93. Used by permission;

American Music Teacher, for permission to reprint essay 47, "The Sense of Immediacy in Singing," originally published in the January 1968 issue of *American Music Teacher.* © 1968 by Music Teachers National Association. Used by permission;

Choral Journal, for permission to reprint essay 19, "The Solo Singer in the Choral Ensemble," originally published in *Choral Journal* 35 (March 1995). ©1995 by the American Choral Directors Association, P.O. Box 6310, Lawton, Oklahoma, 73506–0310. Used by permission;

Journal of Research in Singing, for permission to reprint essay 91, "Vowel Definition in a Performance of Jussi Bjoerling's *Vesti la giubba*";

Raven Press, for permission to reprint essay 70, "The Singing Teacher in the Age of Voice Science," originally published in *Professional Voice: The Science and the Art of Clinical Care,* ed. Robert Sataloff. © 1991;

and to Robert Sataloff, *Journal of Voice* and *Transcripts of the 14th Symposium on Care of the Professional Voice.*

Contents

Part IV   On the Singing Voice and Vocal Function

Introduction

Of all the performance arts, the art of singing is the most complex. Its preparation and its practices are fraught with controversy. Tonal ideals vary. Techniques for producing those ideals abound. A survey of viewpoints found within the vocal pedagogy literature bewilders.

Much of this diversity stems from attempts to unite individual experience, cultural demands, and varying aesthetic goals with the commonality of the instrumental functions of the voice. The wide range of empirical experience described in the literature of comparative vocal pedagogy can be likened to the blind men's diverse perceptions of the anatomy not of a single stationary elephant, but rather of a herd of stampeding pachyderms. A number of these diversities are critically examined in the essays (some new and some old) on vocal technique found in this collection.

However, establishing a proper technical approach to singing is by no means the only concern for the professional singer or for the singer's teacher. Musicianship, style and interpretation, career preparation and development, efficient vocal function, and the conservation of vocal health are all parts of vocal pedagogy. Information on these topics, written by experts, is scattered throughout a wide range of interdisciplinary writing. Much of that literature presupposes familiarity with terminology not readily accessible to every singer. Singers and their teachers do not always have opportunity to explore these literatures and to join the disparate parts of valuable professional information into a total pedagogical picture.

I have attempted to assemble certain portions of data that have been highly beneficial in my own performing and teaching. My aim in this collection of mostly brief essays has been to make such information accessible to other performers and teachers, sometimes through analytical language, occasionally in exhortative mode, and at other times through curmudgeonly anecdote and parable. Several crucial topics are treated more than once from varying perspectives. Only information that I believe influences the art of performance directly has been included.

These observations have been assembled in such a manner that the reader may select topics that seem of most interest. I hope that the courageous will give all of them consideration. Readers should be forewarned, however, that the author has his own set of biases that he seldom attempts to mask, because he deeply believes in them. A certain missionary zeal for the ideas expressed may be detected. Indeed, conversions are welcomed!

A well-trained sailor boy can both tie complex knots and discern whether someone else is tying them correctly or incorrectly, deftly or clumsily. But he is probably incapable of the difficult task of describing in words how the knots should be tied.

GILBERT RYLE
The Concept of the Mind

I

On Training the Singing Voice

1

Imagery and the Teaching of Singing

Singing is largely a subjective action. It results from a *gestalt* that summons up previous experiences of physical coordination, proprioceptive sensation, and vocal sound. Fine singers seldom analyze the things they do in performance. Instead, they depend on recall as to how they have done it well before. They recognize only a pervasive attitude toward performance in which the imagination is freed for artistic expression by motor actions that are consistently repeatable. This constitutes the psychological and physical control of performance.

There is no reason for the successful performer to describe personal processes to others so long as performance remains his or her only field of activity. When, however, the performer turns to giving instruction, communicative, objective language must be developed. In the rare instance in which two personalities, teacher and student, share almost identical experiences and morphology, there may be less problem with the language of imagery. Even then, the student seldom has the kind of unproblematic coordination that may have served the teacher. Many fine performers have never had the kinds of technical problems encountered by the average voice student. That is why a highly successful singer who also teaches may have success with one singer or with a particular category of voice, but not with others. A good teacher must be able to objectify the components of performance and convey them to the student, regardless of the student's vocal category. The teacher who has had to find solutions for his or her own basic technical problems may prove the most useful to students. Valuable preparation for the successful teaching of singing is to have solved one's own personal vocal problems, to have reached a good level of technical and musical proficiency, and to have benefited from the inestimable experiences of a successful public career. (Listening to those of us who teach describe personal sensations and performance attitudes may spark imaginative thinking, but that is not enough. Most singers are in need of precise technical information that goes beyond the language of imagery.)

There is a role for some imagery in the teaching of technique. Technical imagery, however, is mostly of value if it is associated with *already* established, repeatable functional freedom. *After* the singer has learned to coordinate breath management and proper laryngeal and resonatory responses, an *image* may be useful in unifying those functions. The superimposition of imagery on the student beforehand may bring more confusion than assistance.

To be told by one great tenor that during a performance he felt he was winding a golden ribbon around a small wheel two feet in front of his face, and by another famous tenor that he often felt he was singing through an imaginary third eye in the middle of the forehead is of limited value to the young tenor student. Both the world-renowned tenors had long since established the coordinated activities they individually had come to associate with those private images. Just as a word symbol requires common understanding, so technical imaging must be based on the prior experience of more than one individual if it is to convey meaning. It is difficult to describe the taste of an olive to someone who has never eaten an olive, but having once tasted one we can readily recall the flavor.

For these reasons, imagery should not be part of the first steps in teaching the technical coordination of the singing instrument. Singing, with its initially complex elements of vocal timbres, text, and the whole ambiance of performance, is highly personal. The singer will very quickly develop personal, functional imagery. Attempting to superimpose one's own physical imaging on another person is generally less than successful. When teacher and singer later agree as to what the imaginative language may mean as it pertains to established function, there is *then* a role for imagery, even in the technical aspects of the teaching of singing. Unfortunately, much studio *technical* imagery remains a mystical language, one the student is unable to penetrate.

Some aspects of the singing voice respond to conscious control and others do not. The coordination that produces skillful, free singing depends on a psychological attitude—the *gestalt* earlier mentioned—that includes both directly controllable and non-controllable actions. Giovanni Battista Lamperti, as reported by Earl Brown, his studio associate, said, "Thought and muscle are schooled until instinct and reaction develop and take command. Then what was arbitrary becomes automatic." As the training of thought and muscle takes place, the student's own imagination will provide the necessary imaging of what will eventually be automatic responses of singing.

It should be remarked that many outstanding professional singers never use detailed physiologic or technical imagery. For them, imagery occurs *only at the interpretative level*. They maintain a dual channel of psychological and physical orientation in which the technical foundation that has already been established permits imaginative textual and musical projection. Imaging in singing should ideally be directed to the artistic realization of text, drama, and musical content, not to the control of physical aspects of vocal technique. Then the singer is free of the kinds of technical imagery that so dominate many voice studios and that continue to plague many singers during performance. Exempt from technical imagery, the singer is free to use imaging for the depiction of text and drama.

Teacher-imposed technical imaging often unintentionally produces complications that interfere with good vocalism. W. T. Bartholomew, in a paper of considerable historical importance entitled "The Role of Imagery in Voice Teaching" and delivered to the Music Teachers National Association in 1935, expressed the viewpoint admirably:

> when imagery becomes so vivid that it is transferred into the physical field and used to explain physiologic and acoustic phenomena, it becomes extremely dubious, unreliable and even false. It is this misuse which is largely responsible for the bitter controversies over vocal methods, as well as for their often comical expressions.

Bartholomew would be pleased to know that in the past several decades vocal pedagogy has moved away from circling birds, drifting clouds, chimneys on top of heads, purple tones, vocal waterfalls, and gold threads spinning from pyramids that extend from the chin to the frontal sinuses. He would also appreciate that the pseudo-scientific notions about recovering primitive vocal sounds from a pre-existent vocal Atlantis are largely disregarded in contemporary vocal pedagogy. There is an increasing realization that the voice as an instrument can best be trained through exact communicative language. For this we can thank the dissemination of factual information from interdisciplinary sources.

In summary, artistry can be only as complete as coordinated function permits. Free function permits *artistic imaging,* which is not to be confused with performance enslavement to physical imagery. Especially in the early phases of voice teaching, technical imaging should be used with caution. Physical imagery should never be based on misinformation as to how the body works.

2

Five Principles for the Successful Teaching of Singing

Two decades ago, at a meeting of administrators of some of America's leading conservatories and schools of music, all of them offering advanced degree programs, it was felt that the most difficult and precarious position to fill in applied music is that of Voice Professor. Contributing factors were many, but they had mostly to do with the pedagogical mythologies with which many instructors surrounded the singing voice; it was agreed that many singing teachers did not make use of the kinds of observable external maneuvers used by teachers of other instruments. However, in more recent decades vocal teaching has moved in the direction of a more precise pedagogical language. Are there some principles that assist the knowledgeable teacher in ensuring success in teaching the art of singing? Five counsels are suggested here.

1. Teacher and Student Rapport

Any singer who has been admitted to a program of study at a reputable institution of music, or for study with a private teacher who maintains high professional standards, exhibits some degree of potential and at least minimal singing skills, or he or she would not be there. No matter how problematic the voice, some areas of it will clearly be better than others. It is the job of the teacher to identify which sounds are most favorable and to improve those that are not. Frustration over slow results sometimes tempts us to treat students as though they were incapable of discerning the differences between the sounds for which we are searching and the sounds they are now producing. We must also guard against making the student feel inadequate to comprehend what we are saying. Many times it is not the student who is at fault, but we ourselves. How best to proceed?

Identification of even one sound that is better than the others offers the teacher a point of departure not only for bringing about fruitful instruction but also for demonstrating to the student that teacher and student are on the same, positive side of problem solving. Once a student is assured that the teacher is convinced that there is *something* of merit in what he or she does, there is encouragement to try harder to bring other sounds into accord with the more acceptable sound. When the student has been granted an indication of respect for part of what he or she can accomplish, that student is willing to accept almost any degree of specific criticism. The important point is to start with some positive assessment, no matter how disturbing the student's limitations may be. Thereby a comradeship, a teamship, is born.

Establishment of professional rapport is essential to any climate of learning. The problem with the "charismatic" instructor is that he or she may unwittingly come across to the student as the fountainhead of wisdom, the inhabitant of a distant vocal Parnassus. Today's student is far less impressed with the performance credentials of teachers. The sharing of information, not masterful dominance—encouragement, not intimidation—produces the rapport between teacher and student that makes learning possible.

2. Diagnosis and Prescription

After the establishment of trust, which involves the student's realization that corrective suggestion does not mean that everything is wrong, the teacher can begin to pursue the process of *diagnosis and prescription* that forms the basis of all analytical teaching. It is at this point that modern vocal pedagogy either stands or falls. It is not possible to diagnose what is problematic in a vocal technique without an understanding of what is inhibiting function. Any time a teacher of singing suggests to a student that there is a better way of doing things than the student currently uses, the request for change must be justified. Personal preference of one sound over another is not an adequate reason for requesting change. "This is the sound my ear prefers," or "This is the way my teacher taught me," or "This is the way my student who won the Met does it," are equally inappropriate reasons. Diagnosis and prescription, the two chief requirements in teaching the *technique* of singing, can be made only by weighing both of them against what is knowable about the physiologic and acoustic functions of the singing voice. Anything that concerns technique should not take place in the realm of nonsupportable wizardry. Both diagnosis and prescription should be understandable and nonthreatening, and both must be described in clear, functional language if they are to be exactly communicated.

3. Specificity of Language

Language describing breath management, laryngeal function, and resonator response should not be inventions of the moment. These are functions common to all who breathe and phonate, and can be *described through precise language*. Such expressions as "Sing on the breath," "Spin the tone," "Support the voice with the breath," "Sing from the diaphragm," and so forth, are imprecise and often contrary to actual physiology.

The diaphragm is below the level of proprioceptive responses, for example, and can be neither felt nor locally controlled. The process of phonation, being aerodynamic and myoelastic, turns air into tone, and it should not be implied that airflow for singing is induced independently of vocal-fold responses to it.

Similarly, resonance sensations in singing are not the result of the imaginative assumptions frequently offered. In an attempt to convey one's own sensations, the teacher must take care not to confuse the *source* of sound with the *sensation* of sound. "Placing" either air or sound in physical locations where they cannot go accounts for many of the tensions experienced by singers. Only through a clear exposition regarding the resonator tract's filtering responses to laryngeal sound can the teacher avoid giving false information that may lead to malfunction.

Laryngeal function itself is frequently misunderstood. Attempts to "open the throat" may maladjust the position of the larynx and do little to improve pharyngeal space. The response of the larynx to complete inhalation, and the resonator capabilities of the larynx itself, should be understood by the teacher of singing. This information is accessible to all, and must be clearly conveyed to the student. Managing one's own instrument and describing how it feels to oneself is not sufficient for the instruction of others.

4. Efficient Use of Time

The amount of time available to student and teacher is limited. Part of the value of linguistic precision in teaching lies in the efficiency of communicating the specifics of vocal technique within the allotted time. It frequently takes many attempts to convey an idea regarding function when it is presented in the language of myth or poetic invention. Such language may never convey the actual information the teacher wishes to impart, and much time is wasted. Far better husbanding of time occurs when technical language is brought into the world of physical reality. The imagination should be applied to artistic communication, not to physiology. After good function has been established, the singer then relies on feeling, sensing, and seeing the differences between freedom and tension. At that point the singer will find his or her *own* images that make those kinesthetic experiences repeatable. Success in trying to reach these coordinations through the superimposition of personal imaging on the psyche of another is generally limited, and the effort may be counterproductive.

5. Measurable Results

Many technical skills require time to assimilate. The road to a solid vocal technique is not a short one. Today's student is often in a hurry and expects fast results. Notwithstanding, every lesson should aim at the achievement of some tangible improvement. A student should not wander about in a land of the unknown, lesson after lesson, attempting to interpret directions shrouded in evasive language and mysterious aphorisms. Specific tasks involved in vocal technique can be mastered through specific maneuvers. Every lesson a student attends should include the accomplishment of some positive and recognizable goal. Gone are the days when it was the student's duty to penetrate the arcane language and experiences of the teacher.

The mystery of the performance art remains: How does the artistic imagination make use of technical skill to communicate beautiful sound and emotion? The sciences of acoustics and physiology have long been applied to vocal pedagogy; there are far fewer functional mysteries today than there were even a few decades ago. Spectrum analysis and fiberoptic/stroboscopic studies of the singing instrument are currently possible. However, no one can teach another person, through mechanistic means, how the mind assembles technical and musical concepts and brings them into practical realization. Nor does one become an artist simply by achieving good function. The psychological enigma will always remain. Still, it cannot be too strongly reiterated that artistry cannot be communicated if the vocal instrument remains hampered by nonfunctional behavior. A singer can have the most astounding musical sensitivity, native vocal endowment, and poetic and dramatic understanding, but no one will know that if the instrument does not function well. It is the teacher's task to develop a pedagogy that speaks to the student's needs.

The successful teacher of singing will go beyond attempting to pass on to his or her students empirical performance sensations and experiences. She or he will find modes of instruction that develop rapport, that permit the diagnosis of problems, and that supply prescriptions for corrections through specific and communicable language, thereby saving time and producing measurable results. These five principles should form the structure of every lesson.

3

Covering in the Singing Voice

"Cover" is a term common to most vocal pedagogies. Viewpoints as to what "covering" may be, at what point in the scale it should take place, how it differs from one vocal category to another, and even whether it is necessary at all, divide vocal pedagogy into several opposing camps.

Consideration first should be given to what "covering" may mean in the several languages and pedagogical traditions in which the term appears. Further, how do various methods of "covering" relate to actual physical and acoustic events? It is misleading to translate foreign language expressions simply as "cover," as though they all represented the same phenomenon.

For that reason, if one is referring to the most frequently practiced technique of the *copertura* of the Italian school, it may be preferable to use the expression "vowel modification" in English, or to retain the Italian term, because to equate *copertura* with the Germanic technique of *Deckung,* or the French system of *couverture,* is to confuse quite different pedagogical procedures for vowel migration in the mounting scale. The term "cover" is no more specific than is the term "support." Both expressions are part of imprecise pedagogical vocabulary. In addition, the very word *cover* when used with English-speaking singers calls up a variety of subjective connotations that result in very different maneuvers.

In international pedagogy stemming from the historic Italian school, well-balanced resonance throughout the range of the singing voice is described as having *chiaroscuro* (light/dark) timbre, because a balanced relationship is maintained among harmonic partials in all parts of the spectrum regardless of the vowel or the pitch being sung. The singing voice in this internationally accepted model strives for a timbre called *voce chiusa* (closed voice) in contrast to an undesirable timbre known as *voce aperta* (open voice). (*Aperta* and *chiusa* do not, of course, refer to adjustments of the throat!) In skillful singing, this resonance balancing is present from the lowest to the highest notes of the scale. Such a concept of ideal basic timbre must be understood before the technique of *copertura* can be comprehended. (The presence or absence of the historic vocal *chiaroscuro* timbre is verifiable through spectrographic analysis.)

It should be interjected that the long-existent Italian School (which may have only limited relationship to some of the teaching currently labeled Italianate, either in Italy or elsewhere) had on the art of singing an international impact that continued through the late nineteenth century into the early decades of the twentieth. As is evident from the systems of exercises that cover all aspects of singing technique, and from recorded performances and critical commentary, international vocalism tended to exhibit similar features. It could be argued that, despite buffeting from other pedagogical influences, the historic Italianate model continues to predominate to a large extent among singers of international stature. How vowel modification, or *copertura*, fits into that model will be briefly considered, and other approaches contrasted with it.

The basic timbre of *voce coperta* (covered voice) cannot be present in appropriate range without *copertura*. Sometimes designated as *aggiustamento* (although that term has several usages), *copertura* is best described as the process of conscious equalization of the ascending scale through vowel modification so as to diminish register demarcations, not to exaggerate them. It stands in direct contrast to certain techniques of "covering" in which a sudden change in timbre is the aim, as though a pot lid were placed over a pot.

Copertura serves as the agent for scale equalization in upper-middle and upper ranges of the singing voice. It maintains the timbre of *voce chiusa* as pitch mounts. Especially important is its action in the *zona di passaggio* (passage zone), an area also termed *voce media* (middle voice) that lies midway between regions of the voice traditionally designated as *voce di petto* (chest voice) and *voce di testa* (head voice). (For example, it occurs in the lyric tenor between D_4 and G_4.) *Copertura* as a graduated process in the *zona di passaggio* makes possible a scale equalization that avoids the sudden registration shifts in upper-middle voice described by such drastic terms as "flipping over," "hooking in," "slotting," "doming," "shifting gears," and so on. Additional vowel modification then also takes place in upper range *(voce di testa)*. There are no sudden, radical timbre changes at the register pivotal points, and, despite modification, the vowel itself remains recognizable, and maintains its integrity in all but the most extreme part of the upper range. At the same time, vowel modification involves unconscious laryngeal, as well as supraglottic, alterations. *Copertura* is not the avoidance of such changes; it is a process of subtle adjustments *(aggiustamento)* in response to the scale unification demanded by the trained ear. These variations are not induced through consciously controlled changes of larynx or vocal tract.

Each vowel has its own particular laryngeal configuration and its own set of distinguishing formants. Vowel formants result from harmonic partials in the spectrum that determine the characteristic quality of each vowel, making phonetic differentiation possible. Vowels are described phonetically as "front" and "back." Singers often prefer for psychological reasons to call them "high" and "low," or "bright" and "dark." This author's preference is to term them "lateral" and "rounded"; this language removes association with front and back, and up and down, locations, and more accurately describes their acoustic formation.

At any pitch level, some singers have perceptions of unfortunate resonance changes as they progress through a series of vowels. Young singers (and some not so young) complain, for example, that "[ɑ] falls back." In contrast to such a proprioceptive response, the singer's formant (spectral energy in the area of 2500 Hz to 3200 Hz in male voices) and strong acoustic energy in the upper spectrum of female voices should always be present in both lateral and rounded vowels. This can happen only if the resonators (chiefly the pharynx and the mouth) are in tune with the vibrator (the larynx). This balanced relationship among the fundamental pitch, the appropriate vowel formants, and the acoustic energy in the region of the singer's formant, produces the *chiaroscuro* timbre of the historic Italianate model. In order, then, to keep the desired acoustic equilibrium as pitch ascends, modification of the vowel must occur.

When a singer progresses series-wise from the lateral vowel [i] to the rounded vowel [u], certain changes occur in both laryngeal and supraglottal areas (the resonator system above the larynx). The resonator tube, also known as the vocal tract, assumes various shapes in response to positions of jaw, lips, tongue, velum, zygomatic region, and larynx. These are dictated largely by vowel differentiation. In ascending pitch, the supraglottic region alters. This alteration includes subconscious activity in pharyngeal wall movement, at the base of the tongue as well as in the body of the tongue, in the shape of the pyriform sinuses, and in epiglottic movement.

Epiglottic movement unconsciously occurs in response to tongue action. In general, the epiglottis is more erect in the vowel [i] than in any other, with a lowering process occurring in response to tongue movements as the vowel series progresses from [i] through [u], although in some singers the epiglottis again assumes a more elevated position with [u]. Indeed, there appears to be considerable variance of epiglottic movement in response to vowel definition from singer to singer; this phenomenon may have some significant implications for vocal technique, particularly with regard to *copertura,* but the evidence is insufficient for drawing conclusions. However, there is a certain physiologic basis for traditional pedagogical terms that mean *to cover,* because the epiglottis, through its lowering process in vowel differentiation, does play a kind of filtering role within the vocal tract.

As a vowel sequence progresses, subtle adjustments of the larynx and of the resonator tract take place. These adjustments can be moderate or extreme; they constitute the physical and acoustic substance of "covering" (vowel modification, *copertura, aggiustamento*).

In the modern international school, which is clearly a continuation of practices that existed in the historic school, moderate vowel modification is initiated at the *primo passaggio* (the D_4 of the lyric tenor, for example), near the termination of the speech range *(voce di petto),* and additional but gradual modification of the vowel takes place as the scale approaches the *secondo passaggio* (G_4 in the lyric tenor), which occurs at about the interval of a fourth above the *primo passaggio.* These events, of course, are not related to frequency (Hz) designations as determined on the keyboard, the voice being a *glissando* instrument not geared to the semi-tones of mechanically constructed musical instruments; therefore, the *passaggi* events in either male or female voices may occur slightly above or below notated pitches that are sounded on the pianoforte. This upper-middle voice area in the male (frequently located in the zone of $B^{\flat}_3-E^{\flat}_4$, or B_3-E_4 in baritone vocal categories) is the *voce media* or *zona di passaggio* earlier mentioned.

The so-called "mixed voice" (the long middle range) of the female voice of average size and weight is traditionally designated as lodging between $E^{\flat}_4$ and $F^{\sharp}_5$, with a subdivision sometimes noticeable around $C^{\sharp}_5$. (Dramatic soprano and mezzo-soprano registration pivotal points are somewhat lower, of course.) Gradual vowel modification must begin in the upper middle range ($C^{\sharp}_5$ upward to $F^{\sharp}_5$), continuing into upper range (referred to in traditional vocal pedagogy as "head" voice), but is less extensive in the female than in the male voice.

In both female and male instruments, most vowel modification in ascending pitch is in the direction of lateral to rounded vowel. For example, by opening the mouth (lowering the mandible) for ascending pitch, [i] approaches [ɪ]; [e] takes on more of the character of [ɛ], although it may also be necessary to go in the opposite direction with certain voices so that [ɛ] in those cases will actually approach [e]. In some cases, modification may need to go so far as [ɑ], or even [œ]. Decisions in these matters are largely dependent on whether the singer has been trained to use the higher registers as either an [i] singer or as an [ɑ] singer (rather than in a more complete acoustic approach).

Some rigid systems, and some influential publications of the last few decades, maintain that all vowels modify on the same pitch. Such viewpoints do not take into account the individual characteristics of voices, nor differences among instruments within even the *same* category. They also ignore differences between vocal categories. Because of variations in *Fach* (category) and size of instrument, it is false to assume that there is one point in the mounting scale at which all female singers engage in the same degree of vowel modification.

It is equally false, and perhaps even more pernicious, to identify some note in the scale where all male singers experience register events and at which they should "cover." The pedagogical insistence that all male singers modify on the same pitch ["male voices cover at E_4 or F_4"] is one of the major causes of the malfunctioning of a great number of male singing voices. Such simplistic techniques ignore the system of vocal classification that is based on the shifting register events, upon which the entire process of scale equalization depends.

In the process of modifying the vowel, it should be kept in mind that lateral vowels tend to augment high formants and that rounded vowels strengthen low formants. In ascending pitch, it is frequently necessary to avoid the convergence of a lateral vowel (with its high formants in the region of 3 kHz for the male, and 4 kHz for the female) and a high pitch. Otherwise, shrillness will result. By opening the mouth with the ascent of pitch, this natural vowel modification occurs without the necessity to introduce sudden heavy "covering," which is characterized by drastic change of laryngeal position. Though modified, the vowel retains its integrity.

Techniques of "heavy cover" generally are associated with breath management maneuvers that involve muscular antagonism in the hypogastric region of the abdominal wall; these techniques lie outside this discussion. However, the system of *copertura* in the ascending scale is based on the historic *appoggio* model (the verb *appoggiarsi*, to lean on something). During *appoggio* breath management, the inspiratory position of the abdominal wall is less quickly altered than is the case in several other "support" techniques, while axial posture remains unaltered. In the union of the *appoggio* and the *aggiustamento (copertura)* maneuvers, radical changes do not occur at register demarcation points either in the anterolateral abdominal wall or in sternal positioning, nor in the resonator tract, as is the case in some other systems. As a result, the larynx remains in a stable position throughout the *copertura* process, maintaining its relatively low, poised position regardless of register events. Thus the three major parts of the vocal instrument—motor, vibrator, and resonator—are in functional agreement.

At first blush, it might appear that pedagogical expressions that abound in other schools parallel the terminologies and techniques of the historic international model. That this is not the case is clearly to be seen in the following typical procedures.

In the traditional Germanic school, as well as in its Nordic and Middle European derivatives, *Deckung* (cover) demands sudden mechanical registration actions involving laryngeal postural changes, marked pharyngeal spreading, heavy epiglottic lowering, jaw hanging, and resultant radical vowel migration as pitches that lie above the termination of the speech range are encountered. The vowel [ɑ] may suddenly resemble the vowel [ʊ], or even [u], within closely juxtaposed segments of the ascending scale. It therefore must be reiterated that it is inappropriate to equate the traditional system of *Deckung* with that of the *copertura* technique described above. The drastic action of *Deckung* risks a heavy toll on efficiency of production. (It is tempting to describe it as the "ah-ooga!" sound of the old automobile horn!) Whatever its aesthetic results, in matters of vocal health it costs more than it should.

It must here be parenthetically mentioned, and emphatically underscored, that there has always existed on the part of most *major* German, Nordic, and Middle European voice teachers a reaction against the more parochial registration practices of "heavy covering." For these teachers, as in the international vocal community in general, the international model of the *copertura* technique is the aim. On the other hand, because of the nature of its highly organized instructional system and its curricular discipline, the influence of the typical Germanic school has infiltrated its near neighbors and has even gained large numbers of Asian adherents. Nor is American vocal pedagogy immune to its principles.

In the current French School, two dissimilar approaches exist for dealing with the need to equalize timbre in the ascending scale. In the historic French School, *couverture* (cover) was largely modeled after the technique of *copertura,* although there was always the indigenous tendency on the part of many singers trained in France to avoid recognizing the need for *any* vowel modification, thereby sacrificing vocal tone out of respect for vowel purity and for the linguistic interests that are in general so strong in the French School. With these teachers, *voce aperta* is not infrequent. However, French vocal pedagogy has not escaped the influence of *Deckung,* particularly since World War II. This change has been, in fact, partly in response to the charge of "open" singing *(voix blanche)* so often leveled against the French by the rest of the professional vocal world. It is interesting to note, however, that the impact of the French School on the international vocal scene was much greater prior to the second world war than it has since been. There is evidence that in post-war years French vocal technique has moved away from its earlier transalpine tradition. At least in supraglottic vocal matters, the Rhine has receded in its importance as a cultural boundary. The result has not been positive.

Whenever one considers the state of vocal art in Great Britain (and it is in thriving condition), it is necessary to keep in mind the great diversity of tonal ideals that exists within that country. The two extremes are illustrated (1) by proponents of the traditional "Cathedral tone" in which "covering" is not a concern because high levels of breath mixture in the tone have already reduced the upper partials in the singing voice, and (2) by the British-trained opera and concert singer who faces the same options regarding "cover" as do other singers of the international operatic stage. In general, the French and the British, like their North American colleagues (and, increasingly, their Asian colleagues who sing serious Western vocal music) are faced with clear choices represented by the Italianate and Germanic models. (Unfortunately for everybody, claims of adherence to the Italian School, particularly with regard to *copertura [aggiustamento]* can be very misleading.)

In styles of singing in which the vibrant voice is not an aim, questions regarding "covering" or of "modifying the vowel" are not germane. This is clearly the case with many popular vocal idioms, as well as with the unskilled singer who on some occasions appears in specialized "period" literatures and who attempts to recover "authentic" timbres based on questionable musicological assumptions regarding those literatures.

In summary, *copertura* is a technique of subtle adjustment *(aggiustamento)* of vocal timbre that produces the equalized scale in mounting pitch. Within the fabric of the complete scale, a vowel will modify toward its nearest neighbor through acoustic adjustment dependent on graduated mouth opening, while the basic resonator-tract shape for each targeted vowel is maintained. This process avoids heavy mechanical changes at the level of the larynx or within the resonator system. There, are, indeed, changes; they are gradual and do not need to be forcibly induced. Vowel modification avoids the segmenting of the vocal scale that is so often audible in systems of heavy and early "cover." However, "open" singing can be equally damaging to the vocal instrument and is not an acceptable alternative to heavy covering. Through resonance balance, represented by the *chiaroscuro* timbre, the proper relationship among the formants can be maintained while defining vowels throughout the scale.

4

The Open Throat (*La gola aperta*)

At a conference of singing teachers held in Europe, papers that dealt with supraglottal considerations in singing were presented. It was the premise of the first paper that what one does above the glottis (supraglottally) in the vocal tract heavily influences the timbre of the singing voice. The presenter advised that conscious attempts to adjust the muscles of the submandibular region (below the jaw) in order to "open" the throat may remove structural support of the external musculature of the larynx, and thereby induce undesirable tensions. In addition, it was warned that some forms of readjustment of the internal musculature of the throat may upset the natural filtering processes of the vocal tract in such a way as to distort vocal quality.

The title of the next presentation was "The Open Throat." The speaker was not a performer, but did enjoy a reputation as a "voice coach," particularly for choral groups comprising male voices. The presentation began with the dramatic statement, "Of course, we *all* know what is meant by the open throat!" These words were delivered with a hand placed on the throat at the level of the thyroid cartilage near the laryngeal prominence (the "Adam's apple"), in a quality of voice that sounded very much like an advanced yawn. One could feel empathically distention of the muscles between the larynx and the chin. The speaker continued, in the same sepulchral quality of voice, "As I speak, I am now demonstrating to you the universally accepted position of the open throat, which is ideal for singing."

The attention level in the hall zoomed as members of the conference recognized that the two speakers represented directly opposing vocal camps on the topic of "the open throat." The air became electric in anticipation of an ensuing pedagogical battle. That session of the conference provoked more comment in the corridors and out in the garden than did any other. With good reason! What is meant by *gola aperta* (open throat) differs widely from one pedagogical school to another.

The potential for varying the shape of the vocal tract (the resonator tube that acts as an acoustic filter to the laryngeally generated sound) seems almost without end. The position of the larynx itself, the pharynx, the velum, the tongue, the lips, the mandible, all offer innumerable possibilities for modification of the resonator chambers, by responding with behavior determined by techniques for "opening the throat."

The first speaker at the above-mentioned conference had offered a quotation from Sir Victor Negus (*The Comparative Anatomy and Physiology of the Larynx,* p. 199):

> the sounds produced in the larynx are amplified and selected in the pharynx, mouth and nose, and in these cavities some of the overtones can be strengthened while others are subdued or suppressed.

The first speaker further suggested that the sounds the listener hears from the larynx should be the result of the natural phonetically determined acoustic shaping of the vocal-tract filter in match with the laryngeal source. It was also mentioned that, given the cartilaginous nature of the laryngeal housing (the "voice box") and the process of abduction and adduction involved in breathing and phonating, it might be doubted that one can successfully "open" the throat at the level of the larynx through externally perceived muscular adjustments, or by the retention of the yawn position during phonation. With proper breath inhalation, the speaker maintained, the larynx assumes a relatively low posture and the pharynx widens somewhat, but this action does not involve conscious "spreading" of the pharyngeal wall or depression of the larynx. He even suggested that too much sensation in the region of the laryngopharynx should be avoided and that sensations of "openness" might better be experienced in the regions of the nasopharynx and the oropharynx. Methods for achieving such *gola aperta,* he asserted, make use of the "breath of expectancy or surprise," or resemble "silently inhaling, as though gradually filling the lungs with the fragrance of a rose."

The second speaker, obviously unconvinced by the remarks of the first, recommended that the singer "lower the larynx to produce a cave-like sensation in the throat," "fill the throat with resonant sound," "feel like you have a grapefruit in your throat," and "move the walls of the throat outward." This imagery was intended to create and retain a sensation of a widened pharynx and a low larynx during singing.

Clearly, these two *gola aperta* concepts represent one of the watersheds of vocal pedagogy. Some singers avoid any direct attention to sensation in the neck or laryngeal regions, while others attempt a conscious control over the dimensions of the pharyngeal resonator and over laryngeal positioning.

Inasmuch as both camps are convinced of the correctness of their pedagogical positions, how does a singer caught in the middle of this conflict make a decision about how best to "open the throat"? How to judge the arguments set forth? Both ideologies, although presented at this conference in starker contrast than they sometimes occur in the studio, are based on assumptions regarding specific physiologic actions. The singer who wants to weigh the merits of those positions might do well to examine the relationships between the buccal and pharyngeal resonators as they occur in all forms of phonation.

Above all, the musicianly ear of the singer should consider what side effects may result from the vocal-tract management recommended by either pedagogy. Is the sound distorted? Does it sound manufactured? Is it freely produced? Does it cost a lot? Is there comfort in the laryngeal area during singing? Is the voice unified throughout the range? Are language sounds intelligible at all tempi and dynamic levels? In short, if requested to achieve a particular arrangement in "the throat" in order to make the sounds of singing, the singer should take a long look at the physical and timbre results. A good rule might be: a sense of openness, yes; a sound of distortion, no.

5

Breath Management, Diction, and the Vocal Legato

Faulty diction, which is antagonistic to vocal legato (the unrelenting flow of tone), may be one of several debilitating cracks in the vocal edifice. It is often caused by that primary destroyer of legato: an insecure breath process. Legato requires mastery of *appoggio*. Much impurity of vowels, blurring and smearing of phonemes into indiscriminate transition sounds, early anticipation of consonants or heavy leaning on them, exaggerated accentuation that attempts to mask a technique that does not allow easy articulation—all attest to an inability to maintain a coordinated and consistent flow of breath. The relationship between diction and breath management is such an intimate one that only pedagogical scrutiny demands that they be separately considered. When legato singing is mastered, both listener and singer have the impression that words and syllables ride lightly and distinctly on a foundation of secure breath management.

Continuity of Vowel Sound

Vocalization being essentially *vowelization,* it is the vowel that is the real carrier of the tone. Consonants have their own duration requirements that are to be respected, but they must not become predominant within the line; clear consonant articulation can take place without glaring interruption of the vowel. The consonant, whether voiced or unvoiced, need not play villain to the heroic vowel, but can serve as a beneficial agent in delineating the vowel more plastically than would otherwise be possible were one continuous string of vowel sounds to be sung. One of the difficulties in singing extended vocalises of the Rachmaninoff and Ravel sort is the lack of consonant assistance. (Another is a lack of good management of the breath.)

To consider each of the families of consonants at length with regard to accomplishing legato in singing would require a vast opus. A few brief examples of the more prevalent types of error associated with the singing of consonants must suffice.

Duration of Pitch Consonants

Recognizing the relationship between vowel and consonant within a vocal line, some singers hang on to those consonants that have pitch and vibrancy, particularly the nasals [m], [n], [ɲ], and [ŋ], assuming that prolongation of these consonants will contribute to the projection of the word and to the forward motion of the vocal line. They linger over them like the hummingbird poised in midair before a succulent flower. The hummingbird reaps a more generous harvest, because linear phrase movement is arrested as the singer hovers over the consonant. Intensely humming a nasal consonant in the hope of improving diction hinders the legato flow of tone, which is carried chiefly by the vowel. The phonemes [m], [n], [ɲ], and [ŋ], although they are nonfricative continuants, should not be treated as though they were vowels, except when they require doubling (see below). The prolonged humming of nasal continuants also tends to inappropriately emphasize words in which they occur.

Nasalized French vowels must have full rhythmic duration that in no way detracts from the flow of legato, just as is the case with the nasal consonants referred to above. The combination of both mouth and nasal cavity resonances increases the intensity factor in the *nasal vowels* so that during their production there is little loss in intensity. However, many singers, especially non-native French-language singers (but including some native French-speaking singers), make the mistake, in imitation of speech, of too early an introduction of nasality into a nasal vowel that has a long duration. Elegant French singing diction dictates that the nasality of the vowel on a long sustained note not occur at its inception, but be gradually introduced near its conclusion.

Prolongation of *all* pitch consonants produces exaggerated diction. Raising diction to a high level of awareness may be a virtue in some specific phrases, but pretentious diction is to be deplored. "Sticky" duration of consonants produces "sticky diction." Hanging on to consonants because they have pitch (are voiced) produces parodistic language sounds, whether in the solo voice or in choral singing, where they so often occur. Diction-conscious enunciation is not good diction.

In fact, in some languages, the constant doubling of single consonants that have pitch produces amusing textual innovations, since the longer duration of the consonant indicates a doubling of the spelling and results in a different word. This is particularly the case with Italian and German. Indiscriminate lingering over pitch consonants, which is advocated by some coaches, teachers of singing, and choral conductors who do not know these languages well, destroys linguistic finesse in singing.

Unification of Consonant and Vowel in the Onset

An audible separation of consonant and vowel is sometimes requested in the singing of [ts], [f], [h], [k], [s], [ʃ], [θ] or [ð] and the subsequent vowel. Students schooled in this diction technique are taught to sing such a word as *sat* with a quick explosive emission of breath on the consonant [s] achieved through a short epigastric impulse, followed by an immediate second impulse on the vowel [æ]. This diction device, it is claimed, will make the word distinctly audible in the rear of the largest hall, since the listener's ear, it is hoped, will reunite the two sounds into a single sound. This technique might in theory seem appealing, but even though the word may be clearly audible, the flow of tone has been drastically interrupted. A phrase such as "the sad soul sat sighing" produces a series of minor explosions, and is so perceived in any area of the hall. This "double attack" (separation of the consonant from the vowel), as its admirers sometimes term it, on words beginning with plosives, sibilants, or fricatives may be particularly difficult for persons seated in the first few rows to appreciate. With a word such as *peace,* the emotional content evoked by the word-symbol itself is remote from such percussiveness. Application of this principle to both voiced and unvoiced consonants produces a grotesque parody of diction, whether with the solo singer or with the chorister. No matter how fine the basic breath coordination may be, no legato can wend its way through such a battery of eruptions and minor explosions.

Another diction device is sometimes advocated: air retained in slightly puffed-out cheeks is released for the nonvoiced consonant, thus forming the plosive, sibilant, or fricative consonant without drawing on the source of breath still in the lung (thus, it is thought, preserving breath supply for the subsequent phrase). Watching a nationally known choral group follow this advice made several observers wonder if sudden and sporadic attacks of dyspepsia in epidemic proportions had struck the traveling choristers. Nothing is gained either visually or aurally by this somewhat bizarre practice. Legato vanishes.

The Quickly Occurring Consonant

A clean delivery of consonants permits both clarity of diction and continuance of tonal flow. It is accomplished when the singer recognizes that most consonants occur quickly and crisply, with the apex of the tongue touching the inner surface of the lower front teeth. Most other groups of consonants are formed either at the alveolar ridge or with the tongue in contact with the inner surface of the upper front teeth; a few additional consonants use modifications of these postures. Inasmuch as all the vowels are formed with the tongue apex in contact with the lower front teeth, it is obvious that the largest part of phonetic articulation takes place with the tongue contacting either the lower or the upper tooth surfaces, or the alveoli. Even voiceless palatal fricatives, such as *ewig* [ç] or *ach* [x] in German, need not cause the singer to abandon this frontal feeling (because the apex of the tongue is still in contact with the inner surface of the lower front teeth), nor should glottals, aspirants, or consonantal sounds involving contact with the hard palate (such as [ɲ]) dissipate this forward tongue posture.

Techniques of singing that consciously attempt to create space in the velopharyngeal or buccal regions by dropping the mandible and the zygomatic musculature generally negate the phonetic postures that produce clean diction, because the tongue can no longer remain flexible in its frontal maneuvers. Feeling a bit like being at the dentist's in these unnatural phonetic positions, the tongue doesn't know where to go.

The Nondiminishing Vowel Sound

For clean diction and an unswerving legato, it is of utmost importance to refrain from habitually diminishing the vowel sound as it approaches the oncoming final consonant of each word within the phrase. The vowel should continue onward at the same degree of intensity until it reaches the consonant, unless the composer has indicated a dynamic shading, or unless the overall phrase shape requires dynamic change. To achieve this maintenance of the legato, singers must mentally crescendo any note of more than passing duration as the final consonant of the syllable is approached. Otherwise, the tonal level may dip dynamically downward as the consonant is about to make its appearance, and phrase intensity is lost. Native English-language speakers, who are accustomed to the tossed inflection that is so detrimental to legato singing, are particularly susceptible to this coming-and-going dynamic fluctuation on a sung syllable. Although much of the phonetic character of singing derives directly from the spoken voice, resorting to speech inflection rhythms during legato singing does not improve diction, although it is appropriate to *recitativo secco* (dry recitative).

The Unmodified Vowel Sound

It is equally important to guard against allowing the approaching consonant to exercise influence over the color of the vowel that precedes it. Some singers, believing that colloquial diction is desirable, see no harm in this practice. They point out that speech is a continuous gliding in and out of vowels and consonants through various intermediate or transition sounds. They maintain that it is not incorrect to carry over this practice into singing. Since English-speaking singers tend to delineate phonetic sounds more clearly in foreign languages (because those are "learned" languages) than they do in English, the problem is often more crucial when they sing in their native tongue. However, the introduction of these transition sounds in any language tends to alter the timbre of the voice, disrupting both the clarity of diction and the constancy of the legato.

For example, in singing the word *then,* if the untrained singer anticipates the final consonant, he or she will imperceptibly begin raising the tongue in preparation for the approaching consonant [n] before its turn has come, drastically influencing the color of the vowel; this gives the impression of unwanted diphthongation. The resultant *schwa* [ə] ("uh") that begins to creep into the vowel [ɛ] ("eh") is an unpleasant mixture induced by the undesirable position of the tongue as it slowly, and too early, glides upward to rest against the alveolar ridge. In spoken phonation, because of the faster occurrence of language sounds, the journey of the tongue to the alveoli is faster, and reduces the amount of transition sound. In singing, the time element (almost always slower than speech) affects the basic quality of tone; the ear perceives the maneuvers as an alteration of vocal timbre, hence an interruption of the legato. To avoid this, the [ɛ] "eh" vowel must in no way be modified by anticipating the concluding [n]. The tongue must remain in position, in contact with the inner surface of the lower front teeth until the exact moment for the enunciation of [n], at which time it should go swiftly and cleanly to the alveolar ridge. If the tongue is not held in a rigid intermediate position, or series of positions, the larynx (connected as it is to the hyoid bone, to which the tongue is attached) will not need to experience major changes during the production of the syllable. Uniformity of flowing tone will be present throughout the duration of the syllable, and will contribute substantially to a continuous legato.

Dynamic Constancy (Intensity) in Diphthongization

The guiltiest diction agent in undermining the legato line is the unruly diphthong, with its close relative the triphthong. For the native English-language singer to eliminate it from the singing of Italian, German, and French texts is no mean accomplishment. Properly harnessing it for use in English-language singing is almost as great an achievement. When not properly handled, the diphthong is injurious to the legato line, because in speech inflection it usually seeks a lower dynamic level for the delivering of its second component vowel. This is readily observable in such a word as *how,* where the vowels **ah** [ɑ] and **o** [o] are united into one syllable in which the first vowel of the diphthong configuration is of greater duration than the second. Leaving rhythmic considerations aside for a moment (the chief vowel is always longer than the "vanishing" one, of course), it should be pointed out that dynamic consistency must be maintained nearly equally in both vowel components of any syllable that comprises a diphthong. The vowel [o] frequently concludes diphthongs in German and in English, as with *Haus* and *house.* (It should be noted, incidentally, that these words consist of [ɑ-o] diphthongs, not [ɑ-u] diphthongs.) No matter how briefly the concluding portion of the syllable may occur, it should not lose intensity of vibration or fall drastically out of the ongoing dynamic level, unless a musical reason exists for its doing so. It must taper off, of course, but it must not collapse and disappear. Many times, coaches who rightfully insist on an awareness of tonic accents in languages fail to take into account the duration factors in most sung texts, so that the second half of a diphthong falls from the vocal line, thereby destroying the possibility of the perception of legato. This is especially true of the frequently concluding *schwa* [ə] in words such as *Liebe, silent,* or *âme,* on notes of long duration. Clearly these vanishes should be at a lower level dynamically than the main vowel, but they still must "sound" within the legato line.

The triphthong (found in the such words as *fire, lyre, desire, higher*) possibly presents a greater legato pitfall, because in the singing voice it involves a series of three vowels: "ah-ee-uh" [ɑ-i-ə]. Of course, the retroflex American [r], too narrowly termed the *Midwestern r,* plays no role in "classical" singing, although it is much in evidence in musical comedy and pop idioms. In the triphthong, the *schwa* [ə] requires a lower dynamic intensity than its two companions, but it must not be nonvibrantly thrown away simply because it merits a shorter duration. When triphthongs occur in the middle of a phrase, the retention of speech inflection habits in which the second and third portions of the syllable lose intensity and vibrancy (thereby "falling out of the line") wreaks havoc with the legato. In singing, whatever the duration of the note, the "first vowel" of the triphthong gets the lion's share of attention.

Phrase Inflection

Elegant phrase inflection, being closely bound to the legato, cannot occur if forward direction is interrupted by unnecessarily intrusive consonants and debilitating diphthongs. Dynamic level, which together with rhythmic impulse and word inflection sculpts the phrase, should not be dependent on mechanical problems of diction but on musical considerations. It goes without saying that, in stressing the need to avoid dynamic fluctuations caused by faulty diction habits and the lack of a stable *appoggio* technique of breath management, it is not here advocated that every phrase maintain an exact dynamic level from beginning to end. However, true dynamic shading can result within the arch of the phase only when the concertina/accordion effects on individual syllables are eliminated. The contour of no single phrase should be at the mercy of uneven tonal intensity, series of unintentional intensity increases and decreases, or dynamic hills and valleys that vitiate the ascending or descending gesture of the phrase.

Conclusions

During singing, whose very foundation rests on the breath cycle (inspiration, phonation, and breath renewal), breath is turned into tone. When unhindered by clumsy diction, the flow of vibrant sound results in an unrelenting legato line that can be contoured at will. When the artistic imagination is coupled with technical mastery of subglottic pressure, airflow, vibrancy, and skillfully executed diction, the resultant flow of tone will be compelling in its freedom. Communication with the audience—the ultimate goal of the singer—will then be direct and unencumbered.

6

Diction and Vocal Technique

"I am kept so busy building vocal technique that I just don't have time to get around to diction matters," a voice teacher recently confided. This statement is worth examining.

The production of vocal sound deals with the acoustic phenomena of vowel differentiation. Indeed, the terms *vocalization* and *vowelization* share a common etymological source. The singing tone, whatever method may be employed in its emergence, is not the result of a universal, neutral timbre over which is superimposed a series of vowels. Physiologically, laryngeal configuration and vocal tract configuration require correspondence if a sung vowel is to be clearly delineated. To try to "add diction" to pre-existent vocal sound is to violate the processes of both the tone and vowel differentiation.

If permitted, the vocal tract filter (the resonator tube that extends from the vocal folds to the lips) will reinforce the acoustic potential inherent in each vowel by assuming the natural shapes of the resonance cavities appropriate to that vowel. The mouth and pharynx will match laryngeal vowel formation. Good singing is the result of laryngeal action and the corresponding shapes of the resonator tube. Any assumption that there is an ideal mouth or throat position through which all vowels are produced is in contradiction to what is known about physical and phonetic factors in singing; it is the vowel that largely determines buccopharyngeal shapes in singing. In ascending pitch in all forms of phonation, it is also acoustically demonstrable that although the mouth opens, the relative shapes that differentiate vowels basically remain intact. In the mounting scale, vowel, amplitude, and frequency contribute to the changing postures of the supraglottal resonators, but they do not produce a universal shape.

Recently, in an international master class, a soprano sang a well-known aria from the Italian repertory. With amazing control, she maintained throughout the aria nearly the same mouth position regardless of the intended vowel or the pitch. The result was extremely disconcerting linguistic and timbre distortion. When questioned as to her awareness of the degree of distortion, she replied that it was her aim to retain one ideal mouth position in order to ensure a consistent vocal sound throughout her range, regardless of vowel changes. The singer remarked that her teacher held that all great singers keep the phonetic shape [œ] (as in *coeur* or *möchte*) for singing in all languages, regardless of the actual vowels that may occur in the text, to produce a uniform "color." Her teacher had been working so hard on the production of a certain "sound" his ear prefers that he had forgotten the relationship of vowel to timbre. His assumption that all great singers keep one position of the jaw and mouth, has, of course, not the slightest validity.

The soprano made a sound that seemed interesting and rich to some ears but manufactured to most others. All listeners present agreed that seldom could they discern the seven vowels ([i-e-ɑ-o-u] and [ɛ and ɔ]) found in the Italian language. The resistant singer's reply to these observations was, "Well, my teacher says that if you were supposed to understand the words, you would recite them, not sing them. He believes tone, not words, is important."

Tone, not words? Is there, then, a neutral substance called "tone" for singing, which has no relationship to vowels? *Tone* and the individual *vowel,* as has been seen, result from the matching configurations of the larynx and the vocal tract. For the singing voice, as for the speaking voice, neither undistorted tone nor recognizable diction can be superimposed on a single predetermined acoustic posture. As spectrum analysis demonstrates, diction need not be inimical to tone, because it is part of the timbre balance.

As a concluding footnote to this brief discussion of diction and vocal technique, it should be said that clean diction is not produced by exaggerated, heavy consonants, but by quickly occurring consonants (except for consonantal doubling in languages that require it) that do not impede the connected flow of well-defined vowels. Should one then adopt a "diction" approach as the basis of good vocal pedagogy? Only if that approach means that vowel definition and consonant occurrences are produced phonetically, thereby inducing matching laryngeal and vocal tract adjustments. This must result in a complete spectrum in which lower and upper formants (composed of harmonic partials) are in balance, with vowel-defining formants shifting between them. Diction does not exist as a separate entity from tone.

7

The Performer as Voice Teacher

Unlike the contemporary scene in some countries of continental Europe, where with great frequency a noted singing artist retires after a long and successful career and suddenly takes on the new role of vocal pedagogue, most of us who teach singing in North America conjointly pursue, throughout our professional lives, two careers: teaching and performance. Although this is much less often the case in continental Europe, it is more common in Great Britain.

At the risk of appearing chauvinistic, one asks if it is possible that, despite our historical indebtedness to the European cultural heritage, the limited performance arena in North America (in comparison with the far more numerous opportunities available to the European singer) may be partially responsible for the fact that American pedagogy has achieved a generally high level not always present in contemporary Europe. Has the necessity to teach, as a way of maintaining ourselves as performers, given us a pedagogical advantage? In North America, regardless of age or performance experience, a recognized professional singer generally both teaches and performs (with the exception of that small minority of singers who have managed to build "star" careers, or those who have found some special performance niche).

A significant difference, then, separates the continental European teacher and the North American teacher: the North American has not only been listening analytically as a part of the performance experience but has also been applying the same analytical listening to students. By analyzing the performance of one's students day after day, one is enabled to keep a better check on one's own singing; the teacher/performer concurrently teaches both himself and others. Graduate students who begin teaching duties almost always find that their own singing improves because of their diagnostic listening to other voices.

(A parenthetical interjection is appropriate here. No matter how important the teacher may be to the development of a singing voice, no one has ever been taught to sing by anyone other than herself or himself. The singer cannot undertake the construction of a solid vocal technique without the assistance of a fine teacher, but in the long run it is only the singer who puts it all together or who fails to do so.)

Observers of the art of singing are often confused to find that no single vocal ideal is shared by all successful singers. A look at the historic schools of singing indicates that several general vocal philosophies have been generated in response to varying aesthetic ideals. However, although it is true that not all teachers of singing have the same tonal concepts in mind, it is not true that there are as many vocal techniques as there are teachers of singing. The perception of performance values varies, but only within certain boundaries.

Whatever the tonal ideal, the technical means used to produce it should be based on freedom of production. The teacher's responsibility, at whatever level the student may be, is to identify elements of the student's vocal production that are in conflict with freedom, and to eliminate them. How does the performer/teacher identify and diagnose what is in error? By applying to the student the same technical principles by which he himself or she herself has learned to sing—a very different matter from demanding an imitative, uniform studio sound.

It is for this reason that (although there are exceptions) good singers make good teachers, whereas less skillful singers make less successful teachers. Good singers do not have to be possessors of world-shaking vocal instruments; they are persons who skillfully use the vocal material they have, whatever its natural limitations. A person who uses the singing voice well most often has arrived at technical security by having been able to identify his or her own problems, and has come to an understanding as to how those problems were eliminated. That is why some teachers who have worked through personal vocal problems are far better teachers than the person with "a naturally beautiful, unproblematic voice." They have been able to do so because they have been guided by three self-help, "self-teaching," principles:

1. They can *hear* differences between differently produced sounds.
2. They can *feel* the differences in sensations that result from variously produced sounds.
3. They can *see* the physical results of varying technical maneuvers.

Furthermore, it is now possible to make use of some of the newer visual and audio "feedback" aids that augment the perennial "self-help" devices by which every successful singer in the past has learned.

The first two diagnostic tools outlined above—hearing and feeling—are self-evident. However, in anticipation of the charge that I cannot hear myself sing, I offer that although I may not be able to hear my voice as you hear it there on the outside of this sound-producing machine, I very well know the relative differences between "Blah!" (produced by rudely sticking my tongue out) and "Ah!" (made as a cultivated exclamation of delight) with either the speaking or the singing voice. More important, *I can differentiate among all the subtle sounds I am capable of making*. Students often remark that they are able to distinguish three or four different kinds of singing sounds they can make on the same pitch, and they ask which of those sounds is best at that pitch and vowel. They *hear* their own voices!

In response to the question of which timbre on a specific pitch may be preferable, the teacher should never be in doubt as to which comes nearest to the student's requirement at that particular moment: it will be the sound that is most efficiently produced and that matches most closely the emotional demands of the word and music. The teacher/performer who can similarly produce a variety of sounds in his or her own voice, and who is able to sort them out as to efficiency of production and effectiveness of expression, will be best equipped to guide the student to timbres that are right for that student.

Sometimes students question how one can "see" the action of the hidden vocal instrument. Much is visible with a simple mirror, or by using a hand mirror in conjunction with a wall mirror or standing mirror. I can *see* the apex of my tongue, the varying postures of the buccal cavity in the forward portion of the mouth during vowel differentiation, the lips, the movement of the jaw, the zygomatic region, laryngeal position, how the external frame function of the neck relates posturally to the head and the torso, what postures are (or are not) assumed by the sternum and the rib cage, and corresponding actions in the epigastric-umbilical area. I can observe stance, body balance, and equilibrium. Of course, if I don't look, I won't see any of those actions! (Sometimes it is very hard to watch oneself, but inasmuch as we do not spare others our appearance during singing, we should not selfishly exempt ourselves!)

Sensation (how it feels) is an individual matter; it is not the teacher's prerogative to insist that the student feel the same kinds of sensations experienced by the teacher, or to try to induce them. The student will be able to sense differences in the production of sounds, and then, by that kinesthetic sense we rely on for almost all physical action, to unify the parameters of hearing, seeing, and feeling.

Let us turn from technical considerations and look at some other important parameters the performer/teacher will have mastered in his or her own singing, and which will therefore be conveyable to the student singer.

1. *The Musicianly Parameter.* Musical concerns go far beyond the general confines of correct rhythm and pitch that sometimes receive more studio time than other factors. Musicianly matters for the singer involve the subtleties of phrase shaping and phrase direction,

accent and dynamic shading, awareness of how harmonic language molds the melodic line, dynamic nuance, vocal coloration and, above all, maintaining the stabilized basic timbre of the individual vocal instrument.

2. *The Stylistic Parameter*. Stylistic considerations take into account the historic tug-of-war that occurs in vocal literature in every century and period between Romantic and Classical elements, which must be viewed in the light of current scholarly performance practices. To do so, most of us must constantly replenish our sources of information, a time-consuming research activity.

3. *The Linguistic Parameter*. The niceties of language, required for accomplishing musical nuance in the literature of the *Lied,* the *mélodie,* and the art song, make demands that are best attained when the singer understands the structure and rhythm of the language concerned and something of the culture from which it emerges. Linguistic skill and cultural subtlety contribute directly to vocal art, because the art of singing is both a literary and an auditory one. This area is one of the most challenging for the teacher of singing; it is a rare teacher who is equally equipped in several languages (most performer/teachers have some advantage here), yet the need for phonetic accuracy is essential. At least a mastery of the International Phonetic Alphabet is necessary for any teacher of singing.

4. *The Communicative Parameter*. Communication is the most important of all nontechnical skills (it has its own technique), for which all other performance techniques exist. Indeed, vocal technique without the parameter of communication has minimal value. The performer/teacher will have much to convey from his or her own reservoir of experiences.

The art of singing is the art of communication: *sound and literary content; tone and word; voice and drama.* This amalgamation of all the parameters can be achieved only when the singer can *hear, feel,* and *see* (diagnose and coordinate) his or her instrument.

The active performer/teacher (as well as the mature teacher who has been a performer/teacher) is in far better position to assist the student to unify these several parameters than is either the nonsinger coach or the retired artist who comes to such analytical consideration only after his or her own vocal instrument is no longer being actively subjected to such analysis. This is not to assert that the vocal coach, the retired artist or, for that matter, the conductor and the music critic cannot teach. They all do teach, and often astoundingly well, but their function is a different one from that of the teacher/singer. It is because there are so many performing teachers in North America that vocal pedagogy on this continent tends to take the lead in international instruction.

8

Pedagogical Clothing for the Emperor and Empress

Someone should call a halt to the proliferation of so-called "master classes" presented by performing artists who normally do not teach. Incidents from such events could make up a large volume of anecdotal reading. A few examples follow.

Said the artist-turned-momentary-master teacher when the student performer finished singing, "What color were you thinking? I heard green." Replied the young soprano, "I was worrying about making it through the long phrases!" Pedagogical response from the artist: "This time think blue." Subsequently, the colors yellow and purple were suggested, with no change in the quality of the performance.

Another classic example comes from a much publicized "master class" given by a world-famous opera star who advised his singers that they should "pinch the uvula with the tonsils." On another occasion, an equally well-known figure explained to the singers assembled before him that the vowel [i] is good for vocalization because it is small enough to fit into the channel of narrow sinuses that he has found to exist above each eyebrow; further, all other vowels must be made to conform to the same [i] size and shape so that tone can be "placed" there.

At a highly advertised session that took place at a famous conservatory, a superstar in the world of vocal performance suggested to the singers before him that, while singing, they must always hold the epiglottis down. In similar fashion, during another series of master classes, a young soprano was given physiologically questionable advice to raise her eyebrows, because that action would "widen the pharynx" and "place the tone in the forehead." At a comparable level of physiological invention was the comment, from yet another noted performer momentarily turned master teacher, that the diaphragm (indicated as lodging at the navel) plunges downward for low notes (pelvis indicated), and surges upward (sternum indicated) for high notes. Calling this kind of instruction appropriate to a "master class" is illogical.

One grows increasingly weary of the questionable subjective advice proffered young students by successful artists who know how to assemble into one psychological gesture their own personal experiences but not how to communicate that gesture to others. Advice such as "believe in yourself," "listen to your own emotions," "follow your instincts," "just think about the text," and "be carried by the drama" has little value when the young, talented singer is wishing he or she could better manage an evenly modulated scale, or that his or her remaining tongue, jaw, and neck tensions could be resolved. A gentlepersons' agreement to respect professional boundaries should be negotiated between those who teach others the art of singing professionally and those who successfully perform but do not teach. There are major differences between the two disciplines; they are not interchangeable.

Gilbert Ryle, in *The Concept of the Mind* (1949), reminds his readers of a principle not always remembered in academic circles these days:

> First, the capacity to perform and to appreciate an operation does not necessarily involve the ability to formulate criticisms or lessons. A well-trained sailor boy can both tie complex knots and discern whether someone else is tying them correctly or incorrectly, deftly or clumsily. But he is probably incapable of the difficult task of describing in words how the knots should be tied. And second, the ability to appreciate a performance does not involve the same degree of competence as the ability to execute it. (p. 56)

One recalls that much of the excellence in violin playing in this country is the result of study with teachers not themselves noted for public performance. Similar circumstances could be cited from all areas of music instruction.

One appreciates the good intentions of the campus administrator who thinks it would be exciting to have the well-known performer who is to appear on the artist recital series give a "master class." Those who teach in the vocal trenches silently shudder while consenting to what appears logical to those who do not teach. This is because most of us who teach are, or have been, performers, and we have learned that disciplining oneself for the art of teaching requires as much specific preparation and experience as does disciplining oneself for the art of performance.

One does not go blithely into teaching just because one is capable of singing beautifully. Master teaching results from the acquisition of pedagogical information and skill, not from performance career success. Without doubt, the number of premier singers in any generation who have been great voice teachers could be counted on the fingers of a hand or two.

It is worth noting that in the eighteenth century many of the most respected singing teachers were opera composers. (It is also true that many composers of early opera were themselves singers of sorts.) Yet major singing teachers were not often known for performance excellence. Typical is Manuel Garcia the younger, acknowledged as the major teacher of the transition period in vocal styles from the first to the second half of the nineteenth century. He was not a successful performer, although that was his original goal and that of his family for him.

The charismatic presence of an accomplished artist on the master-class stage often provides an exciting performance in itself. Yet when these star performers and dazzling personalities are given teaching forums, one begins not only to feel concern for the kinds of values presented to students as models for success, but also to question what may happen if the art of singing continues to be given over to such "show-business" forums in which the famous performer and a naïve public believe the artist is actually *teaching* young singers, when very little of substance is being offered. The public applauds the performance act, but the professional educator experiences a queasy feeling.

Part of the same great-artist-as-teacher syndrome is evident in the current trend toward hiring the famous performer who has retired from the opera stage as a permanent member of the teaching faculty. The failure of contemporary vocal pedagogy in some European conservatories is a result of this practice. This was not the case several decades ago, when those very artists were themselves building, with their teachers, singing techniques that helped them to arrive at positions in today's performance world. Whereas in the past many famous teachers of today's fine performers were not themselves known as premier performers, currently some American university and conservatory of music administrators, even at institutions that formerly contributed substantially to the development of the pool of young artists, are turning to "names" in order to enhance their faculty listings, often with an eye to competitive recruitment of student talent. Sometimes these "names" then spend limited periods of time on campus. They carry designations such as "artist-in-residence," as though teaching were a demeaning activity lacking in sufficient glamour to seriously occupy the time and talent of an artist. The question then becomes, "When the talented young singers who have been thus recruited arrive on campus, who will actually teach them how to sing?"

It is more complicated to assemble the requisite body of knowledge for solving a wide variety of vocal problems than it is to acquire individual performance skills. For this reason, there are many more fine professional

singers than there are highly qualified vocal pedagogues. This situation can
be remedied if those performers who wish to teach are willing to take time
to acquire information that goes beyond their own personal performance
acumen. The term "master class" cannot be applied to the experimental
public pedagogical musings of an inexperienced teacher who, although an
accomplished singing artist, is as lacking in pedagogical skills as the participating student is lacking in artistic ones.

To confuse performance charisma with masterful pedagogy is to ex-
claim over the beauty of the naked monarch's clothing. Were the performing emperor or empress to take time to dress pedagogically, there
could well be general pleasure over the splendor of his or her instructional garments.

9

The "Tricky" Teacher

"It takes a lot of imagination to teach voice," said the confident and loquacious teacher of singing as we sat across from each other over morning
coffee. "I keep thinking up new things all the time. I have read just about
everything, and I have studied with a number of teachers who had opposing technical views, so that now I have a vast arsenal of ideas that will fit
almost anything I encounter in my studio."

My breakfast companion went on to explain that such ingenuity is essential because "no two voices work the same way," and because "what
is good for one singer is pure poison for another." "Take *placement,* for
example," she said. "Depending on what the problem is, I may have the
student *place* the tone in a half-dozen different locations, changing it from
lesson to lesson. One of the big things to watch for in placement is the
shape of the skull. If the singer has a long 'horse face,' then he has to place
the tone further up in the head than does the person with a broad face.
Or, let's say his tongue is too long—I have him pull it back in his mouth;
or if his tongue curls up, I make him stick it out over his teeth.

"The same thing goes for *support.* Some people have to pull in on the
diaphragm and others have to push it out. It depends on the shape of the
stomach as to which works best. In fact, if pulling in on the diaphragm

doesn't work, I have them push it out. I would describe myself as a 'tricky' teacher with a big bag of little tricks that can really cure vocal problems. I'll bet with your years of experience you're a tricky teacher too, aren't you? Any secrets we can trade?" I suddenly remembered that I had a vocal session in half an hour, for which I had some last minute preparation to do, and hurried away to recover.

Given the diversity of vocal problems and the individuality of the singing voice, it may at times indeed seem that no two voices can be taught in the same general fashion. Are we, however, really to believe that there are no universal principles on which to base a philosophy of vocal production? On the contrary, every voice must obey certain functional laws if freedom is to result. Compensatory "tricks" may randomly be attempted, and on occasion may momentarily serve to correct some technical problem, in the same way that medicine from the medicine chest taken without a medical diagnosis or prescription may seem to alleviate the symptoms of an assumed illness. Just as assuredly as there is danger in "doctoring" without proper diagnosis and prescription, so "tricky teaching" not based on principles of mechanical freedom may cause detrimental reactions in the singing voice.

Imaginative teaching is necessary, but inventive teaching based on chance exploration of adjustments to the singing voice is an abomination. Too often it is erroneously believed that such "creative" teaching is easier than taking time to learn how the vocal instrument really works. However, all technical suggestions must be judged against the measurement of functional freedom. Playing "tricks" on a singing voice is not included in the game rules of any respectable vocal pedagogy.

10

Woofy Baritones and Tinny Tenors

A baritone presents himself in competition with one of the standard arias from the Operatic Anthology, emitting a cavernous, sepulchral timbre. A competing tenor produces a twangy, metallic sound that seems to amalgamate the properties of brass and tin through a catalyst of nasality. (The title of this brief excursion into vocal timbre could just as easily be "Strident Sopranos and Mooing Mezzos," and appropriate examples could be cited.)

Rare indeed is the young low-voiced male who does not, at least at the beginning of his singing career, assume he must "enrich" his sound by making it "spacious" and "warm," qualities generally accomplished through a series of adjustments to his larynx and to his vocal tract that greatly disperse the inherently beautiful timbre of his instrument. Young tenors often mistake the *ingolata* (throaty) buffoesque timbre, character-ized by edginess, for "resonance," "forward placement," or "projection." Within recent memory, one young tenor informed his listeners that for each pitch in the scale above his *primo passaggio* it was necessary to raise his head and his larynx in order to ensure "more brilliance." At about the same period of time, a young bass explained that he had to lower his head for each descending pitch of the scale in order to keep the sound "rich."

These incidents are but prototypes that illustrate the frequently encoun-tered viewpoint that in order to comply with the aesthetics that determine coloration in each *Fach* (category), the basic function of the instrument must be altered. In such pedagogical orientations, tenors use one technique of singing and baritones another, as do sopranos and mezzos. It would be foolhardy to overlook the subtle differences among categories of voice in the accomplishment of scale unification, vowel modification, and in the physiological events that occur at different points in the scale. But given what is now known about vocal function, how can healthy vocalism be thought to result from a series of varying fundamental physiologic and acoustic maneuvers that must be differently produced for each *Fach*, as though there were no functional principles that govern phonation?

It is true that some interesting timbres may be created by momentarily upsetting the coordination that automatically results from controlled air-flow rate, clean cordal approximation, and corresponding configurations of the vocal tract. But to maintain such positions over extended periods of time subjects the voice to inefficient function and results in timbre dis-tortion.

One can only speculate as to the number of sopranos who for technical reasons suffer from short top voices that have been forced into the "mezzo mold" with a bovine-like timbre that only minimally relates to the natural instrument. What must be the count on short-ranged baritones who have not learned to negotiate upper range, and who have therefore been taught to "darken" the voice in order to sound like basses? "Bassitis" is a major contributor to vocal disrepair among male singers, equaled only by the introduction of "bite and brass" into the tenor voice in the hope of making it sound "resonant." Or who can number the legion of *soubrette* voices that have been forced to scream their way into the *spinto* literature, going far beyond their native capabilities?

If a singer is a baritone, and if his instrument is taught to function efficiently, he will sound like a baritone; an efficiently functioning bass will sound like a bass. If one is not a member of one of these categories, and if one tries to superimpose on the instrument a *Fach* coloration that is not native to that instrument, one will have succeeded only in producing a manufactured facsimile. The studio may be impressed, but not the professional world. (None of this discussion should be mistaken as an endorsement of the insipid "unsupported" singing that is sometimes described as "natural.")

Vocal art in the Western world incorporates the principles of beauty, strength, and health that stem from the ancient Greek aesthetic. These characteristics are the result of a freely operating vocal instrument. Any serious look at the historical pedagogical literature of the Western world will prove this viewpoint to be the prevailing one. New methods of vocal production, in opposition to the historical schools, are often far less new than their presenters suppose. These methods falsely claim to improve the vocal instrument through radical adjustments of basic vocal functions.

Vocal coloration is an important part of artistry. Artistic singing requires a palette of varied colors, of dynamically shifting lights and shadows. Yet the essential thing for professional sound production is to first establish a uniform, stabilized timbre of the voice throughout all registers, with a full complement of spectral color (which now can be visualized through actual spectral analysis, and which is the characteristic that distinguishes all great voices from the commonplace). The next essential ingredient is to learn how far a singer may momentarily depart from the stabilized timbre for purposes of expression and musical nuance without violating the efficient function of the instrument.

Woofy baritones, tinny tenors, strident sopranos, and bovine mezzos can in no way serve as surrogates for healthy voices that sound like baritones, tenors, sopranos and mezzos because their instruments work efficiently, and therefore freely.

11

McPedagogy

This is an age of hurry. Fast results are expected in every field. A theologian viewing the popularization of religious concepts worries over the proliferation of McReligion. The political scene, with its avoidance of in-depth discussion of issues in favor of twenty-second sound bites, has become disastrously mired in McPolitics. Education, when it substitutes social adjustment and participation for information, qualifies as McEducation.

Much of what passes today for popular music, lacking form and substance, can best be termed McMusic. (This includes not only the omnipresent, noisy bill of goods sold to the young through adult marketing indoctrination, but the formula music you have to listen to in your dentist's office.)

The art of singing is not immune to nonsubstantive instruction. Vocal McPedagogy lives! It consists of quick solutions, tricks, and gimmicks, largely based on mythological notions as to how the vocal instrument works. *Pedagogy with Ease,* pulled out of a bag of idiosyncratic invention, is an alluring will-o'-the-wisp that entices many insecure teachers and singers. Popular "How to Sing" manuals and articles, with recipes for serving up fast nourishment for choral and solo singers, currently abound.

McPedagogy, the quick fix for the problems of the singing voice, fails to take into account the two basic principles of technical instruction: (1) diagnosis, and (2) prescription. To instruct, there must be a body of specific information that permits analysis leading to solution.

It is insufficient to recognize that a vocal sound may be less than ideal; the correction of any defect requires the ability to diagnose what is interfering with good function. Only then can technical prescriptions be made. Acquiring such information is within the grasp of any voice teacher of average musical training and intelligence. Information regarding the basic physiology and acoustics of the singing voice is accessible to all of us. It can be found in general textbooks and in manuals specifically designed for the singer.

The vocal performer and teacher do not need backgrounds in medicine or the physical sciences in order to comprehend these relatively simple principles. Months, or perhaps a year, of concentrated reading and study of the literature can produce specificity of language that allows a teacher to more accurately convey what the musicianly ear hears and desires. It is not necessary to "take time out to enroll for course work," as is often assumed. Simply, there must be a willingness to take the time to acquire the tools of one's trade. To continue to complain that it is impossible to do so is to admit that the professional goals of the discipline are too demanding, and to play a somewhat dishonest game with oneself and one's profession.

Voice teachers and performers must not allow themselves to be intimidated by the new technology or by persons who fail to make the newer feedback devices understandable. They must resist the obscurantists who make "voice science" difficult. With an honest effort, what at first seemed foreign to all of us will quickly become friendly.

No serious teacher of singing would attempt to give instruction if unable to read music. Anyone who can learn to read music can learn to read a spectrogram, and in far less time. The excuse that it is all beyond one may indicate a more serious defect regarding one's vocal pedagogy: refusal to give up cherished opinions and to risk close examination of private pedagogical territory. (To hide behind the old saw that adding to one's knowledge will diminish artistry is embarrassing.)

Put more charitably, some teachers who have themselves come entirely through the imagery-and-personal-sensation route make the false assumption that everyone else must have the same set of empirical experiences, described through imaginative language. This sentiment is refuted by teachers who have bothered to supplement their good ears and their performance experience with a body of precise information. They universally express great joy in their new capabilities and increased freedom of expression. Vocal pedagogy is only as useful as the specific information it conveys. Regrettably, the value of one's teaching cannot be measured solely by the excellence of one's musicianly ears and the ability to recognize a good sound.

There is no doubt that the musical ear is, above all, the key to vocal instruction. A clear concept of desirable vocal timbre and an awareness of how to make expressive use of it is essential. But the ability to communicate concepts to a student in understandable language is the essence of first-rate teaching. Not just what one knows, but how one conveys that knowledge, leads to successful teaching.

When dealing with a student who is struggling with technical problems it is not enough to play the dedicated role of artistic model, counselor, psychiatrist, musical coach, and close friend. Even the established artist pupil may develop problems that a teacher should be expected to solve— not through personal charisma, but through diagnosis and prescription.

McPedagogy, based on magic-wanding, is on the way out, not only in American but in European vocal circles as well. The artist-teacher who requests that the student think purple or chartreuse, or who requests that floating tones emerge from chimneys on tops of heads, is no longer taken seriously. Today's student wants specific information, not McPedagogy. The successful modern teacher will take time to acquire the means for diagnosis and prescription. Not to do so is to be satisfied with less than what one has the capability of becoming.

12

"What You Need Is More Support!"

Several years ago it was my unhappy assignment to serve as outside consultant on a question of teacher evaluation at an institution where such review takes place. For the greater part of a day, I sat in a studio and tried to sort out the strengths and weaknesses of the pedagogy that unfolded before me. What follows is an accurate account of one of the lessons I observed. Only the name of the student and the title of the song have been altered. (The name of the teacher will remain secret.)

Mark, a nineteen-year-old baritone performance major, vocalizes briefly on a nine-note scale, exhibiting extreme nasality, and then turns to *Già il sole dal Gange*. He sings through the entire composition without interruption, with the same nasal quality that was evident in his vocalizing. Such nasal timbre is the result, of course, of a constantly low velar position that does not take into account the postures necessary for non-nasal vowel and non-nasal voiced consonant definition.

Mark's teacher says, "Well, Mark, something is really wrong with that quality. It sounds very nasal." Mark amicably agrees that the timbre is not a desirable one. His teacher then makes the following series of suggestions, with the indicated results:

Suggestion 1: "Just remain where you are standing but send your voice after my hand." (Teacher stretches his right arm outward, places forefinger and thumb together, and walks slowly backward across the studio floor. Mark, as he moves his torso forward but keeps his feet in place, valiantly tries to make his voice follow his teacher's receding hand.)

Result 1: *Già il sole dal Gange* continues to be sung with nasal timbre.

Suggestion 2: "Get the feeling that you are placing the tone right here in the masque." (Teacher indicates the zygomatic region.)

Result 2: *Già il sole dal Gange* is sung with continued nasality.

Suggestion 3: "All right, Mark," says teacher, "let's try to concentrate on another kind of placement." (Teacher puts forefinger on forehead just above and between Mark's eyes.)

Result 3: *Già il sole dal Gange* exhibits the same degree of nasality as previously.

After a moment's reflection, a new suggestion is forthcoming from teacher.

> Suggestion 4: "Well, perhaps the tone is actually *too* far forward. This time, send the sound out this little hole right here on the top of your head. (Teacher indicates a spot on the dome [the *calvaria*] of the skull.) Have the feeling that the tone goes right up the back of the throat wall, into the head, and out this little chimney on the top."

Mark tries to direct the tone up the throat wall and out the little chimney on the top of his head, this time assisting with furrowed brow and with eyes turned upward.

> Result 4: *Già il sole dal Gange* continues to show nasality as the predominant timbre characteristic.
>
> Suggestion 5: "It still seems too far forward to me. I think we'll go a step beyond now and try to imagine sending the tone out of an inverted cone, a sort of funnel, with the large, spacious end of the cone at the nape of your neck, the little end at your larynx. Just send the sound right out the back of your neck."
>
> Result 5: Despite a courageous attempt to place the tone as directed, Mark continues to sing *Già il sole dal Gange* with extreme nasality.
>
> Suggestion 6: "All right, we've really got to lick this nasality problem. Just send the tone directly down your spine into the center of your body. Sing it into yourself."
>
> Result 6: Mark earnestly tries to follow the proffered directions, but he continues to sing *Già il sole dal Gange* with a nasalized quality.

It is clear that Mark's teacher hears the undesirable nasality that plagues his student's voice, and that he very much wants to help Mark get rid of it. For a moment he is lost in thought. However, having exhausted his "placement" remedies, teacher now turns to the suggestion that tends to be offered as a solution for many vocal problems when all else fails.

> Suggestion 7: "Well Mark, it just *has* to be a question of support. What you need is more support. Come on now! Give it more support!"

Mark is a trusting student, and one sees that he believes himself at fault for not being able to make proper use of these inventive corrective suggestions. So he takes heart that yet another suggestion may trigger his recalcitrant instrument to produce the right action. However, he is unsure as to how he must proceed. He ventures, "Just how should I do that?"

Suggestion 7*a:* Teacher unbuttons his jacket and places Mark's hand on his own ample abdominal wall and distends his abdomen. "Press down and out like this when you breathe in and then hold your breath as you sing the phrase."

Result 7*a:* Mark does so, and *Già il sole dal Gange* rings forth at a slightly higher dynamic level, a little sharp, with the same degree of nasality as before. "It sounds almost the same to me," says Mark apologetically, "only a little louder." "I know," agrees his teacher. "That doesn't seem to be quite the kind of support you need."

Suggestion 7*b:* "So try this: This time pull *in* on your stomach as you sing the phrase."

Result 7*b:* Mark pulls his abdominal wall inward, and he continues to sing *Già il sole dal Gange* with a great deal of nasality.

Mark's teacher appears to be a bit disappointed, but by no means defeated. Indeed, he suddenly seems almost cheerful.

Suggestion 8: "Tell you what, Mark. You keep working on these ideas during the coming week, and we'll hear you again on this piece next lesson. Now what else do you have with you?"

As in so many cases, imaginative "placement" and "support" notions could not be trusted to remedy functional inadequacies present in the singing technique. Mark's teacher has a very fine ear, is an excellent musician, and has had an extensive career as a performer. Without specific information as to the physiologic and acoustic causes of nasality, can he expect to know how to eliminate nasality in singing? Will "you need more support" continue to be his ultimate panacea for all vocal faults regardless of their origin?

13

"Simplicity" in Singing

Singing consists of complex coordinations, as does any physical and mental activity that goes beyond ordinary concentration. It requires special performance skills. The complicated factors that make up artistic singing must have been previously channeled so that at the moment of performance the singer can unify physical and artistic responses. Such performance readiness comes only when technical proficiency is ingrained—programmed—so that the singer can confidently know what to expect under all conditions. Only then can performance be called a simple act.

There is a contrary, naïve viewpoint that learning to sing is simple. This opinion confuses the necessity of cultivated simplicity (the obscuring of the seams of one's art) with a negative attitude toward the acquisition of preperformance skills. It is all well and good to advocate that the teacher or performer ought to regard singing as "uncomplicated and simple" if the performer already is an accomplished technician and artist. To speak of "holistic" aspects of singing may have great merit if the essential components of the art are already in place. Unity, in fact, means just that: the bringing together a number of disparate factors. Recommending "holistic" thinking is meaningless unless the functional details have previously been established. These details depend on knowing how the vocal instrument works.

Students should view with skepticism the teacher who begins by assuring them that singing is "quite a simple matter" and that one's principal attention should at once be directed to artistic and musical concepts. Ignoring the physical aspects of singing would be logical if the student were already perfectly coordinated; since such a student would indeed be a rarity, it is necessary for the teacher to explain the specifics of breath management and resonance balancing to every student. It is patently not the case that the text, the dramatic situation, and the music point the way to technical solutions in the singing voice. The world is full of mediocre performers who have been taught by those assumptions. The end result of vocal instruction must be holistic, a sum of *all* the parts.

Obviously, with regard to time and professional commitment, it is easier for a teacher of singing to ignore the extensive body of information on vocal function and to invent an idiosyncratic system. Reading and digesting the body of available material requires more discipline than some teachers of singing can muster. Much of the insistence on "simplicity" has its source in pedagogical laziness. It takes less ingenuity and factual information to "coach" the singer in musical concepts than to "build" the voice. This may explain why many North American–trained singers occupy continental European performance and teaching posts that might logically go to native singers and teachers.

As a rule, persons who downgrade information on the function of the vocal instrument, or who distance themselves from systematic vocal technique, consider themselves best qualified to teach the high performance level student, not the beginner. Such high-level teaching involves musical phrasing, style, ornamentation, linguistic accuracy, communication, and stage deportment. Clearly, anyone who is hired to teach singing at a fine institution or who wishes to maintain a major private studio should know the performance literature and be able to coach it, and understand the psychology of performance. No one would deny that excitation of the musical and artistic imagination is required. But those factors cannot be accomplished until the achievement of a unified vocal instrument makes artistic responses possible. It is clear that unless the voice is able to operate as a well-functioning instrument there will be no realization of musical or imaginative insights.

Claiming to be a superior musician who cannot be bothered with teaching basic techniques of the instrument is a circumvention of the need to put a singing voice into proper technical condition. It has nothing to do with superior teaching qualifications. Some vocal coaches and teachers of singing assume they themselves possess artistic instincts superior to those of the singer who is unable to achieve the desired musical subtlety. Artistic nuance is dependent on the freedom of our singing instruments, not only on our imaginations. Most of us are not clods; most of us have sensitivity or we would not have been drawn to a field that requires artistry. We are, as singers, not chiefly in need of persons to teach us how to be sensitive; we are in need of persons who will teach us how to acquire the technical means for expressing our own sensitivities. Let it be stated frankly: "Singing, my dears, should be a simple act" glosses over an inability to deal with the admittedly complex problems of many singing voices.

It is remarkable how frequently singers who finally are introduced to factual information regarding the physiology and acoustics of the singing voice suddenly acquire those very levels of musical sensitivity and communication that they had been told are best gained by ignoring function.

"Simplicity" and "wholeness" can only characterize the well-produced vocal instrument. To maintain an "It is all so simple, really, isn't it now?" attitude at any level of performance skill is to close one's ears and eyes to the obvious fact that the *discipline* of singing is not simple at all. That is why so few who want to sing professionally actually succeed. With better information, they might have succeeded.

Singing is as demanding a performance art as any other. Simplicity is possible only when performance has become "simplified" in its reliance on well-programmed technical foundations. There must be a oneness of the whole and its parts. Acquiring a secure basis is not "a very simple thing." To make such a claim is either pedagogical naïveté or an apology for not putting forth the effort it takes to acquire information essential to an understanding of vocal function.

14

Teaching *Hearing* the Voice

During an hour's air flight, you and your seat companion have learned each other's current marital status, number of children and grandchildren, and of course, occupations. What am I? I'm a musician. What's your instrument? I'm a singer and a teacher of singing. "Oh, then you teach voice? But why is it necessary to teach voice when everyone already uses one?" "Well, actually," I say, trying to respond to a very logical lay questioner, "I teach *hearing the voice*." As I heard myself say that, I felt I had put into precise language what I *really* do, which is not to teach voice, but to heighten awareness of the sounds the singer is making, to alert the singer to the wide variety of sounds a voice is capable of producing, and to point out why some of those sounds are more beautiful and more efficient than are others. In the process, I am not teaching that person's larynx but that person's ear. Then the singer must bring together, in a total kinesthetic response, those factors that produce the preferable sound. Although it may seem like dealing in a neat game of semantics, I believe the two definitions of the voice teaching occupation—*teaching voice* and *teaching hearing*—represent essentially different pedagogical orientations. I have personally never taught anyone to sing, nor did anyone ever teach me to sing. Yet I am eternally grateful to four or five people who were trainers who taught me what to listen for in my voice, who pointed to the causes that make one kind of timbre different from another, and who had the patience and persistence to make me pursue those differences until they became permanent. They trained me to hear my voice so that I could teach myself. That is what I would like to do with my students.

Teaching someone to *sing* often becomes teaching someone else to sing the way one sings oneself. Teaching someone to *hear* the voice and to discriminate among timbres and the physical and acoustic maneuvers that produce the differences among them is to allow each individual singer to do his or her own self-teaching. It is not the teacher who must *teach* the voice, it is the student who must develop an ability to *hear* the voice. The discipline of making discriminating judgments between sound *A* and sound *B* is demanding. Surely there must be some new vocal method, some memorizable formula, some sudden epiphany, some shaft of blinding light? Isn't there someone out there who can teach me to sing? No, there isn't.

There are people out there who can point out which sounds are best, but the singer must learn to hear, feel, and see those differences. Routining the right coordinations makes the good sounds permanent.

15

Si canta come si parla?

Si canta come si parla (one sings as one speaks) is a familiar adage from the historic Italian School, the school that for several centuries dominated all serious vocalism in the Western world. Can it really be true that one sings as one speaks? A considered answer to that question might well be, "It depends on which language one is singing, how clearly one enunciates that language independently of regional speech characteristics, and in what part of the vocal range one is singing."

The singing voice does not exist independently of the speech mechanism. Problems of the singing voice frequently are directly attributable to poor speech production. A singer may suffer more fatigue from improper speech habits than from an inadequate singing technique. Yet people who learn to use the speaking voice well may nevertheless sing badly. It surprises some listeners that a "resonant" speaker may not have an equally resonant quality in the singing voice. Most speaking ranges encompass considerably less than half the fully developed singing range. Many pitches routinely used in singing cannot possibly be delivered in speech. Then how does *si canta come si parla* have validity as a pedagogical tenet in the cultivated singing voice?

The acoustic theory of speech production and linguistic recognition is in large part based on an assumption that vowel definition is a product of proper correspondence between laryngeal configuration and filtering processes resulting from the adjustment of the resonators above the larynx (supraglottic). This process is known as "vowel tracking." A vowel is defined by specific phonetic postures. Tracking of the laryngeally produced sound takes place in the filtering resonator tract. In accomplishing such acoustic tracking of the vowel, the physical and acoustic principles that contribute to ideal speech intelligibility must also be present in singing. In this regard, *si canta come si parla*.

A very real problem exists for the singer in that the distinct physical positions of phonemes as described by the phonetician are *not* uniformly present in most spoken language. Further, the variety of vowels in such languages as English, French, and German far exceed the seven vowels found in Italian: [i-e-ɛ-ɑ-ɔ-o-u]. In languages with numerous vowel variations and with a high rate of diphthongization, the precise vowel postures identified in phonetic manuals scarcely exist in practice: transition sounds (on-glides and off-glides) are much more characteristic of speech. By contrast, in singing, because of the duration factor (language sounds generally last much longer in singing than in speech), phonetic precision in vowel definition is attainable in any language. Acoustical exactitude underlies the rubric *si canta come si parla,* with regard to vowel definition but not with regard to some other factors.

There are, however, pedagogical attitudes toward singing based on the conviction that the singing instrument is independent of the speaking instrument; elaborate systems have been erected to *avoid* speech-like coordinations in favor of learned laryngeal and vocal tract positioning for singing. In these techniques, the singer practices methods of avoiding the flexible postures of speech in favor of a pre-set "ideal" uniform resonator coupling.

If the singer has been taught that the voice is best produced in a set mold of the mouth regardless of the vowel or the pitch to be sung, the relationships between larynx and vocal tract during a series of vowels will be drastically different than in a flexible system. In any case, if the conviction is that *one* basic ideal position for singing must be established, whether that position be the lateral [i] ("ee") buccal posture, as in the smile, or by an exaggerated [ɑ] ("ah") posture, as with the excessively lowered mandible, or with the rounded [ɔ] ("aw") shape, acoustic imbalances will exist between the laryngeally generated sound and the vocal-tract filtering system during any sequence of vowel sounds. In these narrow theories of voice production, the notion that *si canta come si parla* is patently rejected. The singing instrument, then, is built independently of the speech mechanism.

To some extent, historic schools of singing can be described by their varying attitudes toward the functional relationships between the speaking and the singing voices. Even the choice of vowels for vocalization purposes (the preference for back as opposed to front vowels, or the reverse, or the predilection for "mixed vowel" sounds) may be traced to the presence or absence of complex vowel formations in specific languages, as well as to aesthetic orientations regarding vocal coloration. These preferences are most telling in the extreme ranges, both upper and lower, of the singing voice.

It is doubtful that teachers in the historic international school ever looked for the establishment of identical postures between sung and spoken vowel formations in any except the lowest ranges of the singing voice. Rigid adherence to imitative buccal opening experienced in the speaking voice was probably never the intent of the admonition "to sing as one speaks." Assuredly, however, retention of the distended posture of the jaw, or of the rounded "pout" of the lips as is seen in some contemporary techniques of singing, cannot be in agreement with the early tenet *(si canta come si parla)* nor with what is currently known about the acoustic process of voiced communication. *Raccogliere la bocca* (to gather the mouth) is closely related to *si canta come si parla,* and is expressly intended as a counterbalance to too much vertical jaw and mouth action during singing; it does not refer to some general constant protrusion of the lips throughout the vowel series, as is claimed by persons who misunderstand the concept.

In the sequence of spoken vowels, from lateral to rounded (front to back) through the neutrals, the buccal posture progresses from lateral through rounded to more opened mouth shapes, the mouth being most opened on the [ɑ] ("ah"). As the level of breath energy increases, and as pitch and volume rise in the speaking voice, the mouth will open farther. In both speech and singing, as the scale mounts the mouth tends to open wider, although the integrity of the vowel should remain. This process is a major device for achieving desirable vowel modification in the upper register of the singing voice, for producing the even scale, and for augmenting volume.

Singing in the upper extremes of the voice will entail the same increase in buccal opening as will other forms of heightened voiced expression, for example, laughter or calling. However, to maintain in the middle and lower singing ranges the same open mouth (low mandibular) positions that are appropriate to the upper range has no more purpose than would such a posture have in the low and middle ranges of the speaking voice. (In singing the very lowest pitches that lie beneath fundamentals of the normal speech-inflection range, additional buccal opening is generally desirable.) Uniform vocal timbre throughout the scale is not achieved by maintaining one set buccal posture, or even something close to it, because vowel definition results from acoustic positions that alter with the changing shapes of vowels and with pitch and dynamic levels. Any "unification" of the vocal scale that avoids flexibility of vowel definition causes a common quality of distortion throughout the scale. If, as so often is the case, a singer experiences jaw tension because of a set mouth posture (generally with the jaw dropped too far in a "hung" or "dumb" position), momentarily lightly shifting the jaw in quick, brief lateral or circular movements will release the jaw from the fixed position. (Such lateral or circular movements are not then continued during speech or during singing, of course.)

To a large extent, with regard to vocal acoustics, the old adage *si canta come si parla* is confirmed by subsequent phonetic findings of the scientific age. That advice is not in opposition to the equally important dictum of the historic Italian School, *portare la voce* (carry the voice), on which the essential art of legato is premised. In a language free of diphthongization and with little percussive inflection, as is the case with Italian, the two historic concepts ("sing as you speak/carry the voice") are ideally wedded. In fact, legato singing is possible only when the enunciatory principle is economically realized (as in *raccogliere la bocca*).

It is possible to sing the many sounds of all Western languages with the same phonetic principles by which the Italian language can be managed. The high incidence of consonant clustering in some languages, specifically German, English, and some Eastern European languages, need not interfere with good vowel definition so long as transition sounds stemming from those consonantal events are avoided. (Good singers have already learned to eliminate regional speech habits from their singing.) Most transition sound is caused by inappropriate attempts to maintain a distended mouth posture or to preserve a fixated narrow buccal aperture (the opposite error). Clarity of timbre, clean diction, and legato line are then inevitably diverted.

Si canta come si parla continues to have important contemporary pedagogical application. The maxim stands in direct opposition to those techniques that endorse nonphonetic approaches to resonator adjustment for the singing voice.

16

How Singing Is *Not* Like Speaking

"Si canta come si parla" (one sings as one speaks); *"Chi pronuncia bene, canta bene"* (who enunciates well, sings well).

These adages have long been a part of the useful reservoir of pedagogical language. They embody the conviction that the mechanism of singing is not an entity separate from the mechanism of speech. They remind us that the supraglottic resonator system is a phonetic instrument that permits vowel definition, consonant formation, and general language perception. These functions are as necessary in singing as in speaking, and the same basic acoustic factors apply in song and in speech. Pathologies may inhibit articulation and phonetic exactitude in either spoken or sung phonations.

Phonetic distortion can be induced by interruption of the articulatory process through abnormal postures of tongue, jaw, lips, velum, or the zygomatic regions of the face. Much attention, then, in vocal pedagogy is directed toward recovering the phonetic postures of speech for the singing voice, through tracking the laryngeally produced vowel sound with the proper shape (largely mouth and pharynx) of the resonator tract.

It goes without saying that in any discussion of the relationship of the speaking voice to the singing voice, differences in regional and individual speech characteristics must be taken into account. The admonition "sing as you speak," even when restricted to the phonetic realm, can only have reference to phonetically accurate ("stage") diction, avoiding regional accents.

An essential fact, all too often overlooked, is that the requirements for singing far exceed the demands of speech. Singing is *not* simply sustained speech spun out over wide-ranging pitch fluctuations, except in the most simplistic and technically limited vocal styles. The tasks of singing introduce additional factors that the vocal pedagogue cannot ignore.

Defining the Vowel

In order to achieve textual communication, general mouth postures associated with specific vowels must be maintained in the singing voice, but the degree of jaw excursion depends on the *tessitura* in which the singer is operating. It is inappropriate to adopt some assumed "ideal" position of the jaw for singing. In mounting pitch, the mouth must open while a relationship to the phoneme as found in the speaking voice is retained. Holding the jaw in the same position while the scale mounts does not produce desirable resonance results in upper range. Further, to equalize vocal timbre throughout the great scale, vowel modification must take place. On the other hand, the assumption that the jaw must hang in a regurgitory position even in low and middle voice, but especially for all pitches above the *secondo passaggio,* is clearly detrimental to timbre, diction, and healthy function. (Vowel modification is an important agent in "covering," which prevents shrill or open singing in upper range.)

The Factor of Phonetic Duration

A major difference between speech and song lies in the *temporal* differences between them. Spoken language is made up of rapidly produced phonemes that fuse into each other through connecting transition sounds. In spoken language, especially in English and in German, the heavy preponderance of diphthongization negates the phonetician's "pure" vowel. During singing, by contrast, one vowel may be extended over several seconds in a single phonetic event. For this reason, the singer must direct attention to constancy of vowel definition for the duration of a sung syllable, and to an avoidance of transition maneuvers on the part of the articulatory mechanism (especially the tongue, the lips, and the jaw). In this regard, the singer cannot take literally the injunction to sing as one speaks.

The Intensity Factor

Energy is a catch-all pedagogical term for the changing levels of subglottic pressure and airflow required in elite singing. There are extreme differences with regard to breath management and dynamics between spoken and sung phonations. Ignoring these essential differences generally leads to *parlando* vocal techniques, and results in swags of syllables, to the detriment of vocal timbre and legato singing. Regions of increased acoustic strength evident in the spectra of a well-trained singing voice indicate that intensity factors also require technical means far beyond those for speech. Many problems singers encounter stem from a false conception that singing is nothing more than an extension of speech, and requires only the same degree of energy as speech.

Clearly, then, because (1) breath management must be of a higher order in singing than in speaking, (2) the duration of the vowel is dissimilar in speaking and singing, (3) the compass of the singing voice exceeds that of speech inflection, (4) sung sound requires adjustments of breath energy to meet the shifting demands of pitch and intensity, and (5) the aesthetics of artistic singing require "resonance balancing" beyond the needs of the speaking voice (even speech usage in the professional theater), only in a limited sense—largely phonetic—does one sing *"come si parla."*

17

Thinking Phonetically (Values and Pitfalls of the IPA)

At least during the singer's formative years, a great deal of technical work in the voice studio is directed toward changing the quality of sound. The supraglottic techniques for altering timbre are highly diverse.

Some vocal pedagogies maintain that there is one ideal position of the mouth and pharynx during singing, only minimally altered in changing vowels and *tessitura,* but they seldom agree as to how that is accomplished. For one group of teachers, that ideal position may be the lateral "smiling" posture of the mouth; for another group, the hung "idiot" jaw is the aim; for others, trumpeting of the lips in a kind of constant [œ] mouth posture; for certain teachers, a lowering of the upper lip to produce "focus" (or with some others, a tight covering of the lower teeth by the lower lip to accomplish the same "focus"); or in yet another system, raising and distending the upper lip to achieve the proper "resonance." All vowels are then produced, as much as possible, within one of these overall shapes of the resonator tract in the hope of achieving uniform timbre throughout the scale by means of a fixed vocal tract position, regardless of vowel or change of pitch. They are patently in opposition to each other.

None of these techniques represents the majority opinion within the voice-teaching profession. In contradistinction to these viewpoints, greater emphasis currently is placed on the phonetic relationships of the speaking and singing voices, and the acoustic formations of phonemes. This information is derived from modern-day linguistics and voice-therapy disciplines, sciences largely unknown (but often empirically understood) to teachers of singing in past eras. The number of recent publications that make use of the International Phonetic Alphabet for singers attests to an increasing interest. It is now rare to find singing teachers in major North American departments of music who ignore the valuable aids offered by the IPA in accomplishing greater language awareness and pronunciation accuracy. (This is not the case, generally, in Europe, where the IPA, despite its origins, remains basically unknown in the voice studio.)

However, the chief value for the singer in thinking phonetically is not in the improvement of language sounds but in the recognition that the

53

constantly changing postures of the vocal tract for vowel definition, represented by the IPA symbols, contribute directly to the timbre of the voice
and participate in producing what singers term a "resonant" voice.

The importance of recognizing acoustic formations, especially of the
vowels, is major to good vocal production. This is made evident when one
listens to the indiscriminate sounds of series of sung phonations when only
laryngeally generated sound is recorded independently of the resonator
system that lies above the glottis. The filtering effect of the supraglottal
resonator tract is dependent on the position of the organs of articulation:
the lips, the jaw, the tongue, the zygomatic region, the velum, and, of
course, the larynx as well.

The source of all voiced sound (as opposed to unvoiced) is laryngeal.
Speech recognition, however, depends on the changing shapes of the filtering resonator tract above the larynx. Students of singing, especially begin-
ners, are frequently concerned about what to do at the sound source itself.
They seek to produce sound by "making space" in the throat, by trying to
"open the throat," by pushing air over the vocal folds, or by other concepts meant to generate improved sound at the laryngeal level. Attempting
to exercise direct laryngeal controls in singing causes the articulatory
mechanism to malfunction. The buccopharyngeal (mouth/pharynx) resonator system is then seldom in tune with sounds generated at the level of
the larynx.

Use of the IPA symbols requires the singer to view "voice production"
in acoustic, not in laryngeal, terms. Such concentration removes attention
from the laryngeal vibrator itself, over which no direct local control is
possible (although the effects of conscious infra-laryngeal muscle actions
alter laryngeal function). The singer's attention is now directed to the resonation system, over which there is considerable conscious control.

If the singer, for example, knows with exactitude which vocal-tract
shapes produce acoustic events that accord with the cardinal vowels [i-e-
ɑ-o-u], that is, recognizes the proper positions of jaw, lips, and tongue, the
undesirable tendency to hold one static acoustic or laryngeal posture for
the changing events of the singing voice will be minimized. An intelligent
singer should be conscious of which vowels are frontal (in which the body
of the tongue is naturally somewhat elevated in the front of the mouth,
with a corresponding lateral mouth posture), and should be aware of
which are back vowels (body of the tongue at a lower posture in the front
but higher in the back, with mouth more rounded). In addition, the neutral
position of the vocal tract should also be identified. Postures of the tongue
and jaw as they relate to front, neutral, and back vowels should be recognized in technical study, especially with regard to their gradated positions.
General admonitions to a singer to open or close the mouth, without spe-

cific supporting information as to acoustic reasons, do not provide efficient pedagogical information. Of course, if a singer perfectly manages resonance balancing and vowel definition, one can forget all these technical niceties. How many of these singers are in our studios? Above all, it is clear that, as with all technical considerations, these comments pertain to the disciplined work needed to establish a well-functioning technique and are not things one thinks about during performance! The International Phonetic Alphabet can be of tremendous value in vocal pedagogy because it directs the mind and the ear phonetically. The teacher who scoffs at the need to incorporate such information most probably does not possess it and cannot therefore assess its efficacy; or perhaps she or he finds it threatening to cherished opinions.

However, IPA symbols must not be considered exact representations of comparative language sounds. For example, the symbol [ɪ] is used to describe the vowel sounds of "ich bin" as well as "it is," although they are far from identical. The symbol [e] is used to designated the phoneme in such disparate words as "chaotic" in English, "Seele" in German, "chanté" in French, and "seno" in Italian.

Further, the symbol [ɛ] represents "mai" in French, "bet" in English, "Bett" in German, and "petto" in Italian; yet contrary to many manuals on singing diction, there does not exist an exact uniformity of timbre among all of them. Similarly, [o] is the symbol used equally for "beau" in French, "goat" in English, "amore" in Italian, and "Tod" in German, although they are not identical. The cardinal symbols of the IPA system are not capable of showing these small gradations. (IPA duration symbols indicate varying temporal values.) The IPA symbol itself does not fine-tune these varying comparative language sounds. Slavish adherence to the IPA in the voice studio can be counterproductive. Skillful singers will need to make precise shades of differentiation among them.

18

A Parable of the Foolish Baker

A foolish baker sets about preparing an elegant cake for a special occasion. He carefully examines a number of cookbooks and chooses a recipe that appears to have had a long history of success. The ingredients are clearly spelled out; the baker selects only the very best for his batter, which he mixes with care. Then he pours the batter into his gleaming cake pan and places it in the oven. Bravo, baker!

The baker has every hope of realizing an excellent product. What a wonderful aroma it will send forth! How well-received his cake will be when placed before discriminating tasters! How exciting to receive the coveted baker-of-the-best-cake award! At the appointed time, the foolish baker removes the cake pan from the oven.

Anticipating his coming success, the baker prepares an excellent icing that he joyfully spreads over the surface of the cake. He fabricates lovely rosettes of delicate confection and arranges them artistically in fanciful designs on the surface. What a masterpiece of informed and sensitive cake-baking! Alas, foolish baker, in your dreaming of success, you forgot to turn up the oven temperature to the level indicated in your recipe!

The cake tasters now assemble, and the foolish baker readies himself to receive the prize. Each cake taster admires the highly embellished surface with its jewel-like appearance. Some tasters comment politely on the wise choice of ingredients and its surface appearance, but suggest that the cake is not yet "ready"; other critics, not schooled in the language of academia, brutally affirm that the product lacks substance and should not have been presented to professional judges in the first place.

Our poor baker, disillusioned by critical reaction to his performance, returns to his kitchen. Recall that he assumed he had found the best recipe and that he selected only the best ingredients. He has been led to believe that these ingredients were potentially of great merit. Further, he has long been convinced of his own discrimination in matters of taste. It can only follow, surely, that the appointed cake tasters were inadequately equipped to judge a good cake.

In time, the baker grows weary of explaining to himself and to others why he lost the contest and begins laboriously to review each step of his preparation. Suddenly, in a moment of objectivity, our baker recognizes that he forgot to heat the oven sufficiently.

The moral, dear reader, is that unless the singer learns to turn up the appropriate energy source in singing—"breath support"—it matters not at all how fine the basic vocal ingredients, the sensitive musicianship, the elegance of phrase or embellishment; the vocal cake will remain unpalatable to the professionally discriminating taste.

Much of the "coaching" in master classes devoted to interpretation and stylistic nuance is, unfortunately, often little more than placing icing and decoration upon an incompletely baked vocal cake. The energy source for singing must be properly applied to the mixture of talent, communication, and musicianship. Until the energy source and phonation are unified in the singing instrument, artistic gloss is meaningless. Until the breath machine and the vibratory machine operate as a unit, all else in the art of singing is mostly in vain.

A fine teacher is not one who begins by decorating and adorning the voice; a fine teacher of singing helps the singer *form* the voice so that it can be put to artistic purposes. The foundation of singing is concerned with the ability to manage the breath so that airflow precisely matches the needs of the vibrating larynx in response to articulatory demands.

To place an overlay of finesse on the unformed and uncoordinated vocal instrument is like decorating a poorly baked cake. Thoroughly bake the cake and firmly establish the substance of the voice before attempting to decorate either of them.

19

The Choral Conductor as Teacher of Vocal Technique

Choral music is vocal music. The most efficient vocalism, whether from the solo singer or from the chorister, produces the most aesthetically pleasing vocal timbre. There is a history of conflict in American academic circles between the training of the solo voice and what is expected of a singer in the choral ensemble. Such conflict need not exist.

An inherent problem for the solo singer is that early choral literature was not intended for solo voices. Most liturgical music was written to be performed not in concert halls and theaters, but in chapels, churches, abbeys, and cathedrals. The vocal demands of the early literature are not modest; its performers were clearly musicians of great skill. But the singers of complex early liturgical music were not expected to give solo recitals in which the unique timbre of the individual voice is valued. The vocal performance major of today's conservatories and schools of music experiences different demands than did the singer of Josquin, Palestrina, or Gesualdo.

The large choral works of the late eighteenth and nineteenth centuries generally call for a quartet of soloists. Nevertheless, the vocal demands for the choristers, who are often amateur singers, may equal the tasks assigned the solo voices. It is clear that the *tessitura* requirements for the soprano choristers in the Bach B Minor Mass or the Beethoven Ninth Symphony go beyond what is requested in many operatic roles. Nonetheless, it is not the symphonic choral literature that causes the chief difficulty for the solo singer, since in that repertory the singer is called on to produce an energized vocal sound to match the orchestral sonority. It is the traditional choral literature, in which voices are expected to "blend" at all *tessitura* and dynamic levels, that most young solo voices find problematic.

Further, there is a problem for vocal performance majors when they are mixed in ensembles with singers of limited vocal resources. Published literature on the care of the professional voice makes a fallacious assumption about the dangers of choral singing when it states that vocal abuse results from attempting to sing as loudly as the person next to you "in order to hear yourself." In point of fact, for the voice major or the professional singer, the threat to vocal health in choral singing lies not in decibel competition but in attempting to submerge the voice into the surrounding bland sound.

Each vocal instrument has its own unique timbre characteristics. The answer for the choral conductor is not to make solo singers emulate the technical level of amateur voices but to work for a more efficient production from the less proficient singers. There cannot be one vocal timbre that encompasses the entire group, unless the choristers are imitating a single vocal model, thereby falsifying their own voices. As Robert Shaw has publicly stated on occasion, it is as illogical for the choral conductor to demand one vocal quality from all categories of voices as for the orchestral conductor to request that all instruments have the same timbre. Balancing voices is far better choral technique than is the unrealizable goal of trying to blend them. A complete choral sound can be achieved only when the singers within the ensemble use their voices efficiently. It is the duty of the choir director to teach the choristers how to become efficient singers, so that they will profit from, and not be injured by, the musical demands placed on them, and so that the quality of sound from the ensemble is of the highest possible order.

If the premise is accepted that choral music is vocal music, the qualifications required of a choral director must be addressed. Is it sufficient to be a good musician, have leadership qualities, possess skills as an organist or pianist, or to be musicologically well informed? It is not necessary to be a professional singer in order to be a fine teacher of singing, but it *is* necessary that one achieve a good level of technical proficiency with one's own instrument. Similarly, it is not necessary for the choir director to be a performing singer, but he or she should be able to lead choristers to improved vocal proficiency. Dealing solely in musical matters will not accomplish that goal. The traditional voice class requirement in most Music Education curricula is insufficient vocal training for a prospective choral director.

Teaching Voice in the Choral Rehearsal

Assuming the choral conductor is properly prepared to work with singers, how can vocal technique be taught in an ensemble situation? Most choir directors do not have time to give private voice lessons to each member of the choral ensemble. Still, much can be accomplished through group instruction by using a brief program in vocal techniques before beginning rehearsal of the literature. These sessions should consist of exercises that, through systematic application, develop good habits in the three main areas of vocal technique: (1) breath management (vocal onset, release, and breath renewal), (2) free laryngeal function (efficient coordination of breath with tone), and (3) resonance balancing (desirable relationships among the harmonic partials).

Onset (often termed "attack") vocalises can be found in every vocalization system of the nineteenth century and in some recent pedagogical publications as well. Silent inhalation precedes each brief onset, which begins with a vibrant tone accurately centered on pitch. The conclusion of this phonation coincides with the immediate quiet renewal of the breath. This ensures that at the cessation of each sound, the vocal folds part and the breath is replenished in a synergistic manner. Then the onset cycle is repeated. Crucial to the maintenance of vocal freedom through the duration of the phonation is the manner in which a singer onsets the vocal sound.

Choristers sing the onset exercises based on standard harmonic chordal progressions such as the traditional I-IV-V-I series, over a two-measure phrase consisting of a measure of four quarter notes followed by a sustained whole-note measure, beginning with the tempo marking ♩ = M.M. 60 (Figure 1). These exercises begin in lower-middle range and progress through several neighboring keys to upper-middle range, using alternate

Figure 1

(any vowel)

Figure 2

series of cardinal vowels. Through this onset procedure the singer induces subconscious activity that produces healthy vocal-fold approximation (neither pressed nor breathy), ensures efficient breath management, and establishes a proper resonance balance.

Such onset exercises, being gradually elongated, can vary in duration. Combinations of short and sustained phonations prove beneficial. Four to five minutes of each session devoted to onsetting trains the singer in initiating free vocal sound and in sustaining well-balanced tone without an early rib-cage collapse. Repetition of these exercises strengthens the musculature of the anterolateral abdominal wall.

Several additional minutes of technical work should be given over to brief agility exercises. These begin as short patterns imitative of quiet laughter, progress to short staccato patterns (5-4-3-2-1), subsequently developing into articulated legato passages in ranges of easy execution (Figure 2).

In all onset, agility, and *sostenuto* exercises, the abdominal wall, although flexible while articulating the laughter-like impulses, remains stable. The singer neither pulls inward nor presses outward at the moment of onset. On notes of short duration, there is minimal change in the abdominal wall from the initial inspiratory position. During sustained phonation, the position of inspiration is maintained until just before the termination of the phrase. This technique of breath management is termed the *appoggio*. Its origins are in the historic Italian School, and it has long been the major breath-management system of international professional vocalism. These group exercises circumvent complicated and time-consuming explanations about breath support, and they avoid nonproductive techniques for "controlling the breath."

Another type of short exercise for groups of singers is directed toward vowel definition. Many of the tuning problems in choral ensembles are the consequence of the singers' inability to clearly differentiate vowels. As an instrument that obeys the laws of acoustics, the resonator tract must assume positions that accurately define lateral (front) and rounded (back) vowels. Choristers sometimes hold the naïve assumption (not physiologically supportable) that opening the mouth by dropping the jaw opens the throat and provides additional space for the emission of sound. Pharyngeal space, however, is not geared to increased buccal room; the pharynx can be equally spacious whether breath is inhaled through the nose with the mouth closed or through an open mouth position. In fact, dropping the jaw tends to narrow the pharynx. The result of the false acoustic premise is distortion of vowels and vocal timbre.

Choristers as well as solo singers need to learn to "track the vowel" by changing the shapes of the vocal tract (including the lips, tongue, mouth, and jaw) to correspond to the targeted vowel. Each vowel has its own laryngeal configuration, and there is a corresponding vocal tract configuration that permits a specific vowel to take on its distinctive form. It is false to assume that there is a single ideal position of the mouth and jaw for singing. The vocal tract (which extends from the vocal folds to the lip bastion, and whose shape depends on positions of the lips, the jaw, the tongue, the velum, the zygomatic arch, and the larynx) serves as filter to the laryngeal sound. Unlike that of some other instruments, the resonator tract of the voice is not fixed, but rather is a flexible system that assumes physical shapes in response to phonetic requirements. It is not the absolute dimensions of either of the chief resonators (the mouth and the pharynx) that produce ideal acoustic conditions for singing. The particular vowel, the *tessitura,* and the intensity determine the degree of jaw opening.

A few vowel differentiation exercises, executed individually or in groups, first slowly, then quickly, bring about an awareness of how vowels can be changed without loss of the consistency necessary to produce a fully resonant vocal timbre. This consistency of timbre can be maintained only if the resonator tract (largely the mouth and the pharynx) is permitted to assume shapes that "track" the laryngeally generated vowel. It is the ability to change the shapes of the resonator tract that allows vocal timbre to remain constant when vowels are differentiated.

One way to accomplish good vowel definition in singing is to choose a sequence of vowels on one pitch, beginning with a lateral vowel, proceeding to a rounded vowel, and then returning to the original lateral vowel posture. An [i-e-ɑ-e-i] sequence (ee-ay-ah-ay-ee) is an example. Once they reach the [ɑ] vowel, many singers have a tendency to retain the more open mouth position appropriate to that central vowel, so that the subsequent [e] and [i] vowels do not match the earlier [i] and [e] vocal tract postures; those vowels are then distorted. This exercise can be done in several neighboring keys; then the reverse vowel sequence is sung: [ɑ-e-i-e-ɑ] (ah-ay-ee-ay-ah). Other combinations of lateral and rounded vowels may be introduced.

A brief exercise making use of alternating lateral and rounded vowels on changing pitch is also beneficial in teaching good vowel definition. A typical device built on a 1-3-2-4-3-5-4-2-1 pattern, uses an [e-ɔ-e-ɔ-e-ɔ-e-ɔ-e] (ay-aw) sequence. The pattern is then reversed with an [ɔ-e-ɔ-e-ɔ-e-ɔ-

Figure 3

Figure 4

Figure 5

e-ɔ] (aw-ay) vowel sequence (Figure 3). Some singers, particularly if they have been told to drop the jaw in the hope of opening the throat to "let the sound out," will retain the same jaw position for both the lateral and rounded vowels, thereby producing vowel and timbre distortion. What was intended as a means for achieving a common quality of vocal resonance despite vowel changes actually becomes the culprit in preventing consistency.

When the ears of the conductor and those of the choristers recognize that clean vowel definition has been established on two vowels—one lateral and one rounded—then a sequence of changing vowels, as in [ɑ-o-i-o-e] (ah-oh-ee-oh-ay) on a 1-3-5-3-1 pattern is introduced. When these vowels can be cleanly differentiated so that no timbre distortion is involved in vowel change, a second combination of vowel changes is introduced, as in [i-o-ɑ-o-e] (ee-oh-ah-oh-ay). These patterns are then sung in neighboring tonalities, moving by half-step, first slowly, then more rapidly. The exercise can also be extended over a longer arpeggio pattern, such as 1-3-5-8-5-3-1 (Figure 4) or a broken-arpeggio pattern, such as 3-1-5-3-8-5-3-5-1 (Figure 5), once again alternating the sequence of the vowel patterns so that sometimes a lateral vowel is the top note of the arpeggio, and at other times a rounded vowel.

Four-part harmony on I-IV-V-I can now be applied to vowel changes—[i-e-ɑ-e-i] and [ɑ-e-i-e-ɑ], for example—with careful attention given to the tracking of vowels and to intonation. These exercises are beneficial in developing the choristers' perception of vowel tracking and resonance balancing.

An even vibrato, the result of relaxant laryngeal function, is an inherent characteristic of freely produced vocal sound. Choral singers should not be requested to remove vibrancy from their voices in the hope of blending them with nonvibrant voices. Rather, the conductor should assist the non-vibrant amateur, through onset and agility exercises, to induce the natural vibrancy of the coordinated singing instrument. Properly produced vibrant voices can be balanced even more readily than can nonvibrant voices. Of course, if voices in the ensemble suffer from oscillation (too wide and too slow a pitch variant, less kindly termed "wobble"), or from a tremolo (too narrow and too swift a vibrato rate), voices will not balance. Additional private technical work with those singers may be necessary.

For every choral director, musical accuracy has to be a major priority. Training the choir to sing accurately requires time. It may seem difficult to reserve fifteen minutes of each rehearsal period to the teaching of vocal technique. Most choral conductors, however, use warm-up exercises with the choir. The systematic technique exercises suggested here could be part of that warm-up process. Improvement in intonation, attacks and releases, breath management, dynamic control, and, above all, basic choral sound, will make such an investment of time pay off handsomely. The solo singer will no longer be an alien member of the ensemble.

20

The Law of Contingency and Vocal Pedagogies

It is rabbit season. An avid hunter dresses in the early dawn, takes his rifle in hand, and drives into the countryside, where he knows there is an ideal location for his potential prey. At the same moment, a country lover takes a last look in the mirror before setting out across the field on a shortcut to the nearest village, where he intends to meet his girlfriend for a wonder-ful day of togetherness. As fate would have it, a rabbit soon thereafter hops out of his warren, and begins a search for succulent nibbling mate-rials.

Unknown to both the rabbit and the hunter, our young lover chooses a path through the very field where the hunter spies the rabbit. Hunter takes aim and fires just as the amorous young man crosses the trajectory of the bullet. Fortunately for the rabbit, but not so for the lover, the buckshot grazes the latter's buttocks. The rabbit runs back into hiding, the young man is transported by the chagrined hunter to the local clinic for the treatment of a superficial wound, and the plans for at least one day in the lives of several inhabitants of village and meadow have been drastically altered by the law of contingency. The rabbit's salvation depended on the contingency of the early morning hurry of a young lover and on an overly eager hunter. The law of contingency required that the young man be shot in the backside because he happened by chance to have placed that part of his anatomy in the wrong place at the wrong moment.

So it is with much of what the singer has encountered in the way of vocal instruction. He or she gets shot by the particular bullet of vocal pedagogy that comes winging that way. A number of other bullets could have reached the same target, but it just happened that teacher *A* and student *B* were in the same pedagogical firing range at the same juncture, and the law of contingency was operative. A different set of circumstances would have demanded another set of allegiances. Inasmuch as the pedagogical technical ammunition is highly diverse—it might even be suggested that some of it is less lethal than some others—an intelligent singer will not simply accept the vocal ideas with which he or she was injected at a moment when circumstances brought a teacher and a singer together. Whatever one has been taught (shot with, if we may be permitted to continue our analogy) should be examined by the rules of efficient function as regards both acoustic and physiologic fact, not by mythological assumptions. Many singers continue to attempt coordinations that are not possible because they do not examine the validity of concepts they have encountered. Sometimes the inability of a singer to pursue a productive career results from a continuing loyalty to an old shot of vocal pedagogy that chanced to land on an unsuspecting target. Reexamination is in order.

21

To Admire or to Teach?

Singers feel the need to communicate emotions and to express dramatic and musical ideas through vocal sound. Despite the frustrations that at times accompany performance, a good singer should love to sing publicly.

The successful exhibition of skill brings tremendous satisfaction, and the exhilaration of reaching and holding listeners is an important performance reward. Singers like being admired. The public gratifies that desire.

The singer then leaves the special aura of public performance and comes to the voice studio, where objectivity ought to prevail. Good singers are confident persons and need to be aware of their artistic uniqueness. They also must be taught.

The teacher of singing is not in the position of members of an audience, who as nonspecialists may be able to distinguish between very good and very bad, but who do not have the ability to differentiate between what is very good and what is truly excellent. By the nature of his professional function, the teacher is placed in the role of discerning critic, no matter what the level of the student. One of the delicate duties of teaching is to find the right balance between letting the singer know what already is admirable and diagnosing what is in need of correction. This task is easier when the singer is a secure and objective person. (Objectivity is an indication of personal and artistic maturity.)

Keeping a necessary balance between correction and encouragement is often particularly difficult with advanced students who have not yet fully reached a professional level. A voice teacher at a major school of music once described her first lesson with a talented graduate transfer student: The first corrective suggestion was met with a look of slight puzzlement but with a polite, "Oh, I see! Thank you for pointing that out to me." The second suggestion received a less warmly expressed "Thank you." The third interruption drew an irritable "Well, just what seems to be the problem?" Plainly, the singer had grown accustomed to admiration rather than instruction.

Every fine teacher is aware of the need to build the student's confidence, but to choose the easy route of making the student feel good all the time instead of the route of analysis and correction is not only nonproductive but involves a question of ethics. Committed teachers are not hesitant to tell students what is wrong. They must also point out what would be better and indicate how best to accomplish it. When the plumber is called in, he is not expected to admire the bathroom fixtures but to repair them. The student is a consumer who is looking for help in achieving a product that will function well and permit artistic freedom. Students do not make studio changes because of objective criticism. The teacher who hesitates to criticize for fear of losing students frequently loses them.

Teachers must be free to teach what they know to teach. The teacher who thinks that the student must always be happy and contented on leaving the lesson has the wrong priorities. The chief aim of a teacher of singing is not to make the student momentarily happy but to provide instruction that makes future admiration possible.

Of course, criticism unaccompanied by proposed solutions can be harmful. It is equally bad pedagogy to assume that problems will disappear if only the teacher is positive and enthusiastic and has a wonderful personal rapport with the student. Although desirable, a fine personal relationship between teacher and student does not substitute for good instruction. The student is not paying for friendship. Approval where appropriate is absolutely essential, but unless teacher can pinpoint what is lacking and can offer corrective suggestions, no instruction has taken place.

Further, it is immoral to charge high fees for lessons that are little more than socially enjoyable encounters during which a few commonplace musical suggestions are made. Despite the desire to be admired, intelligent singers at all levels of accomplishment recognize that they have imperfections (although they do not want them to be publicly known). They want those imperfections removed. However, at first the singer may be hesitant to have problems identified, somewhat embarrassed by them, and unhappy that such faults are apparent to another ear. (Singers often hope that what they know doesn't work well will not be audible to the listener, even to the teacher.) But when a teacher/student team effort is directed toward working out solutions together, there is no resentment, unless the student is so prideful as to be unteachable.

The most successful teachers are those who, as well as building a sympathetic relationship with a student, insist on teaching, not on flattering. A rubric of fine teaching ought to be: "Although an important part of my job is to let you know what you accomplish very well, my chief job is to teach, not to admire." It sets the right tone for both student and teacher in their necessarily distinct professional roles as they work together toward better vocalism.

22

Patching the Vocal Garment

It is a privilege to begin working from the ground up with a vocal student. Many times a singer arrives already having studied for a number of years with several other teachers, and in the process has encountered conflicting technical viewpoints. As a result, the singer comes into the studio with vocal concepts and technical solutions not in accord with the pedagogical aims of the new teacher.

In the academic structure of music degrees, the new student may hope to complete a particular program with its required public performances within some designated period of time regardless of the actual state of technique or of current performance level. It is little wonder that at times the new teacher, particularly at the graduate level, feels reduced to patching up a frayed vocal garment. Quick repairs, sartorial or vocal, are often dictated by necessity. Patching is seldom an effective way of ensuring either the beauty or the longevity of a garment.

We can sympathize with the vocal tailor who must repair an imperfect phonatory garment placed in his or her hands so that it can quickly be respectably worn in required performance circumstances. Too often, however, the results of imaginative restoration techniques are heard in public places, consisting of a patch of "cover" here, a stitch of "placement imagery" for this or that area of the voice, a thread or two of "breath mixture" for musical or interpretative effect, some mending tape of muscular push or pull for "support," or perhaps an overall dyeing of timbre change for "vocal coloration." Corrective patching on one segment of the voice is then often unrelated to other parts of the vocal garment. This "patching up" may become the chief characteristic of the performance sound.

As surely as has any whole piece of fine cloth, the professional singing voice has its own warp and its own weft. The physiologic warp of the vocal instrument, and the weft of vocal acoustical phenomena compose the weave of skillful vocal sound. Honest vocal technique develops from the systematic interweaving of physiologic and acoustic factors.

Even the teacher who deals only briefly with a new student (a year, a year and a half, or two years) must have the fortitude to replace the tangled strands of inept vocalism (threads of habit and false function) with the warp and weft of functionally coordinated vocalism. If not, the result will be a vocal garment exhibiting holes. Patching fundamental errors of vocalism with compensatory threads of colorful imagery only prevents the correction of basic flaws found in a garment that must be publicly worn and publicly judged on its ability to function freely.

No amount of attention to the concerns of audience communication, dramatic interpretation, linguistic exactitude, and artistry and musicianship can mask the faulty weave in the vocal instrument, any more than the addition of red and yellow ribbons can disguise a threadbare coat. A sagacious vocal tailor (the teacher of singing) will make sure that the correct weave serves as the singer's foundation at any level of development, or within any allotted span of time.

23

Mysteries and Miracles

In response to a friend's question about how her voice lessons are going, a young soprano replies, "It's hard to tell, because my teacher uses what he calls 'mystery' techniques that he says will produce miracles." She goes on to say that her teacher understands her voice and the direction in which she is to go, and that he is leading her there without engaging in troubling explanations that would interfere with her artistry. In fact, he says he does not want her to understand the process; she must simply trust in its final outcome. In the sessions, this well-known teacher listens to the student sing, then offers a series of descriptive images to help achieve desired changes.

Does this work? Has the soprano made improvement? Sometimes during lessons new and interesting sounds come about, but she is never certain as to why. She finds it difficult to remember how to reproduce them by herself when outside the studio.

Another teacher of national reputation has a rule that no colleagues may attend lessons. She explains that the reason for excluding all visitors is that her lessons consist of a one-to-one search for the creation of vocal transformation based on a personal, mystical interaction with each student—almost an alchemic happening—which can take place only when teacher and student are alone together. She "unlocks" the personality before her so that artistic impulses can be experienced.

Miracles are, of course, an abrogation of the laws of nature. They cannot be explained through natural causes or processes. Although artistic singing is creative and depends upon imagination, the voice is a physical instrument. Skillful singing depends not on mysterious maneuvers that are magically elicited through Svengalian influences, but rather on repeatable maneuvers that permit artistic imagination to emerge. (The manner in which an artistic personality brings together art and technique remains as mysterious as do the workings of the brain itself.)

The presence of an audience, and the excitement generated by performance circumstances, can at times enhance coordination to the improvement of vocal sound (or inhibit it!). There is, indeed, a kind of magic that surrounds an excellent performance; performer and listener experience a mysterious unity. This is not a chance coming together of artistic, physical, and acoustic factors; it is the result of coordinating technical, musical, and emotional elements in preparation for the tasks of performance. Mysteries and miracles are not the source of performance enhancement.

The teacher who believes he or she is dealing in secret discoveries regarding the technical aspects of singing reveals a lack of information about the voice as an instrument, and knows little of comparative vocal pedagogy. The vocal thaumaturge may occasionally inadvertently stumble upon a physical coordination for the student that appears miraculous because it happens to correspond to good function. That function is neither mysterious nor miraculous beyond the inherent mystery of human communication. Teaching based on mysteries and miracles is at best "hit and miss" teaching. Vocal and psychological tricks do not produce dependable vocal technique. Skillful function does.

Who has the right to substitute mystery instruction for information? (Is the miracle-worker pedagogue free of charlatanism?) In the teaching of singing there is no room for the vocal magician, for technical sleight of hand, for personal cunning. Each of us as teachers is imaginative, and we bring our personal strengths and experience to our teaching; in that regard, we all participate in the magic and the mystery of human contact. We should not, however, assume that we, as opposed to our colleagues, therefore possess a magic key that unlocks vocal mysteries.

It is essential to keep in mind that it is not necessary for the teacher to use precise anatomical or scientific terminology in teaching good vocal function unless the student is versed in such language. What *is* essential is that the teacher's methodology be based on an understanding of how the voice behaves as an acoustical and as a physical instrument. The belief that teaching the singer anatomically correct names of muscles of the human body will improve vocal sound is, of course, patently absurd. The singer should, however, be provided with an understanding of the coordination that occurs within the human musculoskeletal and respiratory systems so that he or she does not ask the body to perform nonfunctional tasks. Most importantly, the singer's teacher should not invent physiology and acoustics in the belief that he or she is dealing in mysteries and miracles.

For each individual, any singing sound that differs from any other singing sound ultimately depends upon a physiologic or acoustic change. The guru teacher of singing who depends on "magical powers" in a student/ teacher relationship occupies questionable pedagogical territory. Miracles and mysteries are not part of communicable pedagogy.

24

The Flat-Earth School of Vocal Pedagogy

Seeing is believing. We know what the physical world around us looks like. We have the right to expect it to behave in certain ways we have previously experienced. By now, however, most of us recognize that things in the natural world are not always exactly as they seem. Looking up at the sky on a cloudless night, we see a vast field of stars which, despite their actual immensity, appear to us as small glittering objects. At times the full moon seems relatively large and calls to mind that childhood family game in which each person describes how the moon looks to him or her. Is it the size of the washtub? As large as a basketball? A baseball? About as big as a dinner plate?

In similar experiential fashion, a young child makes his first trip to the seashore. He is convinced that the horizon represents a termination of the earth, and he assumes that the water, therefore, must be tumbling over the horizon in a huge waterfall. The sun also clearly goes down behind the earth as dusk falls. Based on his powers of observation, his assumptions are entirely logical. The boy is unable to accept his father's assurance that the evidence of the senses cannot always be trusted. "But I *see* that there is an edge to the water where it must fall off the earth, and each evening I *see* the sun fall down behind it!" It will take a few years for the youngster to understand that what one thinks one is seeing is not necessarily so; that what one observes and senses must be filtered through information that is not perceptually discernible.

Illusion, of course, is an important part of artistic representation. The graphic artist may capture the surrounding world in either a literal or a symbolic fashion. Even representational depiction does not literally rely on what is seen but on what is known about how distance and light affect the appearance of an object. Following the rules of perspective or ignoring them for creative purposes makes up much of the visual artist's craft; whether adhered to or ignored, the rules must be understood and mastered.

Theories of voice production that are dependent upon what *appears* to be logical do not always have a basis in physical fact. Many of them are familiar concepts, deeply ingrained in the language of some vocal pedagogies. The more familiar ones follow:

1. Control the breath by holding the diaphragm firmly in one position.
2. Pull in on the abdominal wall so that the diaphragm will stay longer in one place.
3. Pull in on the diaphragm to give "support" for the high notes.
4. Push out on the abdominal wall in order to keep the diaphragm low.
5. Push *down* on the diaphragm for high notes and pull the diaphragm up for low notes.
6. Drop the chest to avoid high-chest breathing.
7. Hold the breath during long phrases, in order to save it.
8. Place the tone on a flowing column of breath that is sent from the lower abdominal regions up to the larynx.
9. Tilt the pelvis forward, move the buttocks inward to straighten the spine, drop the chest, and squeeze the anal sphincter for good support on the high notes.
10. Think of childbirth or difficult defecation when you sing high-lying phrases at high intensity.
11. Involve your sex organs for extra support on high notes.
12. Concentrate on the center of the forehead so that the tone will be placed "up and over."
13. Lift the head and chin to "free the larynx."
14. Pout or trumpet the lips on all vowels to ensure uniform vocal color.
15. Pull down the upper lip (covering the upper teeth) to "focus" the tone.
16. Flare the nostrils to "open the throat" and to increase the resonance of the voice.
17. Cover the bottom teeth with the lower lip to "focus" the tone.
18. Hold the mouth in one position, like a mold, while moving only the tongue, thereby achieving uniform timbre through all the vowels.
19. To open the throat, open wide the mouth by dropping the mandible in the "idiot jaw" position.
20. Place half a cork between the molars, or insert two fingers (or three) in the mouth, to make certain the jaw drops in order to open the throat and to assist in maintaining the "dumb jaw" posture.
21. Imagine a grapefruit in your throat in order to keep it open.
22. Make a spacious cavity at the back of the mouth and in the throat

by pulling the velum upward while at the same time dropping the jaw.

23. Make space in the throat ("open it") by spreading the muscles under the jaw, at either side of the larynx
24. Inhale with a noisy sound, as in snoring, to be sure you can hear the throat open.
25. Wrinkle the forehead upward on inspiration as an aid in opening the throat and placing the tone.
26. Place the tone in the frontal sinuses; they are the chief places of forward resonance.
27. Make all the vowels the same size as the vowel [i] ("ee") so that they can go into the narrow sinuses above the eyebrows.
28. Maintain the [ɑ] position while singing, regardless of the vowel.
29. Throw the sound to the back of the hall.
30. Send the tone down the spine.

All of the above examples are taken from pedagogic sources, oral and printed; most are familiar to singers and teachers of singing. These technical maneuvers hold place in some pedagogies because they seem as though they ought to be true. Their "truth" is in line with what surface observation of the physical world around us might suggest. However, they are not what they seem.

The singing instrument is the entire body, not just the larynx, and is subject to investigative study as is any functioning instrument. The function of the vocal instrument can, in many respects, be measured and accurately tracked. In some quarters it is still felt that factual examination of the singing art should be strenuously resisted because it might undermine artistic impulses. On the contrary, factual information in no way hinders artistic imagination.

False information expressed in the linguistic garb of imaginative physiologic or acoustic imagery inhibits good function and is probably the major source of vocal problems among singers. Faulty singing more often than not is the result of attempts to achieve the physical and acoustical impossible.

Much vocal instruction is patently destructive. Many premier singers are very skeptical of any vocal instruction because they themselves, in order to find the functional aspects of the singing voice that permit freedom in production, have had to jettison much of what they were taught by "flat-earth teachers."

Why similar morphological and laryngeal constructions produce a great singer in one case and a mediocre one in another, although both sing technically well, always remains inexplicable, just as does the nature of human individuality itself. No amount of investigative study can unveil the psychological mysteries that lie behind the production of beautiful timbre and the accomplishment of artistic communication. However, unless the physical instrument can freely function, artistry will suffer built-in limitations.

Most singers attempt to make the body work the way they have been taught that it works. Singers and teachers should not confuse artistic imagination with factual information. Now that the little boy has grown older and has learned that the ocean does not fall off at the horizon and that the sun does not fall into the sea each evening (which even some sophisticated ancient Greeks and Romans tended to believe), he is just as able as before to enjoy the remarkable beauty of seaside sunsets. In fact, appreciation of the beauties of an orderly physical universe enhances his aesthetic response to them.

The above pedagogical admonitions (all taken from recognizable pedagogical sources, it should be reiterated) can be divided into those that deal with breath management, those that affect laryngeal function, and those that adjust the resonator tract above the larynx.

In the first instance, with great frequency the diaphragm is assigned duties that it could perform only under conditions that are not physiologically possible. In some of the above pedagogical admonitions, the diaphragm's inspiratory and expiratory functions—even its actual location—are confused. For example, if a student is asked to commence expiratory abdominal actions during the inspiratory phase of the breath cycle, lung volume will be diminished even before phonation takes place. The limited participation of the diaphragm (although it is not totally passive) in the expiratory phase of the breath cycle is often not recognized, and many attempts to *locally* control the diaphragm result in a more quickly rising subglottic pressure, faster exit of breath, or loss of appropriate antagonism among muscle groups of the torso. Dropping the chest causes the sternum to fall and the rib cage to collapse. Yet probably some 50 percent of identifiable vocal pedagogies are built on false physiologic assumptions about diaphragmatic/chest wall action. Professional singers generally manage to sing despite what they have been taught by us their teachers!

With regard to resonator adjustment, the unhinged jaw (the idiot jaw) may look as though it should open the throat, when in fact the pharynx is almost inevitably narrowed when the jaw is dropped. There is more space in the pharynx on the lateral vowel [i], for example, than in the more perpendicular, rounded vowel [a]. It is the vowel, the pitch level, and the degree of intensity that dictate mouth postures, not some absolute fixed dimension of either the buccal or pharyngeal resonators. Holding the lips or the mouth in some one "ideal" position for singing (such as "the mouth stays open, only the tongue moves") is phonetically and acoustically inefficient. Maintaining one "ideal" position of the mouth for singing can only cause distortion in vowels, because such a fixed resonator position does not correspond to configurations essential to vowel definition, and interferes with phonetic vowel tracking. Flaring the nostrils cannot increase resonance on any phoneme, because the nasal cavity is a nonparticipant in the non-nasal sounds produced by the nonpathological speaking voice and by the singing voice; nasality is the result of low velar posture and is not chiefly dependent on nares action. The notion that tone is a substance that can be placed in imaginary resonance spaces in certain regions of the head, or in sinuses that do not contribute to resonance, has produced a remarkable number of opposing pedagogies. (Sensation, experienced by sympathetic vibration via bone conduction, is quite another matter.) Lifting the head and elevating the chin shortens the vocal tract, raises the larynx, and produces infra-laryngeal tensions. The velum can be raised only to the extent to which faucial elevation and velopharyngeal closure reach their physical boundaries; many attempts at opening the throat and increasing buccopharyngeal space result in pharyngeal tension or in the spreading of the external musculature of the submandibular region.

Perhaps the chief reason for learning how the singing instrument functions is to avoid technical faults that arise from false assumptions. Many technical errors in singing have their origins in pedagogical misconceptions as to what happens physically and acoustically in the singing voice. Most studio time is spent in correcting malfunctions based on such false premises. Vocal pedagogy, as with any discipline, needs to be founded on verifiable information. Historically, the great teachers of singing made full use of all information then available. Should the modern-day teacher do less? It requires time to acquire a body of factual information, but we will then have the assurance that what we demand of the student is based on truth, not on theories of function unknown to the rest of mankind.

Theories about how the body performs form the basis of practically every voice lesson. It is foolish to hold to cherished "flat-earth" assumptions that disturb the coordinated function essential to artistic communication in singing. Given the diversity of technical assumptions, the singer often has to sort through a great deal of conflicting advice about how best to sing. Surely there is no better way to decide what technical advice he or she will follow than by measuring it against that which is functionally most efficient. It comes down to this: what works most efficiently physically and acoustically in the singing voice produces the aesthetic result that is most acceptable to the largest number of listeners, and that ensures vocal health. "Flat-earthing" is no longer a viable way to teach singing.

25

Sharpening Up Some
Old Pedagogical Saws

A number of expressions in vocal pedagogy can be placed under the heading "old saws." *Saw* is a Middle English word that is related etymologically to the modern English word *say* (from the original Germanic *sage*). It has come to mean a saying, a maxim, a proverb, a dictate, or a command; an old saw expresses conventional wisdom.

Old voice-teaching saws exist because they embody concepts held essential or useful to accomplishing the tasks of singing. Many have been around for a long time; some are more recent. Almost all describe sensations experienced by singers or are based on physical actions that look as if they ought to work. Some are useful; some are harmless. Others induce malfunction of the vocal instrument.

Using what is, I hope, a forgivable play on words, may I suggest that if these latter saws cannot be eradicated, they can at least be sharpened up. Some old saws are such a part of the pedagogical language that it is as doubtful the vocal landscape will become free of them as that the front lawn will be rid of dandelions, no matter how hard you dig to remove either.

Consideration of a comprehensive list is prohibited here by space and time, but it may be useful to think about some of the more hardy varieties of old saw that continue to reseed themselves in the pedagogical garden despite all attempts to weed them out. These old saws can mostly be classified into three groups that correspond to the three parts of the singing instrument itself: (1) breath coordination; (2) laryngeal activity; and (3) factors of resonation. First, a few saws related to breath management, or "support," come to mind.

Breath Management

Support the Voice with the Diaphragm

The role assigned the diaphragm in some old saws does not correspond to the diaphragm's actual function, and has little relationship to the reduced role it plays following the inspiratory portion of the breath cycle. The diaphragm has been subjected to imaginative, erroneous physiological assumptions on which entire systems of breath management for singing have been constructed.

The admonition "support from the diaphragm" (or "sing from the diaphragm") may induce certain desirable activities in the torso among muscle groups that play some role in managing the breath for singing, but this old saw is mostly based on misinformation as to the location and action of the diaphragm. The diaphragm is sometimes mysteriously located in the lower torso. The singer then may be told that the diaphragm ascends (or descends) for high notes, or, alternately, that it ascends (or descends) for low notes; that the diaphragm can be held in one position by pulling inward on the lower abdominal wall (or, in other systems, by pushing outward on the abdominal wall); that it can be "filled with air"; and, above all, that it "supports the voice."

Clearly, the diaphragm and the intercostals are major actors in respiration, but much of what is assumed to be the work of the diaphragm during sustained singing is caused by concerted actions involving muscle groups of the anterolateral abdominal wall and of the chest wall. Coordination of the upper and lower torso musculatures can be learned for singing, but conscious local control of the diaphragm, which lies largely outside the realm of proprioceptive responses, would be difficult.

Although techniques of breath management for singing can be subdivided into some half-dozen or so classifications, even the most idiosyncratic adhere to one of two generally irreconcilable notions: first, that the "diaphragm" must move downward and outward during singing, and second, that the "diaphragm" must move inward and upward during singing. Singers sometimes define themselves and others as either "in-and-upper" or "down-and-outer" adherents.

The "down-and-outers" work on the principle that tensions in the lower trunk resulting from hypogastric (pubic) distention favorably inhibit the upward surge of the diaphragm, whereas the "in-and-uppers" maintain that a physically inexplicable column of air must be moved from the abdominal area upward to the larynx in order to provide proper airflow, or that in pulling inward on the abdominal wall while maintaining an elevated torso the diaphragm will "support the voice." Both theories are perilous for the singer, because each is based on false assumptions regarding respiratory function. (Variations of both theories are also to be found associated with breath management techniques that differentiate some regional and national schools of singing).

The old saw about "controlling the diaphragm for singing" dies hard. This is partly because an element of truth remains in that adage: muscular responses that dictate diaphragmatic action *can* be disciplined. But notions of controlling airflow through direct diaphragmatic maneuvers during phonation are largely mythological.

How one takes a "full breath" for singing is crucial to breath management assumptions. The prominent notion that the singer must crowd the lungs with air at inspiration and then use the diaphragm to get out as much air as possible during singing is disastrous. In point of fact, the singer must learn to take a quiet, complete inspiration, without muscular sensation in the upper torso, and without observable upper chest wall movement.

Further, it is not the maximum amount of air that can be expelled that forms the basis of good breath management, but the means by which the singer *paces* the exiting breath. Inducing high levels of airflow through attempting to "use the diaphragm as a driving piston for the larynx" is not productive in managing the breath for the tasks of singing. Attempting to fully expel air in lungs filled to capacity during the expiratory portion of the breath cycle, or at the release of the tone, is inappropriate for efficient breath management in singing.

There is a historical pedagogical approach that drills the coordination needed for the demands of artistic vocalism. It goes by the name of *appoggio*, an international technique of breath management that, despite its Italianate name, crosses all national boundaries. This third approach is in contrast to either the "in-and-upper" or the "down-and- outer" schools of "breath support." *Appoggio*, as admirably described by Francesco Lamperti more than a century ago, had its origins in the pedagogical literature of the eighteenth- and nineteenth-century Italian School: the muscles of inspiration must not surrender too early to the muscles of expiration; this *dynamic muscular balance* results in the *lutte vocale* (the vocal contest) of international classical vocalism. Because of the factors of duration and range, the requirements of breath management for singing are not identical to those of regular speech. The position of the abdominal wall remains in the inspiratory gesture for a longer period of time than is the case in normal speech patterns. The *appoggio* is a specialized method of breath management based on the prolongation of the postures that inhere in the inspiratory gesture and the retarding of the expiratory gesture.

The *appoggio* technique of breath management can be systematically developed through the repetition of onset exercises: following deep, quiet inhalation (abduction of the vocal folds), one begins phonation with a quick, vibrant "attack" (adduction of the vocal folds). The phonation then terminates in the release of the sound (abduction—the vocal folds part again) through immediate silent renewal of the breath. The release is the new breath. These brief exercises are then extended in duration.

Many examples of onset exercises associated with the *appoggio* breath-management technique can be found in standard technical systems published in the nineteenth century—that of Garcia being a prime example—as well as in current books on vocal technique. In the *appoggio* technique, the diaphragm, the intercostals, the rib cage and the musculature of the torso (anterior, lateral, and posterior) are coordinated in a single dynamic, nonstatic fashion that permits adjustable breath management as it is needed to meet the variety of tasks faced by the singer.

Sharpening up information as to how the diaphragm functions during inspiration, phonation, and breath renewal saves teacher and singer much time by eliminating hit-and-miss systems of breathing based on mistaken assumptions regarding the actual events of the breath cycle.

As was mentioned earlier, the voice is a tripartite instrument—motor, vibrator, and resonator. *Appoggio* breath management techniques coordinate the motor with the vibratory and resonator systems. Results can be externally observed through the singer's postural alignment (the "noble" position), the lack of upper chest displacement during singing or breath renewal, and the appropriate delaying of the inward movement of the abdominal wall until the phrase is nearly terminated. As a result of systematic repetition of the onset exercises, antagonism of the muscles of the anterolateral-abdominal wall builds the musculature of that region to the exceptional degree of strength and tonicity demanded by the singer athlete.

Relax and Sing

Some pedagogical viewpoints regarding appropriate posture for singing are based on the old "relax and sing" saw. Many so-called "relaxation techniques" induce a body alignment different from that of the noble posture of the *appoggio*. Students are told to collapse backward in a chair, to relax by dropping the chest or being like a rag doll, and to "breathe with the belly." Then the same "relaxed" posture is retained when standing for singing. Such measures can be successful as momentary corrective devices for singers who suffer from rigid posture, but most proponents of "relax and sing" regard such "posture relaxation" as the standard for singing.

Probably as many fine voices have been ruined through attempts at "relaxing" the vocal instrument as through driving the larynx by too much glottal resistance to airflow. Axial alignment alone permits proper relationships among the muscles of neck and torso that control breath management in singing. The singer ought to be "keyed up and relaxed," as for any athletic event or for activities involving heightened emotion, and ought not to be de-energized under the assumption that the act of singing calls for "relaxed" posture.

Laryngeal Considerations

The functioning of the vibrator is not as readily externally observable as are activities that involve the breath machine. Yet what one assumes to be ideal for the laryngeal area during singing is the second major watershed in vocal pedagogies.

Most amateur singers have serious problems of laryngeal elevation when frequency (which we perceive as pitch) mounts beyond the speech range. Although there is some slight, flexible laryngeal action involved in the production of *speech* phonemes, the larynx should not rise and fall in singing for the production of vowels and for frequency changes.

Open the Throat with the Yawn

Recognizing that laryngeal elevation is a common fault among many singers, some modern schools of singing assume that it must then logically follow that the lowest positioning of the larynx (laryngeal depression), as in a full-blown yawn, is ideal for singing. It is postulated that vocal tract elongation will thereby be increased (that is, the distance from the vocal folds to the velum will be extended), the throat will be "opened," and "resonance" will be enhanced.

Yawning is beneficial to the vocal mechanism as a momentary action, distending the pharyngeal wall in much the same manner that the musculature of the arms and the pectoral region is distended during stretching. Yawning and stretching are often combined. These actions are not constituted to be maintained over periods of time. Just as one can only with difficulty lift a heavy object while stretching the muscles of the arms, so one cannot speak without distortion while yawning. The benefit of the yawn and of the muscular stretch is experienced at their termination, not through holding the distended postures they induce.

The concomitant effect on the muscular support of the larynx during the yawn—the actual increase of tension among muscle groups of the neck that compose the external frame support of the larynx—is often ignored. It is not possible to yawn without putting into a state of tension many of the muscles of the mandibular-lingual (jaw/tongue) complex. Simple experimentation by manually examining the submandibular region (below the jaw) during a yawn attests to the muscular tensions the yawn locally induces. The base of the tongue, as well as the numerous muscles that compose the tongue bundle, are placed in tension.

There are teachers who believe they can "feel the throat opening" when these tensions occur. An illustration from an influential text on vocal technique shows the supposed desirability of the heavily grooved tongue resulting from laryngeal depression, with an accompanying legend that reads "singing with an open throat." The depicted tongue and velar positions could only be achieved by forcing the base of the tongue downward and by a dramatic arching of the velum. Under normal phonatory conditions, it is misinformation to speak of the yawn as a "relaxing" maneuver.

The yawn is a muscular stretch, not relaxation, involving muscles closely related to the external laryngeal muscles and to the body of the tongue. In the preparatory gesture of silent deep inhalation, a sense of roominess does occur in the laryngopharynx, because optimum spaciousness of the vocal tract comes about with complete and uninhibited deep inspiration. This sensation often strikes the singer as similar to an incipient yawn. For that reason, to think of the very beginning of a yawn may be useful in establishing proper laryngeal adjustment, but there is an inherent danger, because once any form of yawning is suggested, the yawn tends to run onward to completion. Better advice is to use "the breath of expectancy," "the breath of joyous anticipation," "the breath of quiet excitation." Although one may involuntarily yawn before action, the yawn and the stretch are generally associated with fatigue, weariness, and boredom. Such psychological states are inappropriate to singing. One does not continue to yawn while engaging in exhilarating activities.

Although it is true that yawning lowers the larynx, expands the pharyngeal wall, raises the velum, and may momentarily widely abduct the vocal folds, the adverse side effects of that maneuver (when sustained over long periods) must not be overlooked. As the initiator of phonation or as a posture for extended phonation, the yawn places the larynx in an unnatural position.

Sigh to Relax the Larynx

What of the sigh as a pedagogical tool for "relaxing" the laryngeal mechanism and the vocal tract? Some teachers who advocate the yawn as a suitable device for maintaining low laryngeal posture, for elongation of the resonator tract, and for "relaxing" the vocal mechanism combine that action with the sigh. The "yawn/sigh" technique had its origin in the Nordic-Germanic School, which reached its American peak in the late fifties and early sixties as the result of widely disseminated, influential vocal pedagogy texts; it still has strong pockets of adherents in the academic vocal community.

The claim that sighing induces momentary relaxation in a rigid vocal instrument is not without factual foundation. When one sighs, breath exits over the vocal folds at a high rate, and glottal closure is far from complete. Thus the sigh can be serviceable in correcting cases of pressed phonation or hypertension. But, as with the yawn, it was never intended to serve as an extended maneuver. It partakes of weariness and exhaustion, reduction of vitality, and temporary loss of muscle tonus. In fact, there is a fair body of evidence to suggest that the passing of excess expiratory air over the vocal folds when whispering or sighing while phonating is deleterious to vocal health. Prolonged breathy phonation is pathological phonation, not simply "flow" phonation, as is sometimes claimed. It negates the aerodynamic/myoelastic precision established by the classic international vocal *onset* in singing. Sighing induces inefficient vocal-fold closure and rapid diminution of the air supply.

Pressed phonation stands in direct contrast to breathy phonation. In pressed phonation, the *closure* phase of the vocal folds during a vibratory cycle is too long, generally in response to excessive subglottic tensions; in breathy phonation, the *opening* phase is too long, and airflow is more rapid. Pressed phonation can be corrected through the occasional use of exercises built on the sighing maneuver, both in speech and in singing. However, when a singing technique is built upon the gesture of the sigh, dynamic balances within the laryngeal musculature are upset. The sigh-to-relax-the-larynx saw fails to take into account its effect on the anatomy of the laryngeal mechanism and on the surrounding supportive external frame.

The vocal folds are housed within a cartilaginous structure (the "voice box") that cannot be altered by attempts to "open the throat" through expansion of the musculature that supports the cartilaginous edifice. Good vocal-fold abduction (parting, or opening) is partly dependent on the avoidance of shallow inhalation; good abduction takes place in deep inspiration. Distending the muscles of the neck does not increase the degree of glottal opening. Rather, the combined yawn/sigh maneuver (1) induces tensions among muscle groups that should afford external frame support to the larynx, and (2) creates imbalances within the submandibular muscle groups. Because this old saw lingers on in some quarters, additional comment may be warranted.

During deep inhalation, as in the preparatory breath for singing, most persons experience slight laryngeal lowering. Silent, complete inhalation induces a natural expansion of the pharyngeal wall, velar elevation, and a widely opened glottis. These actions result synergistically during deep inspiration in concert with the expansion of the muscles of the anterolateral abdominal wall, and of the low dorsal muscles. The sensation of the *gola aperta* (open throat) then remains constant throughout the subsequently sung phrase.

Note that this sensation of open-throatedness can be experienced when inhaling either by mouth or by nose; it has no relationship to the degree of openness or closure of the mouth. Placing the mouth in various postures (for example, dropping the mandible) as preparation for breathing for singing has nothing to do with "opening the throat." Nor does taking the initial breath through some assumed ideal buccal posture, because opening the mouth does not necessarily "open" the throat.

There are several muscles that depress and stabilize the larynx and several that elevate the larynx. A stabilized larynx depends upon maintaining a dynamic equilibrium between the two muscle groups. This desirable laryngeal position cannot be maintained when the musculatures of the submandibular, sublingual, and neck regions are distended. If there is to be free production of the singing voice, the submandibular region must always remain soft, which is not the case in the yawn/sigh maneuver. There is, indeed, a sense of "openness" in the pharynx when one initiates the breath of expectancy, the breath of exhilaration, the breath of heightened emotion earlier mentioned. One does not yawn and sigh at those moments. The "yawn/sigh" has only limited use for the singer as a temporary therapeutic treatment for rigid, pressed phonation.

Raise the Larynx to Free the Voice: The Sword-Swallowing Laryngeal Position

Even less comprehensible from the perspective of efficient laryngeal function is a viewpoint in opposition to both laryngeal depression and the stabilized larynx: in order to free the larynx for singing, chin and head are to be slightly elevated, that is, the head should be placed in the "sword-swallowing" position (as advocated by a recent prominent and prolific writer on singing). Any such elevation of the larynx tends to shorten the vocal tract (inasmuch as the raised larynx reduces the distance between the glottis and the velum). In addition, the larynx is bereft of adequate structural support.

Although there are minimal laryngeal movements coincidental with phonetic definition, a poised, stable larynx, neither rising nor falling with vowel change and breath renewal, is essential to skillful singing. Laryngeal elevation and laryngeal depression are inappropriate as sustained postures for the energized phonation that characterizes the singing voice.

Perhaps one of the most pernicious pieces of advice a singer can encounter is found in some recent vocal research that advises that the larynx may be raised to produce bright vocal timbre (by shortening the supraglottic vocal tract), and that it can subsequently be lowered to achieve greater depth of timbre (by lengthening the resonator tube). Both gestures are then alternately recommended to meet the shifting demands of vocal coloration. This maneuvering results in laryngeal instability and destroys the unification of the scale. Shortening or lengthening the vocal tract at will can alter vocal timbre, but these maneuvers induce laryngeal instability. A high larynx causes hypertension; a sustained depressed laryngeal position produces timbre distortion in the singing voice just as distinctly as does yawning in the speaking voice.

Controlling the Resonator System

We have briefly considered some old saws concerned with the breath mechanism and the vibrator. The third element of this three-part instrument is the resonator system. Mistaking the *sensations* of sound for their *source* has produced an astounding number of old saws regarding "resonance" in singing.

Produce the Tone in the Sinuses

Perhaps the most imaginative theory regarding the sinuses as the chief determinants of vocal tone and timbre is that propounded by the E. G. White Society (which numbers several hundred mostly British and American teachers and singers). Basing his theories on sensations experienced in the head, E. G. White wrote several books whose premise is that vocal sound is not produced by the larynx but by the sinuses. (Investigative study reveals, of course, that as resonators the sinuses contribute minimally, if at all, to vocal sound.) The tenets of the E. G. White Society are of special interest because they are explained through numerous anatomical drawings that purport to be scientific. The misapplication of science can prove seductive.

This raises a general pedagogical question: If results from such theories are positive, does it matter that the functions they describe are patently erroneous? Are there inherent dangers? Indeed there are. In associating what is termed "head voice" with "sinus tone" production, thereby "producing the tone in the head," efficient vocal-fold approximation is modified. The E. G. White followers are somewhat distant relatives of a larger pedagogical group that concentrates on "singing in the masque," at which a brief look should be taken.

Place the Tone in the Masque

Included in "masque" pedagogical orientation are systems that posit the existence of a sphincter unknown to anatomists, located at the bridge of the nose, by means of which tone can be controlled and "placed." A related pedagogy claims that lifting the eyebrows both "places the tone in the masque" and "widens the pharynx."

By bone conduction most singers experience sensations of sympathetic vibration in the bony and cartilaginous structures of the head. These sensations can be relied upon as part of a singer's ability to feel, hear, and see what physical postures contribute to vocalized sound. Clearly, when coordinated action takes place between vocal folds and the flow of air (aerodynamic/myoelastic precision), producing a match between laryngeal configuration and vocal tract configuration, many singers experience some frontal sensation in the head. Yet, concentrating on locally inducing such sensation generally results in upsetting the efficiency of vocal-fold approximation; reduced vitality and intensity of the sound is mistaken for having accomplished the "light head voice."

It is an acoustical fact that *tone cannot be placed*. (Emerging vocal sound is the result of sound waves generated by the vibrating larynx moving the ambient air. Molecules in the air then fly apart as the result of a compression wave and travel at around 1,100 feet per second.) However, sensations of frontal sympathetic vibration are experienced by many singers.

Although the sinuses of the head are not anatomically constructed so as to make a substantial contribution to the basic resonation of the voice, singers have "masque" sensations because of the aforementioned phenomenon of sympathetic vibration by bone and cartilage conduction. Such sensations have given rise to many pedagogical expressions, including the age-old concept of "head voice," because they are based upon empirical sensation, not on the source of the sound. Singers *should* rely upon such sensation as part of the self-monitoring process of the sounds they produce. But those sensations should be the result of coordinated function, not of attempting to "put" sound in places where it cannot go. Any attempt to transfer one's own empirical sensations to another individual is fraught with peril, because individual morphology and perceptual responses vary vastly.

Up and Over!

A more detailed version of "placing the tone in the head" is the resilient old "up and over" saw. Many teachers who use this imaginative language believe it is physiologically possible to send tone up the back of the naso-pharynx into the forehead. However, velopharyngeal closure is present in the production of well-produced non-nasal phonemes, so that *significant* entry into the nasal cavities occurs only in nasality. In non-nasals there generally is an avoidance of conjoining the buccopharyngeal (mouth/pharynx) resonator tract and the nasal cavities. The probable acoustic result of this "up and over" old saw is twofold: (1) to introduce some nasality into non-nasals, and (2) to reduce or deflect airflow efficiency by mentally directing the breath to locations to which it has no actual access.

It is clear that some recognizable aesthetic aim may be achieved through "up and over," which, although not in accordance with what is possible physiological function, produces alteration of sound some teachers desire (described subjectively as "heady," "floating," "fluty" timbre). This is because such imaginative maneuvers produce changes in the velopharyngeal region, and alter airflow factors. However, the forehead—where the frontal sinus is located—cannot serve as a resonating source for the human vocal instrument. (Nor can the maxillary and sphenoid sinuses produce the results attributed to them by "front placement" teachers.) Frontal sensation actually is the result of the coordination involving airflow, vocal fold approximation, and resonator tract postures already mentioned, not of "placement" of sound.

Place the Tone in the Dome

How about the old saw that calls for "placing" the tone in the "dome" at the back of the throat, or into the "dome" in the head itself? Fortunately for all of us who sing and teach, singers do not have holes in their heads where the rest of humankind does not. There is no possibility of enlarging areas that are confined within fixed anatomical structures of bone and cartilage. Trying to "place the tone in the dome of the head" (or in any specific location) can again only mean that the sensation and the source of sound are being confused.

"Placement" experimentation in some pedagogies tries various forms of tone location according to what the "resonance" problem may be: back, forward, in the sinuses, up into the head, down into the spine, out the chimney on top of the head, out the funnel at the back of the neck, progressing backward with the mounting scale like the sequence of "feathers on an Indian headdress," "points on the Trojan helmet," "Nefertiti's hat," or "the tiers of the Pope's tiara," to mention only a few such experimental admonitions. These concepts result in pedagogical systems of extreme complexity, obfuscating what is simple functional acoustics. They may convince the student that his or her teacher is gifted in creating colorful images, but such language conveys little tangible information.

Much simpler is what actually happens to sound generated by the human voice. The reason for recognizing that the voice emerges from a corporeal instrument that obeys physical laws, and that it is an acoustic instrument that obeys the laws of vocal acoustics, is that those laws are simpler and easier to grasp and to communicate than are the fantasized systems of "tone placement." The language of imagery, when applied to the physical instrument, may induce malfunction.

Is there then no room for imagery in coordinating tonal concepts for singing? Indeed there is. But such imagery must come about through the *personal* discovery of kinesthetic and emotive responses. Imagery is best reserved for the artistic imagination, assembling into one mental concept the remarkable psychological complexity that combines art and function.

There is no necessity to invent function or idiosyncratic vocabularies. It behooves voice teachers to forego imaginative theories of either acoustics or physiology, and to give up jargonistic language. The musicianly ear and the aesthetic concept will be free for performance if previous skillful training has coordinated the functioning parts of the physical and acoustic instrument. During performance, a singer should not be struggling with the production of vocal sound through attempting imaginative physical and acoustic controls. Artistic communication is secure only when previous technical work has been based upon efficient function.

Just Sing Naturally

Singing should be based on *coordinated* natural processes. A superior singing artist has that coordination well in hand. There remains confusion in some quarters over the difference between coordination based on good function and on just "doing what comes naturally." It is still not rare to find a teacher of singing who claims that it is not necessary to teach technique at all. Attention to the word, the emotion, and the dramatic situation will solve the problems of the singing voice. "Feel the text, feel the music, feel the drama!" The final desirable result of technical training is here mistakenly substituted for the training itself.

It is not possible to be "musical and expressive" and to "think only of the poetry and the musical line, like the great artists do" when the instrument has not been disciplined. Freedom in artistic communication—making music and words reach the heart of the listener—is not a "natural" attribute. It is the result of skill. Skills based on solid premises are necessary to artistic communication. They can best be acquired through systematic technical instruction that never separates itself from musical and interpretative factors. Indeed, it is impossible to treat vocal technique in a vacuum apart from musical factors. The old saw that there is a conflict between technique and artistry is more often than not a thinly disguised excuse for not knowing how to cope with the technical problems that singers encounter in performing the vocal literature.

Beware of Physiology and Acoustics!

This enduring pedagogical saw, perhaps the ultimate in "old sawing," is closely related to the one just considered: Any attention given to physiologic or acoustic information inhibits artistry or causes the singer to become mechanical in performance. "In my teaching, I would never deal in acoustics or physiology!"

This pedagogical saw is a dodge, because it is not possible to give a voice lesson without dealing in both acoustics and physiology. As soon as a teacher tells the singing student to do anything regarding "support," "tone placement," "opening the throat," and so on, she or he is dealing in the very essence of acoustics and physiology. It is preferable to learn, rather than to invent, how the vocal instrument actually works and to use that information in the teaching of singing.

Old Saws Revisited

Many of these old saws, here selected for discussion from a large reservoir, are in conflict with each other. They are irreconcilable, and they are non-factual. One need not be a scientist, a speech pathologist, or an otolaryngologist in order to understand the basic concepts of vocal acoustics and physiologic function. Such information is surely as essential to the teaching of singing as is the ability to read music. It is easy to excuse oneself on the grounds of being *too busy* to examine what really happens in singing, *too artistic* to need such information, or *too successful* to want additional assistance. (The claim of having *unique* information is surely no longer a possible position for any serious teacher of singing.) Fear of having to change one's concepts may, unfortunately, be what restricts some potentially fine teachers of singing from reaching their full capabilities.

We need to look carefully at the "old saws" we offer the student. Let us sharpen them up so that what we say corresponds to truth. To do otherwise is either to acquiesce to sloth or to flirt with charlatanism.

26

Open Windows

Keynote address, National Convention of the National Association of Teachers of Singing, Minneapolis, Minnesota, July 3, 1983.

Although approximately six hundred musicians have entered this room, there is no problem as to where their instruments should be stored for the next half hour. Six hundred or more carrying cases for the same number of larynges are brought together here, yet you may relax in complete confidence that no one will sit on your instrument, drop it, mutilate it, or steal it. Whereas most musicians can remove from its case the instrument they play, may clear foreign matter from it by blowing into it or shaking it out, tune it, replace worn-out parts of it, sell it, or if necessary throw the whole tiresome thing away, the singer has none of those options. To be sure, these days you may insure your vocal folds, but you may not turn them in for some better model, nor can you exchange them for a sum of money when you finally have finished with them. You, singer, are the instrument. Therein lies much of the mystery and the folderol that surrounds the art of singing and the art of the teaching of singing.

Persons present in this room have collectively traveled great distances to share in the identification of premises most important to singing and to the teaching of singing. We come here to open the windows of our ears and our minds. The National Association of Teachers of Singing as an organization can be proud of its record in opening windows to a broad spectrum of vocal knowledge. Most of the healthy breezes that blow through vocal pedagogy today have been germinated within this organization by openness on the part of its members to the exchange of information.

True, there continue to be some teachers of note who privately maintain that they do not need to associate with other teachers of singing, and who profess to possess information not available to the rest of us, or who remain outside this community of artists and scholars because they secretly fear a loss of their own importance. They refuse to readjust their knowledge to include the expanding gamut of information offered through this professional organization. Those persons continue to operate in small—at times even large—closets, shut off from contact with the developing thought of their colleagues. Their number is rapidly diminishing.

The type of teacher who allows himself or herself to be quoted in a national publication as saying "I am unique" is an anachronism. This comment, appearing in a recent opera journal, created more amusement than amazement within the voice-teaching profession. Anyone who could make such a statement advertises, of course, the limited scope of his or her pedagogical knowledge. Equally amazing is the pedagogue who admits that, having never read a text on either vocal pedagogy or sexual behavior, he or she has not done badly in either field. This brings laughs in master classes, but only attests to the narrowness of the pedagogical viewpoint of the presenter.

In somewhat similar vein, it could be remarked that a number of us have indulged in uncharitable chuckling over the recent exhibition of two pedagogical leviathans who share territorial space in one of our prestigious metropolitan musical institutions, who have become engaged in a war to the death because one of them charges that the other has "stolen my vocal techniques and pedagogical secrets." Apparently, one of these vocal educators carelessly and uncharacteristically opened a studio window and the secrets of singing flew out to nest elsewhere!

Our energies as singers and as teachers of singing are sometimes spent on peripheral considerations about the singing art instead of being centered on the acquisition of technical skills that allow artistic communication. How easy it is, for both singer and teacher, to become caught up in concerns that have little to do with actual artistic accomplishment, to be drawn into private problems of PR concerning ourselves, our students, and our colleagues, or even to become distracted by media-induced warfare between *prime donne* or, more currently, *primi uomini* (today, more precisely, *primi tenori*), and at the same time to lose sight of the substantive pedagogical and artistic interests that ought to be paramount. Later we will look at some of those limiting attitudes.

Rather than build a fortress around our own little heap of vocal wisdom, to guard our own private pedagogical citadel, we need to open outward every window that will permit new information to sweep in and that will allow each of us to offer information from our own performance and teaching experiences, and to learn from those of others. It may prove worthwhile to ask ourselves what some of these windows may be, and for each of us to make certain there are not still some that remain closed. We may need to reexamine old concepts and consider new ideas that drift in from the open windows.

Despite our well-known differences, we teachers of singing occupy the same pedagogical space, joined together in a room with several outward-opening windows. Within this room are identifiable pedagogical proto-types who, though professionally united, are sometimes suspicious of each other. The first window through which we should be able to look out from the chamber of vocal pedagogy appears at times to be covered by a large placard on which is displayed the message, "Only *my* technique allowed in here; keep this window tightly closed at all times." That window may have been shut a number of years ago, perhaps as far back as the last formal voice lesson. When this window is covered over, the assumption is made that by happenstance one stumbled upon the complete vocal gospel through the historical events of one's own career as student and teacher. Whatever I was taught by the teacher or teachers I happened to encounter is unalterably correct, and in my own teaching there is no need to examine any alternative. Blind loyalty requires that I adhere to what I learned dur-ing my formative years. Or, I have constructed my technical edifice largely by myself; no architectural improvements are necessary. On serious con-sideration, it seems highly illogical that some one of the many conflicting vocal pedagogies possesses the totality of revelation. Let us look more closely at the diverse types seated behind closed windows in the vocal ped-agogy room.

Vocal Pedagogical Prototype 1 is the *Technique Mystique* teacher, whose studio is best described as a shrine, an inner sanctum where the precious secrets of the past are charismatically dispensed, and in which the teacher serves as high priest or high priestess of a vanishing art. Much of each lesson is devoted to reminiscences about the greatness of past per-sonal performances and famous colleagues. Guru services are generously dispensed. It is hard work being the sole remaining exemplar of the once fine art of singing. Therefore, mystique technique teaching has to become an egocentric cult that is not student-centered. The novice should not de-spair, however, because one can be initiated into these vocal mysteries and continue the search for elusive perfection for a decade or more, to the tune of $100 an hour.

Vocal Pedagogical Prototype 2, trying valiantly to ignore the other voice-teacher prototypes around him, is the *Technically Intense* teacher, who cannot be bothered with the performance literature or musical con-cerns (after all, there are coaches for such matters!), but only with the voice as a mechanism that functions according to certain assumptions based on early speculation regarding the voice as an instrument. This in-strument has to be taken apart and divided into segments, the functions independently worked, then, at some distant moment, put back together again. The putting-it-back-together may take a considerable amount of time, with the lesson fee pegged at the same rate as that of Vocal Pedagogi-cal Prototype 1.

Type 3, ensconced in the middle of the group (certainly not out of modesty) is the *Interpretation-Oriented* teacher, who avoids all technical specifics in teaching because musical and interpretative suggestions are sufficient to produce the aesthetic stimuli that result in artistic singing. Just portray the emotion of the text and visualize the dramatic situation, and your problems will disappear! The lesson fee remains near the generally established figure.

Pedagogical Prototype 4 has elbows that keep aggressively poking into the sides of her companions. She is the *One-Solution* teacher, who has discovered that the answer to all vocal problems is "posture," or "the upper back," or "the lower back," or "the pelvic tilt and buttocks tuck," or "the diaphragm support," or "the *passaggio*," or "the hum," or "relaxation," or "the sword-swallowing head-and-neck position," or "the idiot jaw," or "building on the soft," or "falsetto," or "skull resonance, "or "forehead resonance," or "spine resonance," or "the masque," or "cover," or "placement," or "So-and-So's method of body positioning and movement." Whichever nostrum, *it* is the universal panacea for the vocal problems of all students studying with the One-Solution teacher. Hourly lesson fee here is also around $100.

Prototype 5 sits quite tall and tries to ignore the others. Why shouldn't he? After all, he alone is aware that the entire answer to singing technique lies in the application of *Voice Science to the Vocal Instrument*. He attends interdisciplinary symposia annually, has read several books on acoustics and physiology, and has learned to read spectrographic analyses. Through all of this, he has discovered *a new, scientific way to sing*. All voice teachers from the past were naïve souls who depended on their ears. Ignore those historical schools. You can't tell if a sound is good unless you measure it with instruments. He has been known to say, "Don't use that imagery stuff around me!" With this pedagogue, music is seldom made, because you don't really have to listen to anything other than isolated sounds to determine vocal values. Despite all of this impressive information, his hourly rate is no higher than the others.

Side by side, these five sit in the chamber of vocalism before boarded-up windows without communicating with each other, each content in the knowledge that the "keep-shut-at-all-times" sign covering the comparative pedagogical window will ward off unwanted invasions into each of the tightly closed systems.

Somewhat removed from the group, not even looking to see if there is a window that might be opened, sits yet another figure, smiling and nodding, obviously without a care. This person, Vocal Pedagogy Prototype 6, is the *Polite* teacher. He certainly cannot be accused of being a dogmatist because he believes that, just as one refrains from mentioning differences in religion and politics, so one avoids taking *any* position on vocal technique beyond requesting good sound. He suggests to his students that they must sing "naturally." He is too circumspect to correct more than superficial matters of diction, style, or sentiment. He repeats two lines of an innocuous litany, by now so familiar that we might have come to accept them for truth, were it not the case that even a quick look at *comparative* vocal pedagogy reveals its vacuity. The Polite Teacher's litany runs this way:

> Well, there are as many techniques of singing as there are teachers of singing, and they are all good,
>
>   and
>
> Well, we all use different language, different terminologies and imagery, but we are all looking for the same thing.

Neither assumption, of course, is true. All techniques of singing can be readily codified into recognizable schools, and there is neither a technical nor an aesthetic universal goal among teachers of singing beyond a generally shared hope for successful performance, even though some techniques have a much higher number of adherents than do others.

We thought we had by now identified all of the persons in the dim light of this pedagogical chamber of horrors, but we are wrong. There is yet another individual at a considerable distance, turned away from the barricaded window. She has precipitously knocked down the wall at her end of the room, and now sits among waves of billowing pedagogical plaster. She is Pedagogical Prototype 7, the *Eclectic* teacher, who keeps spinning like a whirling dervish, caught up in a maelstrom of conflicting pedagogical viewpoints, unable to remain long with any single one, and unable to resist swaying in cross-currents blowing from all directions. With one hand she alternately snatches at bits and pieces of flying pedagogical debris, capturing some fragments in a big bag marked "tricks and gimmicks." With the other she scoops out unrelated pieces of pedagogy from the bag to be pasted on the student's technical problems. She is constantly in search of new approaches. One is reminded of the tale of the miller and the donkey, in which at various moments the vacillating miller was convinced by evidence presented to him by others that instead of leading the donkey his son should ride him, that his son should dismount and that he himself should ride, that both father and son should ride on the donkey, and finally, that he and his son should carry the poor donkey. The pedagogical donkey of the eclectic teacher of singing seldom meets with a better fate than did the miller's donkey, which became so confused it fell into the river. Although her pedagogy is in constant flux, the hourly lesson rate of the Eclectic teacher stays about the same as that of the others.

Is there, then, no hope for the state of vocal pedagogy? Indeed there is, and it is evidenced by our collective presence in this hall. When the "My technique; keep closed at all times" placard is taken down from the window of the pedagogical chamber, while at the same time the walls of that room are kept intact, a balanced vocal pedagogy has every chance of flourishing. The light of intelligence that enters the room from the opened window of comparative pedagogy then removes much of the darkness.

Even with the removal of the offensive placard and the opening of the comparative vocal pedagogy window, the chamber is not yet entirely serviceable. As a result of the influx of light into the room, a second and a third window now have become visible. Although the second window is heavily corroded by rust and dust, it is plainly marked "Open here for current information on the function of the singing voice."

Outside this window lies a body of literature that has grown to large proportions over the past several decades, and whose contributors include otolaryngologists, speech pathologists and therapists, psychologists, voice scientists and researchers, and a growing number of teachers of singing. There remain a few pedagogical hands that struggle to keep this window from opening further. Could it be that it is too much bother to master rudimentary information about vocal function? Do I continue to plead a lack of science background? Have I read transcripts from symposia devoted to the care of the professional voice? Am I aware of publications and professional journals that carry informative articles on vocal research related to the singing voice? Do I read only the vocal literature articles in *The NATS Journal* and skip impatiently over those that deal with function, health, and specific technical information? Further, do I make my students aware of this wealth of material, and have I ordered these publications for my institutional library and for my private collection? Or will it all just go away if I ignore it?

A third window is capable of letting in fresh air and light that will transform the vocal pedagogy chamber into a radiant chapel. It looks out on the field of vocal performance literature. Let me ask myself some questions regarding what lies beyond this window as well. How recently have I opened wide that rewarding window to read through new song literature available to me and to my students? Do I know the current American and British song literature or do I believe that Ralph Vaughan Williams and Charles T. Griffes represent the contemporary English-language song? When did I last buy new music? How many of the 610 Schubert *Lieder* do I actually know and use? How many of the Brahms and Schumann

Lieder beyond those found in Volume I are acquaintances of mine? Do I continue to disregard the exciting and varied songs of Hugo Wolf with the explanation that they are too complex for my students? Do I dismiss Strauss and Mahler as far too advanced for studio use, without actually examining those *Lieder?* What part of the vocal output of Fauré, Debussy, Chausson, Duparc, Ravel, and Poulenc do I know? How much sampling have I done of the lesser vocal composers of the French School, or of the Nationalist Schools, including Grieg, Sibelius, Kilpinen, Smetana, Dvořák, Martinu, Liszt, and the vast Russian-language literature, both standard and contemporary? (Could I even consider taking a diction course in Russian?) Do my students sing the Baroque solo cantata literature, the arias of Lully and Rameau, and the vast chamber music for voice? Am I familiar with items suitable to the young singer that go beyond the confines of the *arie antiche* collections; do I know Gilbert and Sullivan items, or musical comedy materials that might be useful to my singers, or am I above that? Do I look for aria material not included in the operatic anthologies? Have I become narrowly specialized in my literature assignments, often resorting to the same old material year after year? It may be that this window is just as dusty and corroded as is the voice-function pane. I must try flinging it open.

We have looked at three windows in the chamber of vocal pedagogy which, when opened, will provide me as a teacher of singing with a complete set of the diagnostic and artistic tools of my trade. Opening one or more of them is anathema to the self-limiting pedagogical prototypes earlier portrayed. If any one of these three windows remains closed for me, I will suffer serious limitations in teaching the subject matter to which I devote my professional life. Finally, what of substance and specificity do I honestly have to offer my student that should make him or her want to be instructed by me?

Suppose, though, for a moment that I do indeed possess these tools of my trade in some respectable degree (who among us is complete in them all?) Do I hesitate to put them to use for fear I may be offensive to my colleagues or my audience? Do I avoid programming George Crumb and Peter Maxwell Davies because I do not want to be accused of singing and teaching all that contemporary stuff? Am I hesitant to use the acoustic instrumentation available to me for fear my colleagues will brand me with the "science" label? Am I a courageous teacher or one who never rocks the boat? Will I join with those teachers who are not afraid of unknown pedagogical and musicianly breezes that may come wafting in from open windows?

We can take comfort, if we like, in reminding ourselves that we teachers of singing are not the only professional group among disciplines closely related to us that might benefit by prying open a few closed windows. Some of our colleagues in neighboring disciplines have their own hermetically sealed rooms. We are currently at an exciting juncture in the teaching of singing in which persons from other disciplines are discovering *us*. These colleagues want to examine the singing art through their disciplines of medicine, physiology, acoustics, psychology, speech therapy, and phoniatrics. We welcome them with enthusiasm and gratitude. We are pleased that some of them will share their information with us. But all too often they are unfamiliar with the literature of vocal pedagogy—*our literature*. Remarkably few of them have ever read a text on vocal technique. At a recent interdisciplinary symposium, when it was suggested that persons involved in vocal research should consult the vocal pedagogy literature as well as the scientific literature, one nonsinger researcher asked, "*What literature?*" (Open windows?)

One of the reasons nonsingers who wish to write and talk about the singing voice should study the vocal pedagogy literature is so that they can avoid falling into one of the major faults of current vocal research: much of the investigative work on the singing voice carries less authenticity than it might had teachers and singers of stature been subjects and consultants. Research using subjects who live at the periphery of the vocal art, both as regards teaching and performing, does not stimulate productive cooperation between the professional singing community and that of scientists. It surely should be apparent that scientists who are themselves amateur singers should not be considered appropriate subjects for serious investigation of the singing voice, yet that is sometimes the case. Equally appalling is to read that participants in vocal research are professionally trained opera singers when they are students still pursuing voice major degrees, or teachers of singing with limited public career successes.

While the great traditions of vocal performance and vocal pedagogy largely remain unexamined, it is an indulgence to pursue research into nontraditional aspects of vocal sound. It will be so until the sounds of the vocal athlete—the professional singer—become subjects of research. Otherwise, limited value from research will accrue to the art of singing. Perceptual studies of isolated sounds from student subjects are helpful, but singers want to know about the acoustic and physiologic factors that contribute to the vocal timbres professional singers produce.

Collaborative studies, with equal input from related disciplines, are essential. Although voice teachers and voice scientists may inhabit different but neighboring houses, by opening wide their windows they may discover that they share a common landscape.

One leaves the hypothetical pedagogical room with its windows now open. To exit the room, however, we must go through a door over which stands the legend "Tolerance and Generosity." We may have to knock down some heavy cobwebbing to get through that passage, because the threads of cherished pedagogical assumptions are thick and tenacious. In case any of us is feeling comfortable about the answers we have been privately supplying to these rhetorical questions, it might be well for such a faultless one to stand up now and throw the first stone. I suspect that none of us dare do anything other than drop the stone, or, better yet, throw it through an open pedagogical window, and steal away as gracefully as possible.

II

On Musical Style and Interpretation

27

Purely a Matter of Taste

The after-dinner conversation moved to a discussion of the phenomenon of the overnight success of a performing group whose fortunes had rocketed upward on the basis of sudden national exposure from disk-jockeys. Present were guests who lamented the immediate fame and financial return won by these untrained youngsters. People felt an unfortunate message was being given that chance and a hustling agent can achieve in one area of music performance what years of discipline and artistry seldom achieve in another.

One dinner guest questioned that verdict. Who is to say that the product of that "group" was of less merit than that of academically trained performers? What one likes in music, and particularly in singing, is merely a matter of taste. If millions of listeners find a CD worth buying while certain other recorded performances grow dusty on the music store shelf, matters of taste are being objectively registered. Taste is an individual matter, and there is no logic in claiming the superiority of one style of singing over another.

This viewpoint, a minority one at the dinner party, is difficult to combat unless it is recognized that taste is acquired and modified through expanded experience. Taste can equally well be based on ignorance and limited exposure. Harlequin novels may be entertaining and more immediately accessible to readers than Dostoevski's *Brothers Karamazov,* yet few who know the literature of the novel would postulate that critical evaluation is here simply a matter of taste. Reproductions of a popular religious painting may widely adorn the walls of the pious, but the intrinsic artistic merit of the painting is patently below that of the same subject treated by Giovanni Bellini or Raphael. Such judgments may well depend largely on past personal exposure.

Consider the dilemma of the well-trained church musician who must provide music for worship that can be performed by the choir and accepted by the congregation, but which must adhere to the director's own professional standards. Part of the responsibility of that professional person is to educate choristers and parishioners to higher levels of musical taste. Music programs in many churches, under such leadership, have shown a gradual progression from the use of the simple to sublime liturgical music.

The taste argument is being raised with increasing frequency within the voice-teaching profession itself. We are hearing from some sources that if what is popularly termed "classical" singing is held up as a higher aesthetic goal than other forms of singing, we will lose those young singers who are bombarded by other sets of values. Sometimes we are asked why professional organizations, schools, and universities appear so closed-minded about a wider acceptance of vocal sounds. Why, we are asked, does there seem to be so little academic attention directed to lively and popular styles of singing such as blue grass/country and western, jazz vocal, rock and roll, belting, and contemporary gospel?

The answer to that question, although capable of serving as a rippling red flag to those who insist that all forms of music are equally worthy, is that there should be no more lack of discrimination in making professional vocal judgments than in any other area of taste. It is no more possible to claim that all kinds of vocal sound are of equal merit than to say that all wines are equally exquisite. If you don't have the developed palate needed to recognize fine wine, all wine probably tastes equally good or bad; if you don't have experience with cultivated vocalism, all singing may sound equally skillful or aesthetically pleasing.

With regard to vocal taste, there is yet another convincing argument for maintaining that not all styles of singing are of equal merit. Classical vocalism, as practiced in the international historic school of singing, is based on freedom of production and on certain acoustic properties of the singing voice associated with functional efficiency. These techniques permit the singing voice to project easily and to express a full range of timbre colorations and emotions without injury to the vocal instrument. The teacher of singing should no more dilute that heritage than should the server of fine wines pour superb and cheap wines together into a single carafe for the dinner table. If one wants occasionally to drink an inferior wine, one should do so, but one should not diminish the beauty of a superior wine in the process.

The wide range of vocal sounds capable of being emitted from the human larynx are not all equally acceptable, either aesthetically or functionally. Maintaining standards of good taste in singing is not the product of cultural snobbery or intellectual arrogance, as some commentators have implied. Taste in vocal sound is based on the development of sensibilities, as is taste in all areas of discrimination, and it is the result of progressive information derived from exposure to good vocal literature and to outstanding performance. Bad taste in singing is based on the false assumption that objective standards of taste require little background in listening or in information.

Although the controversy that developed around the dinner table may not appear to be of major concern at the moment to all teachers of singing, the kinds of answers supplied to the out-of-step dinner guest will increasingly determine the standard of the teaching of singing, particularly as greater inroads from popular culture continue to be made on the art of singing. Even professionals are subject to erosion of standards by the surrounding environment, and should remain on guard. There is room for all tastes in any society, but professional judgment should not be determined by popular taste. The appreciation of excellent vocalism as opposed to lesser levels of vocalism is *not* simply a matter of taste.

28

The Two Poles of *Bel Canto*

Writing a history of the vocal literature of the seventeenth and eighteenth centuries would surely be one of the most exciting ventures anyone fascinated with the sounds of the human voice could hope to undertake. A number of studies regarding legendary singers, their careers, their managers, their professional battles, the list of roles accomplished, the sums of money received, and the way they were viewed by society offer enjoyable reading, particularly for the opera buff. Seldom, however, do they tell us much beyond superficial descriptions, about the kinds of vocal demands these great singers were able to meet, and why they were more highly regarded than were some of their contemporaries. This is partly the case because we cannot recover the sounds of their voices or see their performances on stage. Yet the operatic literature itself reveals what tasks were called for, and provides a great deal of information on how those tasks were met.

A cursory look at the vocal literature will reveal that the two factors that continue to form the basis of all good technical singing were paramount throughout the period we have come to call "bel canto": they are *sostenuto* and *coloratura*. The form of the operatic *scena* itself (the extended composition composed of two arias, with recitative and bridge material) early exhibited the *cavatina* and the *cabaletta* sections, in which the singer was expected to show the two chief technical facets of skillful singing: legato and agility. Hundreds of examples of such "double arias" abound. They were already well established by the mid–seventeenth century, and later surfaced repeatedly in the early Italian operas of Handel and of Alessandro Scarlatti, on into the works of Haydn and Mozart, and were still very much in evidence among Verdi and his contemporaries. One need only think of such favorites as Handel's *Piangerò*, Mozart's *Non mi dir*, Bellini's *Non mi credea*, and Verdi's *Ah! fors'è lui!* for typical examples.

Part of the value of an awareness of these two constant demands found in all of the *bel canto* and its descendent schools, is to determine their pedagogical implications in preparing today's singers to perform such literature. At the risk of using a somewhat colorful analogy, it can be stated that these two poles of vocal technique are Siamese twins, and that by the nature of their conjoining, each cannot exist without the other. There is a tendency today for singers and their teachers to look for categorization of voices so that a singer is limited early to singing either pyrotechnical melismatic literature or to the dramatic driving line of the *verismo*. In point of fact, if a voice is not capable of moving it is incapable of sustaining; if the voice has not sufficient energization to manage *sostenuto* singing, the velocity factor will not be at high level. An accomplished *Stehbass*, a Sarastro, will sound labored and rigid if he does not possess the ability to sing the melismas of *Sì! tra i ceppi* (as we know, originally intended for a contralto, but kidnapped by all basses). The Violetta who can sing the coloratura of the first act as well as the sustained soaring lines of the third act does so because she has acquired the skills of the two poles of *bel canto*. Today's Duca is no longer safe in assuming he will need to do only the *cavatina* portion of *Parmi veder le lagrime*, because increasingly conductors are reinstituting the subsequent *cabaletta* as well. With the growing interest in authenticity, today's singer cannot make the choice of preferring to sing only those parts of the role most convenient to the instrument; the truncated *scena* came about largely because the inability to master both poles of *bel canto* had become acceptable.

It is clear that a systematic approach to acquiring the agility factor and the sustained *legato* is an essential part of vocal pedagogy. Exercises for developing both capacities abound in the technical vocalization systems of the nineteenth century; modern vocal pedagogy will make vast strides forward if these two pedagogical poles form the foundation of studio instruction. One complements the other. Managing the breath for singing can be accomplished through onset, release, and breath renewal exercises, further expanded into agility vocalises followed by *sostenuto* phrases. Seldom are these technical skills developed simply by singing arias. Materials from the *bel canto* literature can be supplemented by the technical systems of the nineteenth century and by those found in current pedagogical literature. Whoever the singer may be, unless he or she learns the technical skills essential to both moving and sustaining the voice, success will be limited. The two poles of *bel canto* are essential to a complete vocal technique.

29

Singing the *mélodie*

When it comes to singing French music, some non-French singers misjudge both the French people and their song literature. There seems to be a prevailing assumption among North American singers (and their teachers) that the literature of the *mélodie* is precious and fragile, and one should therefore avoid using one's normal singing voice in performance.

This is because of the extraordinary attention directed to poetic meter, to accent, and to the complexities of language intonation on the part of most composers of the *mélodie*. No other song literature is more closely allied to its native language. As a result, the climaxes one has come to anticipate in traditional phrase shapes do not occur where one might expect them, nor at the dynamic levels to be found in some other literatures. In addition, intrusive and obvious emotion has no role in the French song literature. Understatement is a characteristic of much of the *mélodie* literature, but emotional noninvolvement and withdrawal from vocalism are not the ways to achieve that restraint.

The French school of singing is itself historically more closely oriented to language awareness than is any other. Exactitude of pronunciation and enunciation is particularly vital to the singing of the French language. One could make a fair argument that French is the one language in which the singer should have his or her greatest degree of phonetic accuracy.

Fauré must not be treated like Mascagni, Debussy not like Verdi. Yet the *mélodies* of Debussy, Fauré, Chausson, and Duparc are vocally demanding. It is sad to hear an ample voice cut down to a shadow of its natural size, with loss of beauty and presence, because the singer has received the wrong message regarding "French style." Debussy himself complained that some singers did not "sing" his music, but mistook it for a kind of *parlando*. Bernac also reminds us that a *mélodie* needs to be sung every bit as much as does a *Lied*.

Nuance is given high priority by French composers, but so are melodic flow and dramatic impulse. The French, with all their reputation for cultivation, are members of the human race, as are we all; they experience emotion just as profoundly. This does not mean that *verismo* vocalism is to be superimposed on Fauré, but it does mean that singers should not make the mistake of assuming that one doesn't really *sing* French music. No singer should diminish vocal beauty in order to perform the demanding *mélodie* literature. That would diminish the music as well as the vocalism.

30

Self-perception and Performance Reality

A young man comes on stage to perform *Dichterliebe*. He loves its poetry and he deeply respects its music. He wants to convey to his listeners the strong emotion he experiences as he sings one of his favorite works. He perceives himself as the medium for interpreting this wonderful amalgamation of text and musical sensibility. He understands that he must portray an earnest but not entirely happy lover. In his mind's eye, he sees how that person should look, and he is certain that his portrayal is sensitive and moving.

What his audience sees, however, is a young man attempting to choreograph romantic feeling through constant body and head movement, and through distressed facial expression. The musical line shows similar instability, as it becomes lost in correspondingly tortured detail and exaggerated musical nuance. The singer who had intended to display to his audience great depth of feeling and empathy with Heine and Schumann comes across instead as an ingenuous fellow, publicly wallowing in his own emotion. The internal image he has of himself does not match the actual image he externally displays. Why? Because he has never *seen* himself perform. He falsely assumes that he *looks* like what he *feels*.

Some singers refuse to watch themselves in the mirror. "It distracts me to look at myself while I am singing!" Others refuse the aid of the video camera, and cringe when seeing a playback. "But I didn't think I was doing *that*. I look awful on tape!" It is clear that the same singer will "look awful" on stage to viewers as well. The public sees not what the singer imagines he or she looks like while singing, but his or her actual appearance. The singer should know what that is. Performance experience itself will not bring about radical improvement, but will simply make more deeply ingrained those habits.

Visual aspects of public performance are almost as important as the audio. Unlike the instrumentalist, the singer does not bring an external instrument onto the stage, then hold it, or sit before it or around it in order to play. The singer's body *is* the instrument. Physical behavior on stage must be as controllable as vocal behavior; in fact, the two are inseparable. Just as the sounds of singing must be disciplined to produce repeatable vocalism, so must attitudes of the physical instrument. Involuntary rocking, weaving, swaying, raising and lowering the head, elevating the eyebrows and furrowing the brow, gyrating the torso and gesticulating, have direct effects not only on the eye and ear of the listener, but also on the production of vocal sound.

It is for this reason that every singer, professional or student, should have access to video equipment in preparation for public performance. When standing before an audience, the singer will then know with reasonable assurance what the body and the face are registering. Feeling and imagining are insufficient guarantees that the physical responses of the body are properly conveying the intended emotions to the public.

One might ask why contemporary performance preparation should extend beyond the means available to artists of the past. That is a bit like asking why people drive automobiles instead of horse-drawn carriages. Although the eye of the listener has always taken in as much as the ear, today's performer must operate in an arena with even greater visual orientation than was the case in previous decades.

Modern theater avoids the exaggerated histrionics that were often appropriate in the past, because such maneuvers appear excessive and insincere. Good theater, including the concert forum, should not appear "theatrical." A singer must be able to monitor his external behavior while performing, so that it conveys to an audience, through both voice and body, the desired artistic intention.

The video camera is one of the most important pedagogical tools available to modern vocal performance pedagogy. To ignore its potential is to deny the singer a major assist in establishing performance competence and security. Visual feedback makes it possible for the singer to be rid of extraneous, idiosyncratic, and superficial movement, and to avoid appearing self-indulgent or awkward in interpretation and communication. The performing instrument (the body and the voice) are then united in the manner the singer envisions. Performance self-image takes on reality.

31

Liederwurst

Stylistic considerations determine performance practice. A skillful singer does not use identical degrees of vibrancy and vocal intensity in the *B Minor Mass* and the Verdi *Requiem,* yet well-trained singers of the appropriate vocal categories may perform both works creditably, even though the two masterpieces are worlds apart stylistically and emotionally.

Professional preparation requires good coaching from persons who understand requirements unique to the several vocal repertories. Even within nineteenth-century operatic literature, there are clear stylistic differences. One does not sing Donizetti like Verdi, Gounod like Massenet, or von Weber like late Wagner. Just as certainly, to apply a single singing style to the *Lieder* of Schubert, Brahms, and Wolf is to misunderstand the musical and romantic progression of a century.

Yet, not infrequently one hears well-intentioned public instruction in which young professional singers are admonished to sing *Lieder* in a fashion that is fundamentally nonvocal. This approach is based upon a commendable realization that synthesis of word and music is a conscious aim of many *Lied* composers. Unfortunately, it forgets that expressive vocal sound is dependent on the well-functioning physical vocal instrument as its medium, and it confuses desirable nuance with undesirable vocal mannerism.

For example, the tendency to approach the songs of Schubert in *parlando* fashion destroys the essential lyricism that characterizes them. The vocal "miniaturist" is a perennial phenomenon in the performance arena, and each generation has had several singing artists who carved out major careers based on intimacy of expression, as interpreters of a narrow literature. Music and poetry are turned into a personal vehicle. This may be aesthetically viable for those artists, although in some cases one suspects that limitations of the vocal instrument, more than artistic conviction, have determined stylistic mannerisms. There is, indeed, a certain wisdom in turning one's vocal limitations and necessities to artistic advantage. However, to do so under the guise of "correct" style, and to impose such style on other performers, raises a question of professional propriety.

The specific problem with much current *Lieder* coaching is the notion that preciousness of expression is required. This has particularly been the case as a result of the burgeoning commercial recording of much of the *Lied* literature. To hear what takes place in the recording studio and what occurs in the concert hall with the same artist may be revealing. An example might be cited of the famous *Lieder* exponent, with a large body of recorded performances, who then sings a *Lieder* recital in the Grosser Saal at the Salzburg Festival. His festival audience is disappointed because "he doesn't sound like his records." *Voce finta* and nonvibrant singing can be registered successfully in the recording studio, but less so in the concert hall, where the artist must *sing.*

An argument could be made that some early *Lied* literature was meant only for the salon and the drawing room, but internal evidence of the writing itself, and the emotional content of the poetry, indicate that a great deal of the *Lied* literature was intended to be sung by professionally trained voices. One need only recall that the two great Schubert cycles were written during the period when Vogl, a successful operatic baritone and performance collaborator with Schubert on the Schubert *Lieder,* was one of the composer's favorite singers. Vogl himself lamented that there was no German school of singing that could do justice to the Schubert *Lieder.* Schröder-Deviant, the reigning Donna Anna, Leonora *(Fidelio),* Lady Macbeth, "the only singer who could survive with Liszt as an accompanist" (according to Robert Schumann, who dedicated *Dichterliebe* to her), and the singer whom Chorely described in 1822 as "a strong soprano," was a foremost *Lieder* singer into the mid-1850s.

It is in the most frequently performed Lied cycles, chief examples being the Schumann *Frauenliebe und -Leben* and *Dichterliebe,* as well as the Schubert cycles, that one tires of the *Liederwurst* "link-sausaging" of the vocal line, as the singer tries to express depth of emotion and profound understanding of the text through syllabic detail. The flow of vocal sound is interrupted because it is directed not to the musical phrase or the poetic idea, but to constant dynamic altering of each note and syllable. This is an inappropriate stylistic concept, a misapplication of the *messa di voce* principle so essential to phrase shaping and dynamic control. The decrescendo-doing of each syllable as it approaches the next produces a kind of "rock-a-bye baby" vocal effect. The performer's intent is to be artistic, but the vocal line, the essence of the singing style, is destroyed.

The shape of a phrase, like that of a sentence or the formation of a thought, has a continuity that directs it to a specific point or points of importance. When listening to some Lieder performances, one recalls childhood schoolroom experiences when the "Dick and Jane" primers were haltingly read: "Dick! Throw—the—ball—to—Spot! Spot! Bring—the—ball—to—Jane!" With great devotion, Miss Heft, the remarkably patient first-grade teacher, would try to inspire the reader to make flowing sentences, not strings of syllables. We badly need Ms. Heft in some of today's *Lieder*-coaching sessions!

Perhaps the most expressive vocal device is the *legato,* which permits continuous sound that then can be sculpted into eloquent phrases. When the flow of vocal sound has been established, the momentary word emphasis, the doubling of voiced or unvoiced consonants, and the shift of dynamic levels becomes truly meaningful. By contrast, producing *Liederwurst* is neither communicative nor vocally arresting. The potential for communication of the poetry and the music depends upon vocal sound, not on parodistic vocalism.

32

Seit ich ihn gesehen . . . kann ich jedoch singen!

The recording industry has revitalized popular interest in the *Lied* as a performance vehicle. One can imagine the disbelief that might well be expressed by a number of nineteenth-century composers at the wide distribution of *Lieder* recordings in the homes of today's music lovers. This, of course, is true of music composition of most past centuries, a great deal of which was done with an eye to the current season, not the judgment of posterity. More startling for the composers of the past might be the performance practices applied to their songs.

The advantages of so much recorded performance being available to today's young performing artist are enormous, yet this explosion of recorded material is not without its perils for singers. There is much empirical evidence that a recent generation of *Lieder* singers has been led down a pathway of preciousness by attempting to imitate male and female re-cording artists. These singers deliver on close microphone location the ex-quisite dramatic vignettes of Hugo Wolf as though entertaining in a cock-tail lounge, while the pianist is then forced to perform the idiomatic pianoforte accompaniments as though they had been written for harpsi-chord. The poetry of the *Lied* (including the Wolf *Lieder*) mostly deals with engagingly vital or warm and noble sentiment, and seldom whimpers. Even the most highly romantic and personal expressions in the *Lied* litera-ture need to be seen within their historical literary and musical settings.

Which brings us to *Seit ich ihn gesehen.* No matter what one may think of von Chamisso's male expression of how females should properly regard their (in Chamisso's case) much older male partners, or of Schumann's setting of such maudlin poetry, for a contemporary female to sing this literature as though she were undergoing induction into penal servitude is simply too much to bear. Even Robert Schumann, with his idealization of what marriage could mean (which, in his own case, failed to turn out perfectly, although there was no lack of offspring), did not write music to be moaned through and groaned out as a result of female adoration of the male.

The tiny bellows-like straight-tone crescendoing and decrescendoing of each syllable in *Seit ich ihn gesehen* in the breathless, nonvibrant fashion found in some recent recordings, becomes caricature-like. Viewed from a purely harmonic basis, it is apparent that, in this first *Lied* of the cycle, Schumannesque "lyric declamation" does not imply sexless whispering. It is also evident, from the unfolding emotive basis of the entire cycle, that Schumann had in mind a young woman of character and will, not an enslaved concubine. His inspiration for the cycle—the woman he fought so hard to marry and who later pulled him through a number of emotional crises—was not wimpy. She was a highly stable individual, a very de-manding teacher (she made all her female students dress in black in accor-dance with the seriousness of their work), a remarkable concert pianist, a composer of merit, a matriarchal figure who ran her household with a firm hand.

Who sings *Frauenliebe und -Leben* must be a sensuous, not an ectoplas-mic, personality. This cycle is not literature for the shy and retiring female singer of limited vocal resources. The singer dare not circumvent vocalism that includes good resonance and balance or fall into a form of detached *Sprechstimme.* She can say, with pride, "Seit ich ihn gesehen, kann ich jedoch singen!" (Since having seen him, I can nevertheless sing!) The woe-ful example of some singers, both male and female, who moo and sigh through the literature of the *Lied* should be identified as the faddism it represents, and as stylistic distortion of vital, living literature.

33

Words or Sentences?
Notes or Phrases?

Communicative language is not formed by stringing isolated words together. We express ourselves by organizing words into sentences that permit the progression of an idea. Groups of such sentences develop the initial
thought. There is a direct correspondence between the role of words and
sentences in spoken language and of notes and phrases in singing.

A singer presents musical and literary ideas spread out over longer periods of time than does the speaker. This duration factor allows the elements
of vocal and musical expression to exceed those of normal spoken communication.

Because a word, or even a syllable, may last several seconds during
singing (whereas it would be quickly disposed of in speech), there is a risk
that sung syllables will assume an individual existence detrimental to logic.
It is just this literary pitfall that may cause the singer to stumble. The
singing of individual syllables and words often interferes with both vocal
timbre and phrase direction. A false assumption is made that it is artistically desirable to customize each syllable or word in order to enhance it.
Some singers treat syllables and words like long swags of link sausage. In
place of vocal line and dramatic sensibility, the vocal sausage-maker gives
us *words, not sentences; notes, not phrases.*

Just as the spoken sentence must be inflected and shaped in order to be
communicative, so must the sung phrase. However, the tendency to make
a *messa di voce* on every syllable, in the hope of being artistic, produces
naïve musical results. The crescendoing and decrescendoing of each sustained pitch characteristic of some singers generates a cloying, mannered
style. Legato, which is the most basic element of expressive singing, is lost.

Of course, there is no room for maintaining only one dynamic level
throughout a song or aria. But the imaginative singer needs to be reminded
that there is a danger that "fussing" over every word or syllable in such
detail may destroy the totality of the phrase.

This brings us back to the initial question: Notes or phrases? The intelligent communicator will need to sing phrases even if the musical setting of
the poetry is largely syllabic. Syllabic settings frequently have rhythmically

percussive keyboard or instrumental accompaniments. Singers must learn not to be unduly influenced by them when the vocal line clearly indicates a contrasting legato. Of special difficulty is the avoidance of "notiness" in the singing of fast-moving texts in compound rhythms (6/8, 9/8, 12/8). The tendency to chop the short notes into small nonvibrant units of sound and to accent and sing vibrantly the longer notes must be corrected. A good device to use when working on songs or arias with quickly occurring syllables is first to sing the phrase on nonsense syllables, filling each note with sound. Use "ra-di-da-da," or "ra-la-la-la," or something similar. Follow that by singing the same single phrase on one vowel, then with just the vowels inherent in the text. Finally, the text should be sung with the same linear character of the continuously sung sound. This process should be done phrase by phrase, not by singing the aria from beginning to end.

In singing, one often overlooks the inflections of speech that most composers have taken into consideration when setting texts. Speaking the text at a relatively high dynamic level suitable for stage delivery, in the tempo of the musical setting, is useful in eliminating series of individual notes, while it also points out the important words that shape the phrase. Another useful device is to sing the text with the same rhythm and tempo on a single pitch, beginning at a lower level than the actual musical phrase and arriving at the *tessitura* of the written phrase through gradual pitch elevation. This is a valuable practice, because unwanted syllabification and the breaking of legato in singing are both often related to intervallic leaps, both large and small.

The question of notes or phrases does not directly relate to problems of diction in singing, although it is clear that diction will be cleaner when constant legato and quickly occurring consonants permit a flowing singing line. Many techniques intended to improve diction are built on percussive enunciation that has no place in either singing or speaking. They produce notes, not phrases.

Above all, the singer should not confuse heavy syllabification with expressive singing. Every phrase must have direction and an overall shape that is undisturbed by excessive attention to the detailing of individual notes and syllables. These considerations do not involve the general aesthetic question of which comes first, words or music, or of the way in which composers achieve synthesis of text and music. They are concerned with practical performance techniques that permit the singer to be musically expressive and vocally secure while interpreting the poet and composer.

34

Sentiment or Sentimentality?

For the sake of argument, let us say you are judging a vocal contest that holds high-level performance expectations. It is your hope that you are a thorough musician capable of determining competence based on style, phrase shaping, general musical nuance, dynamic variation, linguistic accuracy, and overall communication. Although the beauty of the vocal instrument and its technical skill are assumed in any singing contest, you are also looking for the kind of total performance that makes the artist.

In fact, voice teacher though you may be, you have grown weary of hearing technical singing machines with stunning sustained Fs above high C, and rapid-fire melismas that never seem to stop. You also know that the audience will respond with wonderment to such feats. But you recall having heard, over the years, several hundred others with similar range and technical prowess, all of whom seem to have been cloned from the same technical cultivar. The score sheets in front of you begin to all look alike, and a general sense of the blurring together of performers sweeps over you.

Suddenly there emerges from this plethora of pyrotechnical gingerbread a singer who begins to show some understanding of the relationship of text to musical phrase, even to language inflection. You settle back in your adjudication chair and look forward to some real music-making. You will always remain convinced that it *could* have been fine music making, but early disappointment sets in. Our "musical" singer has not yet fully understood the difference between sentiment and sentimentality. *Abendempfindung* is pulled apart at the seams by miniature crescendi and decrescendi on each syllable, by "word-painting," and by exaggerated dynamic contrasts, to the point that the general shape of the phrase is lost. The Debussy *mélodie,* sung with undesirable heavy speech inflections and straight-toning detrimental to the center of intonation, comes across like a *chanson.* An artless listener might further conclude from this performance that Brahms had only a limited concept of how to spin out a long vocal line. The singer's hill-and-valley approach to arching phrases permeates all the *Lieder* as though syllabification were an artistic goal in itself. The oratorio selection comes across as an exercise in *parlando.* These attempts at sensitive style result instead in revolving-door auditory responses for the listener. Now we begin to wish the contestant would really sing!

Sensitive singers avoid the unimaginative concentration on sound solely for tone's sake that characterizes some singing. An opposite peril for the singer, however, lies in trying to prove to audiences and to judges how "musical" one is. Distortion of the music by putting on it one's personal stamp, in "underscoring" each nuance, is just as disturbing as monotonous vocalization.

There is a fine line to be drawn between true sentiment and superficial sentimentality. Unfortunately, some well-schooled singers have not yet found that important distinguishing border. Part of the problem comes from attempting to put into practice the subtle stylistic suggestions offered by some coaches and teachers of "interpretation," principles that the singer has taken to excess and thereby diminished the intrinsic instrumental beauty of the voice.

It is fair to estimate that a number of substantial prizes have been lost at major national and international competitions by talented young singers who mistook sentimentality for subtlety and finesse. One sometimes hears a contestant complain that the contest judges were interested only in big operatic voices. Had he or she only known, the judges were very much hoping the musicianly singer would distinguish between sentiment and sentimentality, and do some honest singing.

35

Singing the Recitative

The origins and the development of the recitative as a distinct vocal style offer an intriguing historical view of the art of singing itself. It is not possible to speak of performance practices in the recitative without taking into account its existence over a period of four centuries and its integral relationship to those more static moments in opera served by the *aria*. It is apparent that the term *stile recitativo* has its etymological source in the verb *recitare*, properly translated not only as "to recite" but also "to perform."

As all singers know, the Florentine Camerata made use of speech rhythms in its musical/dramatic experimentations, and even earlier liturgical music tended to be built on speech patterns and inflections, but without the use of exact rhythmic notation. Overlooked today is the fact that the separation between recitative and aria was not always clearly defined during the first years of their inception. It is also the case that in the early years of the seventeenth century, the recitative and the aria were frequently less well delineated than in some later periods. There even existed, at times, the *aria recitativa*.

By the eighteenth century, the recitative had become the dramatic link between arias (and ensembles), often in modulatory fashion. It existed in two basic forms, one occurring with keyboard accompaniment (generally harpsichord) and the other with orchestral accompaniment. A number of eighteenth-century treatises on performance practice deal with the harmonic realization of the recitative and its proper cadential embellishments, subjects not germane here.

Although *recitativo secco* became ubiquitous in the eighteenth century, it was not until the nineteenth century that the term was applied to recitative accompanied only by keyboard, to differentiate it from *recitativo accompagnato* (or *strumentato*), which had orchestral accompaniment and which was already widely in use by the early eighteenth century. In fact, because of the need for its slower musical realization, the orchestrally accompanied recitative frequently has an *arioso* character about it. Although during the early years of the nineteenth century, dry recitative *(secco)* was still retained in the *opera buffa,* accompanied recitative became the rule in *opera seria. Recitativo accompagnato* tended to follow two distinct pathways, one being the substitution of orchestral chords for the previously simple keyboard support, in a kind of orchestrated *recitativo semplice,* the other consisting of more extended orchestral material of considerable melodic and harmonic importance. Examples of these two kinds of recitative can be found extensively in Mozart, as in *Le nozze di Figaro,* for example. Rossini still used *recitativo secco* in *Il Barbiere di Siviglia,* but he and his contemporaries Bellini and Donizetti began to abandon it in favor of the orchestrally accompanied recitative. Twentieth-century composers as well have made occasional use of *recitativo accompagnato,* but seldom of *recitativo secco.*

Our reason for taking a cursory look at the several forms of recitative is to help clarify confusion that sometimes surrounds contemporary performance practices of recitatives that cover such a wide span of history. Early Baroque opera (from the first works of Monteverdi to the period terminating around 1650), opera and cantata literature from the second half of the seventeenth century, the works of Handel and Telemann from the first half of the eighteenth century, and the culmination of operatic vocal styles with Mozart in the several forms of operatic media in which he excelled do not all require identical performance practices. An in-depth look at these recitative styles as they relate to the singing voice would constitute a major musicological study yet to be undertaken by experts, and the subject is here mentioned only in passing.

Our aim of the moment is the practical one of determining how today's singer should approach the singing of the recitative as it presents itself in much of the "standard" performance literature. Having already taken a rapid look at the differences between the two major types of orchestrally accompanied recitative, it seems most logical to deal first with the kind of recitative that introduces the eighteenth-century aria, in either opera or oratorio, reserving for a moment comment regarding the performance of dry *(secco)* recitative from the same period.

Consider as a classic example the relationship of the recitative *Giunse alfin il momento* to the subsequent aria *Deh, vieni, non tardar (Le nozze di Figaro)*. Here present are the typical pitfalls singers may encounter in performing such a recitative passage. Although the opening vocal line of the recitative that follows the brief orchestral introduction is unaccompanied, it must not be sung in *secco* or *parlando* fashion; it has about it an *arioso* character that mirrors the orchestral commentary that precedes and follows it. There is a tendency among even some established artists to treat this recitative as though it has a *parlando* existence separate from what comes before and what follows. This is because the singer tends to confuse *secco* and *strumentato* musical styles. To throw aside the next phrase, beginning *timide cure,* as though it were not a part of the integrated musical whole, is to misunderstand the style and to destroy the composer's finely spun emotive moments. When *Oh come par* is frivolously and hurriedly tripped over, its entire musical fabric has been shredded.

The major stylistic error in performing not only the *operatic scena* of Mozart but also the concert aria is in treating all recitative as though it were *parlando* in nature. Some vocal coaches appear unclear in their own understanding of the two distinct styles involved in *recitativo secco* and *recitativo accompagnato* passages. This fault is found not only in performances of Mozart; Handel suffers equally, as do later composers such as Bellini. When the extended accompanied recitative, *Eccomi in lieta vesta,* that so wondrously leads into the aria *Oh quante volte (I Montecchi e i Capuletti)* is rushed in imitation of speech rhythm, no music remains.

What, then, of the *recitativo secco* itself as the medium for rapidly unfolding dramatic action so often realized through dialogue? Mozart, the master of extended recitative passages, as in *Don Giovanni* and *Le nozze di Figaro,* offers the finest examples for consideration. Leporello and the

Don must expeditiously deliver dialogue that catches the excitement of the dramatic situation, often *sotto voce,* but with sufficient vocal energy and intensity to carry in large theaters. Once again, the recording industry may do a disservice to a young Leporello and a young Don. The kind of breathy chattering that can be heard on studio recordings is often not *parlando* singing, but the result of intimate whispering into a microphone. Skillful recitative can be audibly delivered in the hall with rapid-fire speed at all dynamic levels only if a center of energy and vibrancy is maintained in the vocalism. Breathy "stage whispering" is stylistically inappropriate, except in rare conspiratorial moments when word communication is not an essential.

As is often the case when it comes to practical musical performance that aims to be appropriately historically informed, too much of a good thing can be detrimental to music-making. Of course, the recitative must be performed as a theatrical convention that closely adheres to the natural rhythms, inflections, and accents of speech; the manner in which it is rhythmically paced gives it its life and its credibility. However, when coaches and conductors (and above all, nonmusician stage directors!) demand wispy phonatory noises on the operatic stage under the impression that such sounds constitute recitative style, the singer must learn to protect himself or herself. Extended stage whispering is not healthy for the vocal instrument, is largely inaudible, and is not recitative style.

A singer who is serious about stylistic authenticity will keep in mind the differences between the several types of recitative, and will not forget that they are all written for the *singing* instrument.

36

Reality and Art

"But you don't understand! I am an artist, and singing is how I express myself!" said the moderately successful soprano, who had managed to fight her way through *Sempre libera* in a European master class, but who was not happy with the instructor's suggestions about working on vocal onsets, breath management, and agility exercises. Although the possessor of an impressive vocal instrument, she was clearly neither technically comfortable nor artistically expressive. Why? Because she assumed that the emotional involvement she experienced from singing the text, and her understanding of the dramatic situation, would allow her to communicate her innermost sentiments to a responsive public. She had not yet learned that art is not reality; art consists of the disciplining of reality for the portrayal of emotion without succumbing to emotion.

If Otello were to feel the rage expressed musically and dramatically in Verdi's final scene, one would need to engage a new Desdemona every night, and the *tenore robusto* would face charges of homicide. Otello could not successfully accomplish strangulation and high vocal *tessitura* simultaneously. Nor can Violetta become a wild, inebriated woman while accomplishing her melismatic tasks at high levels of vocal intensity and physical energy. A genuinely weeping Rodolfo will find it impossible to deliver his final, heartbreaking, sustained $G^\sharp_4$ vocal cries of "Mimì!" Andromache cannot move us with her decision to throw her royal son over a precipice if she is as torn apart emotionally as she would be by such a horrible act in real life.

It simply is not possible to experience deep levels of pain, joy, or sexual arousal in public and to sing about them at the same time. Art is knowing how those experiences would feel and how to translate them into communicable representations. It is of no interest for an audience to watch a performer wallow in her or his own emotional bathwater while floundering to keep vocally afloat. In fact, the true artist-singer has long since learned to pull the private emotional plug, to climb out of the bath of personalized sentiment, and to dress raw emotion in the clothing of skillful artistry. The singer's task is not to experience emotional highs in performance but to transform sentiment through artistic means so successfully that the audience can share with the performer in the portrayal.

Operatic singers learn not to allow the stage to rob them of their vocalism. A seasoned observer of so-called "master classes" soon grows weary of public teaching that attempts to induce high emotional responses to text and drama when the student is not yet capable of phonating through the material. Student participants in such circumstances may momentarily be stimulated to new levels of emotional response through the increased flow of adrenalin, but seldom in the process do they receive the technical tools for continued safe application of performance excitation.

Indeed, many of the situations encountered by singers in both the operatic and the song literature could not possibly have been experienced by the performers themselves. Who among us has fallen in love with his own legal mother, or thrown her child into the fire, or strangled her newborn baby, or been forced to emigrate as punishment for pursuing prostitution, or had his heart eternally eaten by eagles? The artistic imagination learns to *simulate* dramatic situations never experienced in life.

Don José probably needs to control and pace his emotions, not fall prey to them, as he assays the vocal tasks of *La fleur*. If he hasn't already learned to manage his breath, achieve an even resonance balance as he moves from one register to another, properly modify his vowels, and accomplish the dynamic control Bizet requests, staggering about the stage in a state of excitation will not help. The voice will function as a communicative instrument only when its technical problems have been solved.

By no means is this an argument for nonexpressive, noninvolved singing. The dramatic singer needs to assemble every ounce of concentration, every shred of flexible mental and physical energy, and all of his or her athleticism and direct these abilities to the dramatic portrayal at hand. This can be done only if artistic objectivity can control the highly emotional content of much of the dramatic literature. In so doing, the great singer transforms reality into art. Raw emotion is not art. Art is not raw emotion.

37

Pop Music, Non-Western European Vocal Styles, and Efficient Vocal Function

Much of Western art owes its characteristics to a commitment to beauty, strength, and health stemming from classic Greece. It is true that at various periods stylization and conventions modified those principles, at least until the rediscovery of the ancient classical aesthetic at the time of the musical Renaissance. Since the appearance in the West of significant solo vocal literature at the close of the sixteenth century and the beginning of the seventeenth century, the human vocal instrument has consistently maintained that philosophy, at least until recent decades, in which the pop music culture has largely forsaken the historic precepts of timbre and musical structure in favor of other values. That aesthetic commitment becomes apparent when one looks at the history of the solo voice as it has developed in the Western world over the past four centuries.

The technical skills mandated by serious vocal literature (and even of much traditional popular music) require excellent physical coordination of the vocal instrument. Demands of range, *tessitura, sostenuto,* agility, dynamic control, and vocal coloration can be met in this literature only by healthy vocalism in response to an ideal of beautiful timbre undergirded by physical strength.

In the Americas and Europe, some forms of current entertainment that make use of the vocal instrument are no longer oriented to those classic goals, as any otolaryngologist who must deal with today's singing entertainer will attest. The extent of vocal abuse that accompanies much of the music that "untrained professional voices" (a medical designation) engage in today keeps the otolaryngologist's appointment calendar crowded. There are a number of teachers of singing, themselves "classically" trained, who do yeoman service in attempting to modify the effects of misuse and abuse that many young entertainers experience by tempering the more extreme phonatory aberrations of those singers. (So long as there is a lucrative market for such sounds involving the human voice, there will be performers to meet the demand.) The major concern of the voice teacher of the popular performer is no longer whether "the Broadway voice" can be kept in healthy condition; it is how to avoid aphonic episodes with singers who ignore the canons of beauty, strength and health. This has become a Western-world entertainment problem.

Another area of vocal performance is of considerable interest to persons who are drawn to the study of World Musics. With the burgeoning Western world interest in non-Western cultures comes the question of how ethnomusical vocal sounds are produced, and whether the Western ideal of skilled vocalism has not been too narrow with regard to matters of function.

Because the subject is vast and involves many disparate sources and diverse cultures, and because as of this moment there exists insufficient research into the vocal health aspects of such phonations, raising the question may seem purely academic. Nonetheless, for those teachers of "classical" singing who have long been convinced that there is a relationship between vocal efficiency and vocal aesthetics, the question is intriguing. Until vocal practices found in non-Western liturgical music, and in the musics of the Orient, of Africa, of Polynesia, of Eastern Europe, of folk-music enclaves on several continents (such as native American dancers/singers, Andalusian gypsies, Transylvanian peasants, Portugese urban Fadoists, Bulgarian farmers, Berber villagers, and primitive tribal groups) can be subjected to investigation, no definite answers can be given. It is a subject that will offer interesting research rewards in the future.

However, some personal impressions and experiences may be allowable.

It was this author's privileged experience some twenty years ago to exchange information on singing techniques with a muezzin whose duties
took place at a large Cairo mosque. My colleague was an exceedingly large
person, tall, of tremendous girth. In his demonstration for me, he tied a
large rope (perhaps it was part of his liturgical costume) around his waist,
raised his head at a tilt, and began very loud phonation. He pushed force-
fully outward on his rope-belt, and he carried what the Western world
would call "chest voice" (heavy vocalis action) into the upper-middle and
upper ranges of his ample voice. He produced the melismatic portions of
the call to prayer with shakes of the head, and perhaps of the larynx.
The musculature of his neck was distended, and his complexion took on
additional color. The sound was quite remarkable and not unlike that of
certain operatic baritones in trouble at aria's end (although it is patently
unfair to judge his performance by Western criteria). When asked if he
would kindly repeat the exercise he informed me that he could not do so,
because it was so strenuous for his voice that he could manage the brief
call (a few minutes in duration) only five times per day. In short, vocal
efficiency was not an aim. One could assume that he occupied his position
as muezzin at a major mosque because of his professional qualifications.

Unfortunately, these days the calls from minarets are almost entirely
electronic replays, so that one wonders if the art of Muslim liturgical song
has much of a future. Twenty years ago, one could still walk the hills of
Sarajevo to hear live muezzin calls resounding from mosques small and
large. The unintentional polyphony that results from the simultaneously
reverberating, all-pervasive recorded muezzin calls from competing
mosques in the center of Istanbul would have delighted Charles Ives. The
popular singers of present-day Turkey (as can be heard on radio and cas-
sette tape) often include some of the melismatic characteristics related to
the Muslim liturgical style, delivered with a timbre not unrelated to the
muezzin call.

The cantorial styles of various parts of Europe (Eastern as opposed to
Western) are at times near the "operatic" sound, and at times quite far
removed from it; Slavic folk elements seem to vie with "classical" vocalism
in this European Jewish liturgical singing.

Other personal "ethnic" listening experiences confirm the impression
that the aforementioned "classical" Greek ideal is not universally accepted
(certainly not among most of today's singers of popular idioms). The popular vocal music of Malta is not like that of nearby Italy, although it may
be influenced by neighboring North Africa. Listening to the vocalism involved in hymn singing twenty years ago in a church in Sicily, with its
crossroads mixture of Western and Eastern singing sounds, remains an
unforgettable memory. The singing/dancing/acting tradition of the young

boatmen of the upper Sudan (who take the roles of both males and females, using the timbre of their male speaking voices as well as imitative female vocal sounds in falsetto) was still remarkably untouched by Western influences some thirty years ago.

Singers of traditional music that stems from the Orient do not look for the same kinds of "efficient" vocalism as do Westerners, and make use of timbres and colorations that strike the Western ear as thin and nasal. On the other hand, although listening to Polynesian musical performances arranged for Western visitors to the South Pacific may not be the best way to determine vocal traditions in those island regions, the use of full-bodied vocalism is unmistakable; it is what the cultivated Western ear would describe as "chest voice" production carried beyond the point that Dame Nellie Melba, in an early decade of the twentieth century, advised was safe.

Even within our own culture, there are a few teachers of singing who believe that Neapolitan street cries in "chest" form the model for good vocalism, especially in "belting"; and from the other side of the Alps comes the *Urkraft der Stimme* (primitive strength of the voice) of Georg Armin, who, it is reported, had his students, as a vocal exercise, shout upward from the central courtyard to his third or fourth floor apartment. The primal scream, as a means for removing vocal inhibition and for recovering "lost vocal functions," periodically surfaces in England and America. A small fraction of the North American pedagogy community recommends carrying "chest" voice into the highest ranges (as an exercise in register separation meant to develop the vocal instrument), much beyond the region reserved for that timbre in traditional literatures and vocal pedagogies.

So, shall we chuck all this nonsense about vocal efficiency and declare it simply a cultural characteristic of European-oriented society, transplanted to our own American continent? As one might expect, this author's answer is a resounding "No!" There is no reason there cannot be many strands of artistic vocalism from many sources, and there is no need to subject them to aesthetic criteria that do not pertain to them. But it is safe to predict that future research into their function will support the Western ideal, stemming from our Greek heritage, that that which is the most efficient vocalism is the healthiest vocalism, and that what we call "beautiful timbre" is its logical result.

38

How Is Legato Achieved in Singing?

Legato is the result of binding one sound to the next. The term stems from the Italian verb *legare,* meaning to bind or tie. There is a strong conviction among vocal *cognoscenti* that excellence in singing can exist only if the art of legato has been mastered. Traditional vocal literatures call for a high degree of stable legato singing.

As with any musical instrument, in the singing voice it is the progression of uninterrupted sound that permits legato. If the segments of a sung phrase go forward in contiguous fashion, legato is the un-induced result. Vocal legato depends upon continuity of vocal sound.

Many standard pedagogical suggestions for achieving legato do not get to the heart of the problem. For example, the suggestion to "bind" one note to the next often results in rigid vocal timbre, because the singer holds back airflow in an attempt to achieve legato; held, nonvibrant, straight tone is erroneously elicited by an increase in subglottic pressure in order to control the exit of breath. If, within a phrase, the singer produces vibrant vocal timbre followed by nonvibrant timbre, the legato is interrupted because vocal quality has been altered. (There are times when, for expressive purposes, some interruption of legato is desirable, but the habitual negating of the legato is another matter.) Extraneous technical maneuvers for achieving legato would not be required if each note were filled with equal dynamic levels of vibrant sound. Although legato results from binding together the sounds of singing, it is equally dependent on the consistency of vocal quality attained by connecting one sound to the next. Interruption of stable vocal timbre and the constant intermittent fluctuation of dynamic level destroy the perception of legato. Legato need not be so induced; it will result from the continuous flow of vibrant vocal sound.

Much non-legato singing comes from marked syllabification, in which each syllable is permitted to diminish in intensity as it approaches the subsequent consonant. This peril is especially present when singing non-Romance languages such as German and English, with their high incidence of diphthongs and consonantal clusters. In the musical settings of most poetic texts, rhythms and inflections of phonation are extended over longer periods of time than in speech, but the residual habits of rapid speech (particularly regional speech tendencies) often militate against legato. Perhaps the most treacherous of the numerous obstacles to vocal legato is the assumption that in order to be perceived as "musical" the singer must dynamically vary each syllable within the musical phrase. "Expressively" torturing individual notes and syllables is no more appropriate in singing than in speaking. Some singers italicize each emotive word through a kind of crescendo-decrescendo *(messa di voce)* technique that results in vocal instability, not in legato singing. Phrases then become segmented, resembling broken strings of beads, to the detriment of both timbre consistency and honest communication. The distortion of vocal sound under the assumption that artistry is thereby enhanced should be resisted. The substitution of the inflections of "emotive speech" for sustained singing is counterproductive to the musical and textual needs of elite vocal literature, including the song literature.

The sophisticated singer does not mistake personal emotional indulgence for artistic communication, or imitate those few successful artists who do. Rather, if the singer allows one sound to move directly into the next, that singer now has the means for playing with expressive dynamic control and ensuring both vocal and artistic integrity.

A frequently encountered pedagogical expression used in the hope of furthering legato is "Shape the phrase." Its good intentions, and those of the companion request "Sing a line," are quite clear. Yet a singing line is possible only when vocal sound fills and connects adjoining notes and syllables. Because phrase shaping (the trajectory of the musical "sentence") is an essential in artistic singing, singers are often urged to conceive of the totality of the phrase at the moment of its inception and to push that phrase forward to some climactic point, or onward to its conclusion Yet it is vocal sound that shapes a phrase, not superimposed controls set in motion by complex intellectual gyrations. Continuous vocal sound will of its own accord "move" the phrase and give it its "direction." Trying consciously to contour the phrase, to sculpt it in minute detail, may destroy the very phrase shaping the singer hopes to realize. The greater the reliance on free-flowing vocal sound, the higher the capability for successful rhythmic and dynamic shaping of the musical phrase. What is here intended is not the granting of license for insensitive uniformity of vocal sound produced without cognizance of textual and musical nuance, but a reminder to the singer that syllabically bumping along through a musical line in hope of realizing poetic sensibilities is a naïve way to interpret both music and text.

Legato is essential to all cultivated vocalism. It is fundamental to both efficient vocal production and artistry. Continuity of vocal sound is the substance of legato. Communication of musical and textual values best occurs when *sound,* not interpretative mannerism, is the medium of their conveyance.

39

Rhythm versus *Beat*

Singers are sometimes accused of being oriented to a single musical line, and of ignoring the harmonic movement that underlies the flow of vocal melody. It is true that most singers need to be reminded that phrase shaping results from harmonic progression and from overall rhythmic movement.

When one sings, the temporal aspects of speech are generally greatly extended, even with some *Lieder* composers who purposely follow speech inflection in lyrical declamation. But syllables have greater duration in singing than in speaking, and they are not usually accented as in spoken patterns. A common error among unskilled singers is to retain speech-inflection rhythms even when a melodic contour stretches out the phrase duration to several times that of speech. Such speech-retention practice belies the concept of the *bel canto* style, in which moving the voice and sustaining it are paramount. *Sostenuto* requires a deft legato in which the linear aspects of phrase direction are not diminished by the perpendicular elements of reiterated beats. Even in agile coloratura singing, linear direction should not be lost.

Yet today's young singer is surrounded by the current obsession with the "beat" in music, and may mistake it for the musical parameter that brings life to any musical score: *rhythm*. It is often the beat, not the musical line, that occupies the singer's attention. Much popular music is based on an incessant beat, the most primitive of all musical elements. At times musical form, melody, and timbre are reduced to near nonexistence as the verbal message is pounded out. When turning to classical song literature and arias, many young singers continue to favor the perpendicular movement of popular singing styles over the linear movement that is the basic requirement of the trained singing voice.

Singers seldom forget melodies, but textual and rhythmic elements are likely to suffer from memory lapses. As a preventive measure, rhythmic tapping with text repetition is often recommended to the student. This can be a helpful device in securing text and proper note values, but singer and teacher must be certain that strong rhythmic accent is not carried over into final performance preparation.

The basic pulse of the music, the *beat,* is the chief enemy of the melodic flow that characterizes most finely written vocal literature. Accented movements of hands, head, legs, and torso often mark the amateur singer. The accomplished singer is free of the need for constant physical movement, which works against vocal legato.

Both recitalist and opera singer must avoid repeated body impulses that negate the dramatic situation. If the drama is to remain believable, a singer/actor should learn to walk and move independently of the beat. This contrasts starkly with the current pop-culture scene, in which physical gyration is thought to be expressive and emotive. It is not easy for today's young singer (who may be involved in both performance worlds) to keep the differences in mind.

Rhythm, dictated by phrase contour, melodic excursion, and harmonic movement, is essential to artistic singing. The *beat* is detrimental to it.

40

Large and Small Strokes

Examine the brush display at the art supply store. Brushes come in all sizes. Some are made up of just a few hairs so that the painter may produce minute detail. Others are almost as broad as brushes meant for painting the back fence. Unless the artist deals exclusively in either miniatures or grandiose canvases, a good supply of various-sized brushes is requisite.

Comparing the art of the painter with that of the singer may, at first blush, appear something of an absurdity. This is not the case when one recalls that there are miniaturists and muralists among singers as well as among painters. Some singers work for small detail, whereas others aim to present spacious, sumptuous sonorities. The latter are concerned with the impact of resonant vocal sound; the former conceive vocal sound chiefly as a vehicle for musical and textual communication. The knowledgeable listener regrets both extremes.

There ought to be some relationship between essential detail and overall design. The singer who only "goes for the sound" offends our musical and stylistic sensibilities. Indeed, a large part of vocal instruction is necessarily devoted to developing style and musical nuance. Singers are not generally less musical than instrumentalists, but they often are behind in musically matters because they come late to the discovery that they possess an instrument of merit. They may not have had a long association with music and its traditions, and they may not yet be aware of some musical niceties that instrumentalists usually discover in early study. Singers are, then, often more in need of musical coaching than are instrumentalists. Yet there is a danger in applying an overlay of vocal filigree before the vocal structure of the singing instrument itself has been secured.

Tiny brush strokes are essential to miniature portraiture, partly because the genre is intended for intimate perusal. The advent of recorded vocal performances has introduced a relationship between performer and listener that normally does not exist in a concert situation, but that always exists between painter and viewer, even in the museum. It is interesting that some noted singing artists who have made lucrative careers in the recording business as vocal miniaturists have learned to modify that style of singing when they face the spaciousness of the average-sized hall. Such acoustic differences present a solid argument for keeping in mind that the "studio tone" is limited to the studio ambiance. The miniature vocal brush stroke is often inappropriate to the demands of the concert hall. What seemed very effective when recommended in the studio by the sophisticated vocal coach may well come across as cloying and mannered in actual performance circumstances.

There are, in the two extremes, a kind of aesthetic jousting. Some singers have little concern for the inherent timbre of sound, regarding timbre only as a supplementary part of communication. Others find the visceral nature of vocal sound to be emotive and expressive, and it is their chief concern. This latter viewpoint sometimes seems to downgrade the text or the poetry, as it conceives of the inherent *instrumental* timbre of the singing voice as being equal to that of any other instrument that arouses emotions by virtue of the quality of its sound, as, for example, the violin.

Both graphic and musical artists need to bring imagination to any performance, but it is not a singer's prerogative to forgo sound in an attempt to be "artistic." Some few prominent vocal performers feel compelled to stamp the music with a personal hallmark as proof of the degree of sensitivity and musicality they are capable of expressing. Generally, the result is a performance in which the listener/observer recognizes only self-indulgence, not true communication. The aim of performance should never be to prove to the audience how artistic one is but rather to communicate the essence of the music (including beautiful timbre) and the text to the listener.

In addition to having available a wide variety of brushes, the painter has license to create privately conceived visions. That is not the province of the singer, because the constraints of the re-creative artist are quite different from those of the creative artist. The singer brings new perspectives to already existent works of art, but has no right to turn them into vehicles of self-aggrandizement. The singer who, in order to enhance herself or himself, changes the composer's work into something never intended by that creative artist is a fraud, not an artist. Temperament has little to do with such distortion; ego, a great deal.

The brush display at the art store reminds us that large and small strokes are needed in the technical reservoir of the skillful painter. We know also that the re-creative singing artist must depict emotion, word, and musical idea while submitting to the constraints of the musical idiom, the poetry, the accompanying instrument or instruments, and even to ambient performance circumstances. Like the painter, the singer should have at hand a wide variety of brush strokes and should use all of them in balancing detail and overall design. Only in such fashion can performance completeness be realized.

41

The Gilda-in-the-Sack School of Singing

The ability to occasionally color the voice and to control a wide range of dynamic levels is an artistic necessity. To hear a singer produce one constant volume of tone, with no variation of timbre throughout an aria or an evening, is not a rewarding listening experience.

Poor last-act Gilda, having been brutally stabbed by Sparafucile, packaged up, and delivered to a duped Rigoletto (who may drag her around roughly, thinking he has hold of a tenor, on a stage set made up of several levels), must finally peer out of her sack and sing pathetically before her spirit floats heavenward. One may forgive the muted, straight tone Gilda may feel she must produce at this point. Although the greatest Gildas have always managed to achieve appealing timbre in these moments, Gilda's final singing must not sound as though her sack has served as an ideal vocal warm-up chamber for brilliant vocalism.

But let us go back to act I, garden scene: Soprano Gilda has been en-

tranced by the tenor lover she believes to be Gualtier Maldé. She may wish
to convey a feeling of the innocent, dreamy ecstasy of love, but there is no
reason that she should sound as though she has, at this point, just been let
out of the sack. Yet *Caro nome,* that war-horse of every vocal competition, often is sung with a disembodied vocalism that makes one suspect
Gilda is either ill or already dying, has an aversion to tenor suitors, or
does not understand the difference between the first- and last-act situations.

Nor should Mimì (despite the stairs) deliver her autobiographical first-
act aria as though consumption had already nearly completed its work.
Our other great consumptive, Violetta, is seldom guilty of lifeless vocalism
until it is called for in the last act; yet, a few Violettas of recent memory
have come perilously close to making this error in vocal characterization
with *Ah! fors'è lui* in act I.

It is not even chiefly in the operatic literature that the temptation to be
publicly sensitive and artistic at the expense of true musicality and style is
to be found. Why should the literature of the *Lied* and the *mélodie* be
delivered as though the performer were exceedingly weary with life when
the texts say otherwise? It requires a voice to sing the literature of both,
and although momentary aberrations from stable timbre can occur, no
singer can afford extended departures from good vocal timbre in an attempt to be "artistic." Style and artistry should not rob one of good vocalism.

"Softness" *(morbidezza, Weichheit, douceur),* a vocal timbre not necessarily related to *piano* dynamic level, when occasionally introduced in contrast to stabilized timbre can be exceedingly effective in shaping the character of an aria or song. But except for those instances where imminent
death *(Der Jüngling und der Tod)* or psychological devastation *(Das ver-
lassene Mägdlein)* is to be portrayed, no singer dare continually reduce the
innate beauty of vocal tone in the hope of becoming more expressive. It
should never be forgotten that the balanced timbre of any worthy singing
instrument, when coupled with understanding of textual nuance and musical line, is already emotive and expressive. The timbre of the violin is emotive; the violinist (who is often urged to "sing") does not need to distort
quality in order to shape musical and artistic phrases. The singing voice is
equally an instrument, with the added advantage of text and dramatic situation available to it. It is a *musical* instrument; its timbre *is* emotive!

Musical young singers, and at times their teachers and coaches, too
often believe they are producing a "sensitive" sound when they are actually only removing energy from the voice. Inexperienced singers sometimes
mistake lack of physical involvement for easy production. Of course, the
opposite error consists of bulldozing one's way through all styles of litera-

ture in the hope of knocking everyone over with sound. One of the main tasks of vocal pedagogy is to teach the student how to be vital and free simultaneously.

Producing tone appropriate to the dying Gilda is not the way to sing publicly unless you wish to sound as though you are already dying in the sack.

42

The Demise of the "Studio Baroque" Vocal Sound

Twentieth-century "Baroque vocal sound" has come a long way since its inception several decades ago. As in the early stage of any movement, it was to be expected that certain excesses would accumulate. There was a sudden burst of article-writing advising that performance "authenticity" required singers to forget what they had been taught about singing by their voice teachers. They were to "color the voice early Baroque" to match instrumental timbres; vibrato was forbidden; straight tone became the rule; and legato singing disappeared in favor of *détaché*, in imitation of instrumental styles. The human voice was treated as an extension of the Blockflöte and the Krummhorn. The end result most often was amateur vocalism in which patently *cantabile* vocal lines were treated like *recitativo secco*, and melismatic passages as spasms of aspirations. So much attention was directed to embellishing the vocal line that little remained of the structure of the music itself. *Inegale* excesses finished off what remained of the legato. The demanding vocal lines of Monteverdi, Cesti, Cavalli, Caldara, Marcello, and Alessandro Scarlatti were reduced to series of syllabic events. Lully, Rameau, and Handel, even in their pyrotechnical writings, were not viewed as intended for voices of size or substance. In this challenging vocal literature, the distinctive *cavatina* and *cabaletta* styles (which were later to develop into the *bel canto* style) became blurred.

There are several contributing reasons that the performance of "early" vocal music went through a period of distortion under the assumption that "authenticity" was being established. First among these is that although there is a substantial amount of documentation regarding instrumental performance practices for the several periods that fall under an "early music" designation, there is much less information about performance practices for the singing instrument. The second reason stemmed from an assumption that whatever the instrumentalist was requested to do must be imitated by the singing voice, regardless of differences in technical and musical demands. A third reason was a narrow reading of the acoustic circumstances surrounding the performances of many major Baroque works, especially operas. The fourth, and perhaps most overlooked, factor was the failure to take into account that the voice was the same physical and acoustic instrument in 1639 that it is today, although the orchestral instruments were not. The fifth and most compelling consideration lies in the internal evidence of the vocal writing itself.

Comparing the vocal requirements of *Orfeo* (1607) with that of *L'incoronazione di Poppea* or *Il ritorno d'Ulisse* (whose performance dates were 1640 and 1642, although they may have been of earlier composition) makes an interesting study, both from a musicological standpoint and in consideration of the technical demands placed on voices. Although possible, as has been suggested, that other hands may have also been involved in versions of these works, these dramatic compositions clearly represent the virtuosic vocal writing of the period. With the "invention" of opera and of the somewhat earlier oratorio style, the solo voice began to emerge. There is no doubt that the music of several centuries prior to the end of the sixteenth century was vocally demanding, but it was not chiefly for the *solo* singer; it consisted largely of ensemble music in service to the chapel, to the monastery, to the cathedral, or to the court. A radical change is apparent beginning with the seventeenth century, developing throughout the period of Monteverdi's long creative life. Range and *tessitura* already show the modern singing instrument. To sing the demanding roles of *L'incoronazione di Poppea* in detimbred straight tone, in imitation of the recorder, is to ignore the technical requirements of phrase management and dynamic levels and, above all, to negate the dramatic impact of this ample work.

It is equally impossible to conceive of nonvibrant singing of *bravura* tenor and bass arias, which were often written to be performed in competition with trumpets (a combination beloved by Handel). Handel, above all other composers of the period, made vocal demands of his singers that require the ultimate in breath management, laryngeal flexibility, and balanced resonance. These factors cannot be realized by an inefficiently functioning vocal instrument. The emasculated treatment of the Handelian vocal literature in recent decades was perhaps one of the more painful developments of mistaken "authenticity" in the performance of vocal music from the past. Hearing demanding Mozart opera arias from *Don Giovanni, Idomeneo, La clemenza di Tito,* and *Die Entführung aus dem Serail,* not to mention some of the dramatic concert arias, sung in "tube-tone" vocal timbres was equally distressing.

Never mentioned by the over-zealous of the early "authenticity" movement were the Italian organs of the sixteenth century that had ranks of pipes constructed in such a fashion as to produce the *vox humana* vibrato, or comments from composers like Praetorius that the human voice must have vibrancy, or Mozart's comments on the subject. Based on what the ear had come to enjoy, there was a conviction that the vocal sounds being asked for were those desired by composers and listeners of previous centuries.

A supportive argument that convinced some researchers was the belief that the hall acoustics of the earlier periods demanded miniature vocalism, and that the modern vocal instrument would have been out of place in such surroundings. This argument is, of course, quickly dispelled when Baroque opera is performed in some of the locations for which seventeenth-century and eighteenth-century operas were written, or in comparable modern performance spaces; it becomes eminently clear that reasonable resonance and intensity levels would have had to be maintained for vocal projection. The argument that the music of the Gabrieli and of their pupil Heinrich Schütz, when writing in the Venetian style, was to be sung with a small, straight tone is belied by listening to a vocal performance in San Marco today. Even when not accompanied by four Baroque trombones or other brass instruments (as was often the case, either in consort or antiphonal style), the immensities of space do not tolerate vocal miniaturism.

In the few serviceable opera houses that remain from the eighteenth century, with their more limited seating capacity than modern houses, one looks at the tiers of balconies and the complex of boxes, sings a few notes from the stage to check the acoustic, and must conclude that nothing less than a well balanced, vibrant, and projecting voice could ever have been appropriate in such ambiances. To employ the "salon" sounds that several decades ago were considered by some persons to be "historically informed," and that sold many record copies, would not have been possible in actual Baroque theater settings.

Fortunately, a new professionalism has modfied the practices of the past few decades regarding authentic Baroque vocal style. Monteverdi is now being produced in circumstances not far removed from the original conditions, with authentic "period" instruments whose players are skillful and who play in tune, and with singers who can legitimately manage his very difficult writing with the kind of elite vocalism it takes to sing any demanding literature. (One will surely be forgiven for having never forgotten a review carried in a large metropolitan newspaper during the early days of HIP [Historically Informed Performance], in which it was commented that the instrumentalists had appropriately played out of tune, thereby adding to the perception of authenticity!)

Gone is the period when the players of period instruments were amateur music lovers who, although recognizing the beauty of the Baroque litera-ture, mistook lack of technical skill for authentic performance practice. Today's professional Baroque instrumentalists are as capable of skillfully playing on their older instruments as they are on modern ones. Indeed, some early-music players bypass the modern instrument entirely, and ap-proach the study of period instruments with the same seriousness of pur-pose they would bring to a modern instrumental discipline. The result, in both cases, has been to raise the level of much current Baroque music performance to heights of excellence.

Along with this new professionalism has come the awareness that the singers for whom much of this music was written were not amateur music lovers but accomplished vocal technicians with pyrotechnical skills and dramatic instincts of the highest order. Anna Renzi, Monteverdi's Ottavia, was known as one of the great singers of her day. Today it is possible to hear both early and late Baroque opera performed with stunning vocal skill. Singers use their own instrumental voices and no longer try to sound like recorders. As a result, Baroque vocal music can now be performed skillfully without complaint that it is not "authentic."

The continuing substitution of male falsettists for contraltos, in the as-sumption that they sound like the *castrati* (a sound the unaltered adult male could not possibly accomplish), may be a cause for some skepticism, especially when it is done under the guise of "authenticity." Whoever likes countertenor voices has a right to make use of them, but not to tell us they are recovering the sounds of the Baroque. The castrati had prepubertal larynges located in oversized male bodies, often with immense torsos and correspondingly enlarged lung capacities. They were frequently of great height and with long vocal tracts stemming from larynges that could pro-duce the *bomba;* in contests with trumpets they won for both durability and decibels. Prepubertal castration inhibited bone growth but did not per-mit hormonal changes that produce masculine vocal and sexual character-istics. Techniques of producing the *musico* (also *evirato*) differed. What-ever their procreative deficiencies, some castrati were involved in amorous scandals. The often sweet sound of today's countertenor can result in a pleasant listening experience in some early literatures, but it is not the recovery of the castrato vocal instrument, which was known for its power and penetrating timbre. Nor can the castrato sound be recaptured by imitating the large female voice by means of the driving, reinforced falsetto of which many males are capable

It is, of course, nonsense to claim that the countertenor voice is produced by a rare laryngeal construction to be found in only a few male singers. Most countertenors are baritones, and some of them make more beautiful sounds in their falsetto voices than they can make in their baritone voices. They also can make a living doing it, and they should continue to do so, so long as there is a public demand for that sound. But to speak of the countertenor's rapid agility skill, subtle dynamic control, and three-octave range not matched by other male voices as remarkable feats is ingenuous. Falsetto singing, in imitation of the female vocal sound, does not require the same muscular activities in the laryngeal mechanism that *voce completa* (complete voice) timbre requires. Vocal-fold approximation, vocal-fold elongation, and vocal-fold mass diminution (which are the contributing laryngeal factors in the mounting vocal scale) require far less energy to accomplish in the falsetto voice, as every well-trained male singer empirically knows. (Some recent research on the falsetto voice confuses the issue, because the subjects were producing traditional *voce piena in testa* [full head voice] sounds in *mezza-voce,* which the researchers assumed to be falsetto production.) Critics who wax ecstatic over countertenor skills might be amazed at how many males can imitate those skills if they choose to negotiate the range in the same falsetto voice as does the countertenor. The professional male falsettist must have a fine sense of musical style, and is frequently an accomplished musician in nonvocal areas as well. Most countertenors will readily admit that they use a developed falsetto technique.

A countertenor generally learns to incorporate his own lower range male voice into the descending scale as he leaves the falsetto range, and this requires special technical skill. There are many kinds of countertenoring, and some of them are more efficient than others. Because of the tendency toward laryngeal gapping (the presence of some degree of open glottal chink, with escaping breath not turned into tone), the performance life of many countertenors is not extensive. Others continue for a longer period of time because they have found ways to compensate for this built-in hazard. Reinforcing the falsetto to produce a large driving sound, however, is as detrimental to the countertenor as is pressed phonation to any singer.

Some of the most exquisite writing for the *solo singer* stems from the seventeenth and eighteenth centuries. Longtime devotees of Baroque performance admit today that, in the recent past, personal preferences in tonal vocal ideals often were mistaken for historical accuracy of style. The fact that neither the heart nor the larynx has undergone radical physical change over these few centuries, the realization that there is little contemporary commentary to dictate how one should *sing* the music so far as timbre considerations go, the improvement in the quality of instrumental sound in support of professional vocal sound, the acknowledgment that some assumptions regarding acoustic conditions for the performance of Baroque music were arrived at without sufficient investigation, and, above all, the internal evidence of the vocal writing in the scores themselves are moving the demanding Baroque vocal literature back to an important place as performance vehicles for the well-trained modern singer. As the vitality of that music is recovered, the demise of the "studio Baroque" vocal sound is not to be lamented.

43

Vocal Coach or Vocal Technician?

Stories of instructional failure that students of singing tell each other are often based on having had wrong expectations regarding the kind of expert with whom they chose to study. A common complaint is, "She doesn't teach voice, she only coaches," or, equally widespread, "All he wants to do is to work on breathing and do a lot of vocalizing." Waste of time, energy, and money is a normal part of the building of a professional singing career, but many of these losses could be avoided if the singer were to recognize what mode of instruction is appropriate at each moment in career development, and if the singer were to take sequential steps in the process of preparation by being aware of what is out there in the way of instruction.

If Mr. Martin is a highly touted coach of the French *mélodie*, it makes little sense for a young soprano to expect to get her money's worth in instruction if she is unprepared to handle the linguistic and musical nuances Mr. Martin will undoubtedly demand. *Lieder* coaching with a great recording artist can end up being an invitation to psychological disaster for a student if the student's technical facility, linguistic capabilities, and coloristic skills have yet to be developed. Why do students enroll in expensive *Lieder* courses when they do not yet possess easy association with the complexities of sung German?

The assistant conductor or coach at the opera house may be just what the soprano with a solid vocal technique now needs, but this may be something of a disaster for the *tenore spinto* who is still trying to consistently negotiate the *secondo passaggio*. The performance experience of the noted diva is not going to help Gloria manage the Mad Scene if Gloria does not already have her melismatic house in order; no amount of "coaching" will make it possible. Both Gloria and the noted diva will end up in a state of frustration.

A talented young singer often assumes that coming to the big metropolitan area where successful singers perform will, perhaps by osmosis, further career ambitions. Better she or he had remained back home with the teacher who has already helped in solving technical problems and in developing performance readiness. If the singer has made the decision to move to the big city to pursue study, and if there are technical problems remaining, a vocal technician should be sought out. That may not be an easy search, because many noted teachers of singing accept only those students whose technical difficulties have already been solved by someone else.

Assuming a stable technique and a proper musical foundation that permits profitable coaching, it is probably a better idea to begin with a vocal coach who has the patience to drill language sounds and assist in developing musical accuracy than to seek out the coach who deals only with the fully established artist, and whose fee is double that of a lesser known person. As in all parts of the marketplace, bargains with equally serviceable results may sometimes be had by avoiding name-brand products.

One of the saddest career-preparation syndromes can be seen in the singer who believes that a high-priced coach or voice teacher whose time the singer has bought will provide contacts for entrance into the professional world. In almost no case does it work that way. These teachers' expensive studios and apartments have to be paid for, and acceptance into the studio doesn't mean the teacher believes the student is at the same professional level as established singers on the studio roster, nor does it mean the student is at the same time hiring an enthusiastic agent.

The roles of vocal coach and voice teacher are not identical, although they frequently overlap. The coach may have a highly developed ear for vocal sounds and be able to identify the need for improving areas of technical weakness, but seldom will have the know-how for correcting vocal problems. A coach is not there to teach the singer the music, but to help him or her find freedom of musical expression through proper linguistic flow, phrase movement, textual insight, and stylistic security. A less positive situation is brought about by the vocal coach who knows what the great artist does with a particular *Lied* or *mélodie,* who knows all of the aria traditions, but who makes the same demands of the young singer without due regard to levels of performance competence. Lamentably, such "coaching" causes conflict for the young artist because the singing teacher is trying to establish vocal stability while the coach is looking for final performance finesse. Both parties have valuable information, but this information is not helpful to the student when it is at odds.

In the best of all instructional worlds, the voice teacher and the coach are combined in a single individual. Certainly, the teacher of singing who knows the repertoire, who has studied musical style, and who is able to balance textual and dramatic content with musical considerations is of great help to the young artist-singer. As a practical matter in career building, the young professional singing artist should know where to go for which services, and not waste time and money expecting certain results from the wrong specialists. If you are in need of a voice teacher, don't hire a coach; if you are an established artist with no problems, don't go to the teacher who "builds" voices. The way to find out is to question singers who work with those specialists, to observe their work itself (if that is permitted, as it certainly should be), and to listen to the results as evidenced in the performance of singers themselves.

44

Vocal Tea Parties of the Private and Public Sorts

The accomplished vocalism required by the literature of the opera, oratorio, *Lieder, mélodie,* and the art song demands a solid technical foundation. Acquiring the skills for secure vocalism is not always an entirely pleasurable endeavor, but technical work cannot be bypassed if one is eventually to enjoy the rewards and satisfactions of public performance. All this notwithstanding, the very process of learning to sing can itself be a source of much joy, particularly as the student sees the elimination of problems and begins to experience greater freedom. Public singing should be full of joy, but it is futile to speak of joyful singing when the technical means for expressing emotion are not present. "Feeling joyous" does not result in joyful singing if breath management is insufficient to the accomplishment of sustained phrases, and if maintaining the resonance balance is a struggle. It is difficult to experience joy in singing while undergoing discomfort. Vocal instruction should convey the information that makes performance become pleasurable.

Having a good time at private or public instruction is commendable, but the teaching of singing is at its best when teacher and student have specific goals in mind. Pedagogical generalities, vague suggestions, and personal pleasantries bear a certain resemblance to the old-fashioned tea party held on the lawn in the lazy midafternoon of a mild summer day. Tea parties are not problem-solving forums but rather provide the setting for light banter and cozy communication. They are often fun, but usually of little substance. Voice lessons, whether private or public, must be treated as matters of consequence, not as vocal tea parties. Studying singing means acquiring the technical means for singing, and as soon as any student seeks professional assistance, professional responses are in order.

Perhaps the most typical occurrence of public vocal tea parties takes place these days at international conferences and symposia, in the form of teaching demonstrations. The attempt to overlay style and finesse on singers who have not yet learned to manage the singing voice may mislead us into assuming that this is what vocal pedagogy is all about. Fortunately, most well-informed teachers of singing who attend such public teaching sessions are aware of the superficiality that generally characterizes these events. Public coaching may have value in introducing new insights into a familiar *Lied,* a new pacing of an operatic recitative, or a needed reminder as to why the composer set the text as he did. Firing up the singer's imagination is part of the job of every person who teaches voice, and it is always of interest to see what someone else has to suggest.

However, the singer is seldom a feelingless person, and might well be able to offer his or her own viable interpretation of the material being coached if sufficient vocal technique permitted. In short, the substance of vocal technique must be assimilated before any high level of artistic expression is possible. Public teaching, it sometimes appears, starts from the opposite premise: "Be musical and you will solve your vocal difficulties!" Serious teachers of singing know how minimal are the results of such instruction. Although momentary distraction from any problem may have temporary value, sentiment does not solve functional problems.

Because vocal pedagogy is not a monolithic structure with a uniform set of concepts and techniques, there is always the temptation for the invited master teacher to avoid conflict in public gatherings of voice teachers by offering "tea-party coaching" and "interpretation," no matter what the technical level of the singer. Good showmanship, wit, charm, and charisma will provide entertainment, but they do not encompass the essential elements of successful voice teaching. Public or private teaching that does not clearly identify problems and offer specific solutions is not "masterful." In public teaching demonstrations, we need to be shown helpful approaches to problem-solving with students. Voice lessons, private or public, should not confuse the teaching of singing with the serving of pedagogical tea.

45

"As the Old Italians Said—"

The advertisement below appeared in a popular nationally distributed music magazine more than seventy years ago:

> Voice placing, interpretation, coaching in opera and concert. Students prepared for professional careers according to the best traditions of the Italian School of "Bel Canto." Appointments made by mail.

This was not the first, nor will it be the last, advertisement to lay claim to the teaching of *bel canto*. Current notices in major metropolitan newspapers are often but variants on the same promotional theme. We encounter articles and books that assure us we are about to be introduced to *bel canto* vocal methods. Indeed, the title *Bel Canto* was given to a book on vocal pedagogy published some years ago, in which were advocated vocal techniques difficult to find described in any of the pedagogical literature of the *bel canto* era.

Widely varying singing techniques are frequently introduced during lessons with the phrase "as the old Italians said." In some twentieth-century pedagogical literature of the Northern European School, *die alten Italiener* are called upon in support of nearly every typical vocal tenet.

On the other hand, there are some North American singers who feel that unless they study in Italy with a *maestro* or *maestra,* or on this continent with an American who bears an Italian surname, all of whom purport to teach *bel canto,* the art of singing has not been mastered. A young American baritone once confided that he had gone to Germany to get "*Lieder* technique," and had then come to Italy to pick up "*bel canto* technique," mistakenly viewing vocal technique as the assimilation of layers of stylistic information.

Are there then no present-day ties with the *bel canto* practices of the nineteenth century? There are indeed, and they are to be found within the literature of the period itself—in the published nineteenth-century vocalization systems—and in the vocal traditions passed down literally from mouth to mouth for at least the past one hundred and fifty years. There is little quotable technical material to be found in early written historical pedagogy, but a great deal of circumstantial evidence is present in the operatic literature itself. It is this absence of extensive, precise technical language that permits some current teachers to make unsubstantiated assumptions about the "technique of *bel canto*." Whenever one hears remarked, in justification of some technical suggestion, "As the old Italians said," the listener would be wise to ask for some specific source.

Specifics regarding function abound in the writings of Garcia, the Lampertis, and a number of their contemporaries, and in the writings of their students. The literature designation *bel canto* only came into being around 1860, as it became clear that the newer school of *verismo* writing was making increasing vocal demands on singers.

The term *bel canto* should not be misused as a mystical incantation muttered over a host of contradictory contemporary pedagogical assumptions, in which case it ceases to have any historical meaning. Beautiful singing—*bel canto*—must be based on beautiful vocal function associated with beautiful artistic imagination. There is much to be learned about both in the literature and the tradition of the historic Italian School. Fortunately, no one has a corner on it.

46

The Lively Dying Art of Singing

Gentlemen! Masters! Italy hears no more such exquisite voices as in Times past, particularly among the Women, and to the Shame of the Guilty I'll tell the Reason. The ignorance of the Parents Does not let them perceive the Badness of the Voice of their Children, as their Necessity makes them believe, that to sing and grow rich is one and the same Thing, and to learn Musick, it is enough to have a pretty face. "Can you make anything of her?"

PIER FRANCESCO TOSI (1723)

In Italy music is decadent, there are no more schools, no great singers.

GIAMBATTISTA MANCINI (1774)

Today one hardly ever hears a really beautiful and technically correct trill; very rarely a perfect mordent; very rarely a rounded coloratura, a genuine unaffected soul-moving portamento, a complete equalization of the registers, a steady intonation through all the varying nuances of crescendo and diminuendo.

RICHARD WAGNER (1834)

Singing is becoming as much a lost art as the manufacture of Mandarin china or the varnish used by the old masters.

MANUEL GARCIA (1855)

There has never been so much enthusiasm for the singing art, nor have there been so many students and teachers as of late years. And it is precisely this period which reveals the deterioration of this divine art and the almost complete disappearance of genuine singers and worse, of good singing teachers.

GIOVANNI BATTISTA LAMPERTI (1893)

On every hand we hear the question: "Why have we not more great singers? Are Americans unmusical? Are there no good voices in this country?"

D. A. CLIPPINGER (1929)

There is a serious shortage of really fine operatic voices these days. It is compounded by teachers who do not know how to teach, singers who refuse to admit that there is anything they cannot sing, and opera directors who think every soprano can sing every soprano role, every tenor take on the entire tenor repertoire, every baritone launch into the whole baritone list. If the situation is not altered, the present problems of casting Aida, Trovatore and Turandot will quickly multiply.

PAUL HUME (1978)

For an art that has been dying for more than two and a half centuries, singing remains remarkably alive! Nearly every commentator since Tosi has bewailed the deplorable condition of singing and the teaching of singing despite contemporary sources that ecstatically describe specific singers from all the periods concerned. No matter how willing the astute listener may be to blame technical limitations of the early recording industry for some of the less-than-stellar recorded performances of the past, the ear cannot ignore some of the remarkably off-key singing from many a golden voice of previous eras. Indeed, although we are at times moved to astonishment at the demonstrated technical skills, we are as often presented with evidence that the art of singing probably never attained some universally exalted niveau.

Without doubt there are singers lacking sufficient vocal endowment, adequate technical training, and essential musicianship who make auditions and who advance in major competitions. Yet anyone who frequently adjudicates or attends today's singing contests must report that the general level of artistic singing has improved over the past thirty years.

Herbert Witherspoon's perspicacious comment of more than three quarters of a century ago is an equally appropriate perspective for the singer and teacher of the present decade:

> There have always been few good singers and fewer great ones. So a tirade about present-day conditions in comparison with the glorious past is of no use. Let us take the world as we find it. Perhaps if we heard the singers of a century or two ago we should not care for them. We do not know! Our task is with today, not yesterday.

47

The Sense of Immediacy in Singing

When the poet, in a flash of insight, finds the right combination of syllable and symbol, presenting in one terse line what we would falteringly have needed a paragraph to express, we experience a moment of truth that becomes all the more meaningful to us for the sense of immediacy it conveys.

If we stand in the Brancacci Chapel before Masaccio's great wall, or find ourselves in Borgo San Sepolcro, face to face with Piero's *Resurrected Christ,* we encounter the figures on those walls in a heightened manner. They are more real to us than flesh and blood, more perfectly in the round than the very figures standing beside us, because the painter through his art has made them plastically immediate. He has taken the essence of being and purified it into an otherworldly ambiance. In a moment we have been granted a conception of being that we did not previously have. We are enriched through instant perception.

Although the singer's creativity is more modest by the nature of its transitoriness, the performer must bring to words and music a similar plasticity that lifts an audience into a world of heightened perception.

The singer has not authored the text; the melody on which the words spin forth is not of the singer's creating. In all probability, language and music have been given shape and form by combining the genius of a great poet with that of an eminent composer. Yet no matter how familiar the song, how great the original conception, it must project from the singer with a sense of immediate creation. In an act of re-creation, the singer becomes surrogate poet and composer. The text must be born again with the same freshness and reality that inspired the poet; the melodic line, with its particular grouping of intervals and rhythmic patterns, ought to spring from the singer's consciousness at an intensity level at least as strong as that which motivated poet and composer. The singer's art is a re-creative art. Only the singer can give life to the song. By so doing, she or he renews its existence in time. The song has life only if the singer endows it with life.

A creative act is subject to a limited degree of analysis. Attempts to describe the process of creativity serve only to point up its elusive character. The classic mystic in setting forth a series of metaphysical exercises does not claim to explain, but rather to experience, the ground of being. God is encountered, not defined. In like manner, a creative act cannot be explained, but the skilled performing artist has a system, just as surely as does the mystic, for engendering the creative process. It would be presumptuous to set forth "artistic exercises" to spur on the creative performance instinct. It is possible, however, to offer suggestions that may be helpful.

One of a singer's chief assets is the ability to visualize, to see clearly and distinctly with the inner eye the dramatic and emotional situation of a song. This mental picture must be sharper than reality itself because it transcends reality. Serving as intermediary between the creative artists (the poet and the composer) and the listener, the singer becomes the means by which the original artistic experience is conveyed.

A generally vague atmospheric feeling of the poetic situation is insufficient. The creative inner vision must emanate a third-dimension intensity, be bathed in light and color, be sharply outlined. If the inner realization is to have a forceful impact on the hearer, the performer's awareness of the text and music must be as vivid as a stereoscopic scene. Reality becomes transformed by art.

This vision of the spirit can be more vivid than the vision of the physical eye. It should not be bound by the static limitations of space or by the physical properties of reality. Kaleidoscopic fluctuations of images, of shapes, of masses, and of color are the stuff of the mental vision. Long before the psychedelic age, the re-creative artist knew how to bombard the senses through excitation by the artistic imagination.

If, in the song, a performer explores a lonely forest pathway, a specific woodland trail is conjured up. Its aspects can be viewed from many angles all at once, or intermittently in quick succession. Images swirl in and out of perspective, sometimes close up in great detail, sometimes at far distance. The promenade is not bound by solid flesh striking firm ground. No single physical view limits this artistic musing. The pathway turns, the foliage is alternately brilliant or muted, the light bathes it, the heat of its surroundings or the coolness of the night engulfs it. All are the more vivid for not being limited by actual location and by real time. Images tumble in as the scene evolves from the textual description. This world of the imagination is nearer to us than is the world of material things. The whispering reeds described in the text are more material than the stage on which the performer stands, because they have come to occupy the center of consciousness. The performer breathes not the atmosphere of the concert hall but a purer, more refined air. Communication will be as complete as the performer's concentration on this inner imaging.

While one level of the consciousness is operating imaginatively, another serves as monitor, seeming to stand off to one side, looking on with detachment at the unfolding process of creativity. To visualize and inwardly experience the drama is not to give way to unrestrained emotion. In view of the possibilities for distraction during performance, the singer must train his or her instrument to the same level of concentration by which the ascetic cuts out the noisy beatings of the surrounding world. This visualized conception remains constant in the inner eye.

It is probable that the re-creative act may be even more intense than was the original act of creation itself. The composer, as well as the poet, conceives, alters, revises, and meticulously applies the rules of the craft to an emerging work of art. The re-creator brings to the artwork a greater degree of immediacy, fires it in the heat of instant artistic imagination, and presents it fully formed, giving it life in the present moment. Although the performer's calling may seem to be a lepidopteran one compared with that of the poet and the composer, those creators must themselves remain in chrysalid dormancy until that moment when the re-creative artist supplies wings for flight. For that reason, the ephemeral art of re-creation may be more intense, requiring a greater sense of immediacy than does the act of creation itself.

At the risk of over-explanation, further comment on what the singer may experience during performance may be in order. Hugo Wolf, who was remarkably sensitive to his poetic sources, offers a wealth of material to the singer who is a strong communicator. Each song is a miniature drama, a marriage of word and music. *Denk es, O Seele,* both descriptive and philosophical, is such a song. The original German of Mörike is here followed by a free English translation:

Denk es , O Seele

Ein Tännlein grünet wo, wer weiss,
im Walde,

Ein Rosenstrauch, wer sagt,
      in welchem Garten?
Sie sind erlesen schon,
      denk es, O Seele,
Auf deinem Grab zu wurzeln
      und zu wachsen.

Zwei schwarze Rösslein weiden
      auf der Wiese,
Sie kehren heim zur Stadt
      in muntern Sprüngen.
Sie werden schrittweis gehn
      mit deiner Leiche;
Vielleicht, noch eh an ihren Hufen
      das Eisen los wird,
Das ich blitzen sehe!

O Soul, Consider
A fir tree grows, who knows where,
      in the woods;
A rose bush, who can say,
      in which fair garden?
They have already been chosen
      on your grave
To take root and to grow.

Two little black horses graze
      on the meadow,
They turn homeward to the town
      with gaily springing steps.
They will go, step by step,
      with your corpse,
Perhaps, even before their horseshoes
      are replaced,
That I see sparkling!

With the sound of the opening pianoforte chords, the singer is transported to a specific spot, to an enigmatic world. It exudes the atmosphere of a different time and place. The musical figures unfold and repeat themselves, leading us through chromatic harmonies into a mysterious land as yet unfamiliar to us. Suddenly, the diatonic harmonies spring upon us like a light being turned on at dusk. We stand in the woods before a fir tree in bold relief. We feel the texture of its needles not with physical fingers but with the inner eye. For one moment in time, the little fir tree with its deep color and its fresh aroma, has become the center of our existence. A split second later *ein Rosenstrauch* comes whirling into the consciousness, more vividly than could the rose bush of any real garden. Once again the kaleidoscope shifts. We enter a new time frame in which the fir tree and the rose bush take root and grow upon our grave. In this moment, that small plot of ground contains all of existence.

Swiftly, new motion occurs. We are swept away to a place where joyous primitive animal energy abounds: two little horses fill the meadow with life. We empathically experience their springing step as they bounce homeward to the town. Then suddenly we are pulled up short by watching them draw the wagon that contains our own corpse. Although an active participant, the performer stands off and watches the scene, experiencing a new understanding of the relationship of death to life.

Another artist singing the same *Lied* will invoke other visions. Each re-creator varies the vision with every performance, but the imaginative process remains the same. With every song, the singer creates a role just as surely as he or she would when in costume on the stage. In fact, the imagination has even freer rein in the song literature than in the literature of the theater, because it is not restricted to a single character, to a specific dramatic moment. The performer may play several roles within one song, and be commentator and active participant within the span of several measures.

Building on the heritage of Franz Schubert, and influenced by the aesthetic of the nineteenth century, most *Lied* composers attempted a synthesis of word and music. The singer can intelligently re-create the worlds of Goethe, Eichendorff, Mörike, Rückert, or that of Rimbaud and Verlaine, or the cosmos of e. e. cummings and James Joyce, only by some acquaintance with the cultural ambiance that gave rise to each of these poetic expressions. Such information supplies the singer with material for the inward vision. A singer who exists in a literary void is as limited as one without knowledge of musical styles. Communication, the ultimate goal of performance, depends on the singer's ability to immediately envision the poetic and dramatic situation.

III

On Preparation for the Professional Life

48

The Seven Pillars of
Performance Success

What makes a successful performer? What factors dictate degrees of success? What specifically determines why some singers are successful while others are not? The answer attributed to Rossini, that the most important requirement for success in singing is *"voce, voce, voce,"* is generally assumed to be true by most aspiring young singers. Rossini's answer is sometimes embraced by their teachers as well. Vocal talent, it is thought, is the number one requisite for success. Without an astounding native endowment, it is believed, career possibilities are limited.

A clearer look is in order. As a starting point in this assessment of the factors for successful performance, we might ask why it is then that some persons who possess beautiful voices and who have learned to use them well have not been able to achieve the career status they so much desire. The opposite side of the coin poses an equally interesting question: Why are there some singers on the performance stage whose vocal talent is clearly less remarkable than that of some others, who can only envy them their position? Providing answers to these questions must take into consideration overlooked elements that go into career building. A clever singer will take into account *all* the requirements for a successful career, and will concentrate on developing equally those aspects that add up to success.

The First Pillar: Musicianship

The foremost of the essential supports for the professional singing career edifice is *musicianship*. If the singer is to arrive at a high level of performance success, she or he must be *first a musician and second a singer*. This message causes outbursts of protest from many young singers, who cite great singers of the past who could not read music, or who had to be taught their scores through constant repetition. It cuts to the quick those singers whose preparation consists of imitating style and nuance from recorded performances. Whatever the standards of the past, today only the superior musician, the person who understands vocal line and phrase direction, who knows how to listen to the harmonic language supporting melodic excursion, who is able to learn music quickly, will succeed. That does not mean that the singer has to be able to write four-part chorales, take melodic and harmonic dictation (none of which, unfortunately, contributes directly to actual performance skills), or play a second instrument, although all of those abilities are helpful. It means that the musicianly ear (not necessarily the acquisition of basic music-skill facility) must be highly developed. One of the saddest of the numerous cosmic ironies that exist in the musical world is the young woman or the young man with a superior vocal mechanism attached to a nonmusical mentality. If the singer is not willing to come to a deep understanding of what the music itself has to say (not just how he or she *feels* about it), chances of performance success are diminished.

One of the problems in being a singing musician is that the instrument itself is already a given. It is there. Whereas other musical instruments are constructed by master builders (theological speculation about the singing voice will be here avoided), the vocal instrument arrives in its physical carrying case, the human body, already constructed in its basic form. One even knows something about how the instrument functions because the voice already accomplishes communicative speech. To a certain extent, one has the "hang" of how to use this particular instrument in at least a limited way even before beginning to train it. The vocal mechanism is the "natural" instrument. This phenomenon is as much a curse as a blessing. Many singers mistakenly believe that the instrument they possess will ensure them success. They expect to ride to stardom on the merit of their vocal potential.

The Second Pillar: Vocal Technique

For these reasons, singers are far less accustomed to approaching the training of their instruments in the same systematic way as do their instrumentalist peers. In part, this is the case because it is not possible to spend six hours per day using the vocal instrument, a practice quite common among serious string and keyboard performers. Realizing that much less time can be spent in phonation than is possible in practicing other musical instruments, a whole generation of singing students currently tends to avoid the practice room in favor of singing in circumstances where they can be publicly self-expressive. This was not the case with successful singers of the not-so-distant past, many of whom devoted most of their waking hours to the acquisition of musical skills, role preparation, and dramatic training, in addition to several hours of technical work per day.

The second pillar, then, among the columns of support essential to performance success is a *stable vocal technique*. Technical requirements of the singing instrument are as complex, and as simple, as those of all musical instruments. As with every physical skill, coordination comes about through the repetition of kinesthetic responses conditioned by mental awareness. Such skill is not acquired through bouts of emotional indulgence during which the singer "feels" the text and the music and experiences cathartic emotional bathing. No matter how gratifying such sessions may be as forms of self-expression, they contribute little to the acquisition of technical proficiency that permits true communication. At moments of visceral indulgence, the vocal instrument momentarily responds to the excitation of the emotions; there are some things to be learned from those experiences, but enduring technical security is not one of them. A singing personality, and there is such a thing, can be the most imaginative and expressive in the world, but if the vocal instrument is not at a high level of technical proficiency, the world will never know those qualities.

All of this is currently of particular pertinence, because today's young singer lives in an age, created by her or his elders, where great importance is given to self-realization. Current educational philosophy has been rightly concerned with tailoring general knowledge to individual interests and propensities. Yet the universally shared aspects of that physical instrument known as the singing voice have not appreciably changed in several centuries. The search for individualism, so highly prized in this age, when applied to the physiology of the singing voice is detrimental to vocalism. People who want to "do their own thing"—that is, who believe they can assemble their own set of compensatory measures for dealing with technical problems, or who attempt to avoid solving technical problems through emotional end-runs around them—are doomed, long-range, to vocal mediocrity.

It is essential for the individual performing artist to take advantage of that body of information common to, and available to, all singers. This information concerns the effective cooperation of the functional aspects of the singing instrument, including management of the power source (the breath), the vibratory source (laryngeal freedom), and the resonator system (the vocal tract that extends from the laryngeal lips to the external lips). The coordination essential to singing is not "naturally" there, because the tasks of the singing voice far exceed those of the spoken voice.

Just as some people are congenitally more athletic than others, so some singers can more readily adapt to the coordination essential for singing. Yet myths about the self-trained singer are quickly exploded if the true histories of noted singers (including some currently famous performers who claim to be self-taught) are closely examined. While it is true that every singer must put his or her own psychological performance house in order, it is just not true that any great singer has done it entirely on her or his own. Egocentricity often clouds perspective in autobiographical reports.

Indeed, the singer need not search for idiosyncratic physical and acoustic procedures, nor try to invent private systems of physiology and acoustics, because there are none. The laws of vocal acoustics and physiological function are universally present. This is by no means to deny that there are individual perceptions and proprioceptive responses, but the argument is here presented to warn the aspiring vocalist that individualism, highly applicable to *artistic* expression, is not appropriate to efficient *physical* function, even though individual differences in morphology and psychological orientation inevitably play their roles.

Individuality in the singing instrument stems from structural differences and from the uniqueness of the individual artistic imagination, not from mysteries regarding the functional aspects of the singing instrument. The second priority then—the second of the principal pillars of the professional singing voice—is to acquire a skillfully operating instrument, trained and schooled in the same kind of exactitude to be found among performers of other musical instruments.

The Third Pillar: Artistic Imagination

Singing machines are uninteresting. The only reason for developing a stable vocal technique is to be able to communicate sound and emotion to the listener. It is true that beautiful sound, in and of itself, can be emotive. But beautiful vocalism separated from the artistic imagination is not sufficient for dramatic and textual communication.

Much speculation has taken place regarding the psychological factors that produce imaginative performance. Yet these processes remain as mysterious as does the diversity of human nature itself. How the psyche is able to externalize internally sensed emotion within the confines of an art form is not subject to exact analysis. The means for its realization can be identified, schooled, and technically repeated, but the spark of creativity that unites technique and artistry cannot be captured and described.

A beautiful vocal instrument placed within an unimaginative personality is yet another kind of cosmic joke. However, the imagination is also capable of development. Sometimes teachers and coaches write off a singer because "she has no imagination," or "he lacks an artistic temperament," without realizing that hidden under that noncommunicative façade lies a reservoir of emotion waiting for release. Part of pedagogy consists in assisting the singer to lower the barriers of inhibition, to be willing to publicly reveal the private person, to risk sharing oneself with others.

More times than not, the lack of communication stems not from the inability of the singer to feel the emotional impact of text and drama, but from the lack of technical means to deliver those emotions. Artistic communication, in fact, is as much a part of performance technique as is skillful vocalism. An actor is not simply an individual who feels more deeply than those around him and can therefore enter into emotional states more readily than the rest of us; he or she is trained in the techniques of emotional portrayal through quite specific means. So must be the singer. It is as essential for the singer to learn the language of the body and the impact of facial expressions as it is to learn how to accomplish the even vocal scale.

The importance of physical freedom in singing has always been at the heart of vocal pedagogy. Techniques for achieving such freedom predate the current surge of popular methodologies that direct attention to the whole body as the singing instrument. Physical movement, and the equally important ability to achieve physical quietude, play important roles in releasing body and voice for emotive expression. Dramatic training is as essential to the singer as to the actor. Before dismissing any vocally talented singer as lacking in "imagination," the teacher should explore the technical routes available for the externalization of internal emotion.

The Fourth Pillar: Objectivity

The fourth pillar needed to support the professional singing edifice is often the most difficult of all to construct and maintain. It keeps falling down, and it has to be constantly repaired and braced. That pillar is *objectivity*. Singers generally are extroverted personalities, or at least become so when they are involved in public communication. Although introspection may be one of the most valuable assets of an artistic personality (and its total absence a major lack in some otherwise interesting performers), singers generally display high levels of skill in communicating on a personal level—not always a verbal one—with those around them. It is clear that a successful singer must eventually have a strong ego and a firm belief in himself or herself. However, when strong self-conviction has not been founded on an undergirding process of objective examination, foolish results abound.

One of the most detrimental and destructive factors in the performance world is the false notion that work in any artistic medium can be done entirely one's own way. At this moment there is more than one person on the roster of a major opera house who, although chronologically at the peak years of performance, is now hanging on for dear life to contracts that embarrass Management. Those singers remain convinced that the art of singing is a totally unique experience and that they must continue on in what they do technically, no matter how negative the results, because they "believe in themselves." Objectivity is as much a necessary part of the art of singing as are musicianship and technical proficiency.

This objectivity is often especially problematic in the early years of preparation. It is not unusual to encounter the imaginative young person eager to enter the performance world who insists success will be obtainable simply as a matter of willing it, when all professional judgments indicate otherwise. Not confronting reality has produced innumerable frustrated personalities, who hover around the fringes of the professional performance world. Just as the person who stands five feet tall and weighs 128 pounds who has a burning desire to be a fullback with the Cleveland Browns must learn to direct his athletic abilities into some other aspect of the world of sports, so must the singing personality of lyric vocal proportions who dreams of singing *Amfortas* at the Staatsoper adjust his performance goals. Objective assessment of one's capabilities is often an exceedingly difficult matter for the singer. Part of the role of the voice teacher is to help build objectivity with regard to career potential. Teachers have an ethical responsibility to assess potential and to point out what a long process career building entails, even when considerable potential is present.

Because the pillar of objectivity depends not only on one's own impressions but on the judgments of those around one, it is incumbent upon persons who mentor young singers with professional goals to proceed with much caution. Because of the variable factors that go into career building, it is not ethical to say to any student who has demonstrated enough talent to be admitted as a performance major to a respectable institution of music, "You are going to have a career," or "You will never have a career." To tell a twenty-year-old bass-baritone that he will be the next great Wotan, or the *leggiero* tenor that he is slated to be *the* Rossini tenor, is as unrealistic as it is unethical. The teacher and the student should objectively assess together both the demonstrated level of talent and the practical requirements of career building. Such assessment cannot take place if the student is unable to organize time and energies so as to discover what the possibilities may be.

But as a practical studio matter, what does the teacher of singing do with the student who lacks objectivity about the learning process, and who believes that his or her own experiences are unique and all that matter, and who therefore makes limited technical progress? What of the student who looks in disbelief at a teacher when he or she insists on detailed work to establish good function, and who says, "But you don't understand, this is the way *I* feel it, this is the way *I* do it"? Often the assumption is that whatever is habitual and therefore familiar—whatever is "my own thing"—constitutes natural function. The teacher, in the process of being supportive and positive, dare not back away from demanding professional levels of skill. Perhaps it is at the very moment when outstanding talent stands before one that the teacher must exercise his or her own greatest degree of objectivity.

A common problem of the motivated student is to confuse ability and self-esteem. This confusion must not deter the teacher from objectively teaching such a person. Strong self-image is part of the perception of talent, but an aggressive student who is disproportionately ego-centered should not be allowed to mistake ego for talent. Unless egotism can be rechanneled into objectivity, career goals will go unrealized for that person.

The Fifth Pillar: Perseverance

This leads to the fifth essential pillar in building and upholding the career edifice: *perseverance*. The good race must be run to its conclusion, and the two participants, student and teacher, must run as a team. This is a distractible age, both for teacher and student. We live in a period when taking the shortcut is almost a necessity in order to manage daily schedule demands. Fast food preparation, fast food ingestion, fast learning devices, fast communication of information, fast career preparation, fast transportation, fast entertainment, fast sound bites: all permit the rushed patterns that typify contemporary living. Traditional studies have been revolutionized by new technological advances. It is not now necessary to assimilate most information, because much of it is readily available in the electronic library. A glaring exception to this burst of already accumulated information is that which makes up the discipline and coordination required for achieving professional levels in the world of artistic performance. Awareness of the extent of perseverance required in the building of performance skills often separates the successful from the unsuccessful aspirant.

The Sixth Pillar: Talent

The sixth pillar is the very one that often is considered the most essential: *natural vocal talent*. Talent, properly understood, embraces all of the other factors mentioned, yet normally the term "talent" is used to describe the beauty of the native instrument. However, it simply is not the case that the best voices are the most successful. Vocal talent is an essential, as are dramatic talent and artistic imagination, but it is not the overriding factor in the determination of success. Today's young singer needs to know that the world is full of beautiful larynges, but that only a small percentage of those remarkable instruments will ever realize a professional goal. The assessment of talent varies, but the means by which talent is put into play do not vary. Those means are identified above.

The Seventh Pillar?

The skeptical observer, having seen careers that seemed certain to bloom then fail, and having marveled at the flowering of some others based on lesser talent, is tempted to add yet a seventh pillar essential to career success: *business acumen*. The same kind of devotion that is needed for the building of a business career is essential to the building of the performance career. Practical matters such as self-organization, objectivity, and perseverance make the difference between success and failure. Having the energy and the courage to prepare and follow through with auditions, to find the appropriate agency to represent one, to risk time and money on a precarious profession, to maintain an even emotional keel through adherence to disciplined living—all are central to career success. No one will discover you. It is you who must build the career. "Who you know" and "the breaks," contrary to what many frustrated performers believe, are far less vital to career building than the other personally controllable factors cited earlier. Building a singing career requires a total commitment that many young people are simply not willing to make. A singing career should be undertaken only by persons who are willing to sacrifice much in order to pursue an irresistible goal.

49

Wrapping Up the Performance Package

"What a beautiful natural voice you have! You should become a professional singer!" a singer is told. After a few years of exploratory study, the singer enrolls in a professional training program at a reputable conservatory or school of music. Friends and family say, "John is becoming a professional singer," or, more probably, "John is learning to be an opera singer." That is what John himself most certainly believes. What are his chances?

The consistently beautiful sound John may eventually learn to emit from his larynx and his vocal tract is not the crucial factor. Nor is his desire to sing, although both are necessary to the realization of a professional singing career. John must assemble the *total package.*

Voice teachers sometimes marvel at what might unkindly be termed "cosmic mischief" in the world of vocal endowment. John or Jane possesses an instrument of exceptional beauty but does not have the innate ability to master basic skills essential to the art of singing. He or she may lack an exact rhythmic sense, an understanding of phrase movement, an awareness of the subtle shades of vocal timbre, the ability to repeat consistently a concept of tone or to distinguish among the niceties of linguistic exactitude, the facility for quickly learning music and for memorizing it readily, a sense of drama, a genuine feeling for communication. Coordinating the elements of artistic singing may forever remain an unattainable goal, no matter how intense or how long the training period; despite favorable attributes of the larynx and physique, the other essentials of a professional singing career are inherently lacking.

Can it be assumed that if the singer has natural vocal endowment, a musicianly ear, musical skills, and an artistic imagination, a career will follow? Even if he or she does, chances are small. Why should this be? Because nature is profligate in her gifts, and the world is full of beautiful vocal instruments housed in persons of musical sensibilities. Something more than the basic components is needed.

What makes the difference in career success among persons of similar endowment? Conventional wisdom speaks of "the breaks" and of "contacts," both of which are important along the road to a professional career but neither of which makes the compelling difference. Singers themselves often attribute lack of success to poor technical instruction, and too many times they have reason to lament what they have been taught. But that, again, is seldom the cause of a lack of success. A clever singer will eventually find the help necessary to solve remaining technical problems.

The "package" itself must be in place, and the difference between having it and lacking it lies in the extent of the singer's *self-organization.* (This used to be termed *self-discipline,* but such language is now out of style.) A singing career has to be built with the same concentration of energy that is directed toward any successful enterprise. This is particularly difficult for the young singer in a world full of distractions. It comes down to a matter of immediate priorities. A person who, after acquiring the essential musical skills, hopes to have a singing career must systematically devote large amounts of time to the aquisition of technical skills, to listening to successful artists, to gaining familiarity with the literature of his or her *Fach,* to the long process of role coaching and memorization, and to an orderly lifestyle that contributes to vocal health. Excellent studio training does not obviate the need for these factors.

One is often astounded when talking with gifted young singers to realize how limited they are in their knowledge of the professional field and its requirements. Hopefuls are frequently unfamiliar with the voices and artistry of past and current singing artists, and are unaware of the competitive nature of the profession. They have little information on the practical aspects of career building, and harbor an assumption that they will be "discovered." The need to work aggressively at finding performance outlets, and the essential role of agents and representatives, are unknown to them.

Many of today's performance majors complete their musical education with little knowledge of the standard art song and operatic repertory. They are in command of only the literature learned for the required public recital appearances associated with their degree programs. Even within these limited repertory expectations, it is not uncommon for the student singer to assume that if the material is memorized a week or two in advance of the dress rehearsal, adequate preparation has been made. They are like unsuspecting persons who begin the ascent of a mountain without knowing how high it is and without appropriate mountain-climbing gear.

Most of these problems stem from the social milieu within which today's young singer moves. It is not possible to spend long hours watching television, "playing house," or accepting the duties of the "normal" life style of the young adults around one while building a career base. Peer pressures to do so are strong. But unless there is singlemindedness about career building, there will be no career.

This means foregoing many pleasurable activities, accustoming oneself to long work days, to a tightly organized schedule, and to "woodshedding" and "slogging away" at career preparation while one's companions appear to be having a great time partying. It comes down to the basic recognition that "if you do this, you can't do that," no matter how interesting or even commendable "doing this" might be. The value and limited nature of time available for attending to the many aspects of career building must be understood. Daily adherence to a work schedule that embraces all facets of that training is essential. During the preparatory years, immediate gratification cannot be a high priority.

The advertising world attempts to persuade that "you owe it to yourself" to have a good time, which obscures the fact that there is far greater pleasure to be found in the satisfaction of permanent accomplishment than in momentary entertainment. The counterargument being made here may well smack of a call to an out-of-date "work ethic," of "holding one's nose to the grindstone." It is clear that a call to *self-organization* does not readily fit into current social attitudes. However, the professional classical singing voice requires the same amount of preparation in time and commitment as it did in previous epochs.

This is not to say that there is no room for socializing or recreation in the life of an aspiring young singer. As in all occupations, some respite from work is essential to the healthy maintenance of equilibrium. But because of the nature of the singing instrument and the need to approach the art of singing creatively and imaginatively (and because of the gregariousness of most singing personalities!), it is easy to unwittingly assume that things will happen of their own accord as a kind of natural phenomenon, and therefore to expend one's energies in undirected fashion in nonprofessional areas.

No doubt self-indulgence has always been as much a characteristic of established performing artists as of the world in general, but the successful artist early learns to channel that self-indulgence into professional preparation. A true artist, at any age, is consumed with his or her art, and perceives such complete commitment as self-indulgence, not as sacrifice. Still, much of the exacting process of professional preparation is *not* fun. This fact goes contrary to the current assumption that to expend such amounts of time and energy is to place oneself in thrall to the "bitch-goddess Success." Although she may not be best described by such a pejorative appellation, the Goddess of Art is a demanding mistress.

It may well be that a professional career is not worth all the effort. So be it. Then the singer should face that fact and not invite the later frustration of nonaccomplishment that dogs so many would-be performers. A gifted young singer must decide if a professional singing career is more important than anything else in the world. An understanding of human needs and emotions is essential to artistic expression, but it is not necessary to experience all that life has to offer if it means dissipating one's time and energies on life's numerous distractions. In fact, that may be the best way to ensure failure.

Wrapping up the professional package consists of a conscious attempt to husband one's time and energies and to direct them to specific career goals. Otherwise, one should forget about singing and turn to some other field of endeavor.

50

What To Do on a Performance Day

Pity the poor student Mimì who is expected to attend classes all day and tonight sing the campus premiere of *La Bohème*. Student performers are asked to take on tasks that would floor a seasoned professional. Even though tonight is Tom's senior recital, the choir director expects him at today's rehearsal, because with the concert coming up this weekend he is badly needed. Voice teachers should take all means within their power to protect students on performance days. They should initiate institutional policies that permit absences from classes on days when major performances are to take place.

Although the student may not be able to control his or her performance-day schedule, the professional singer generally can. Curiously, there are a number of professional singers who have yet to find an acceptable pattern of performance-day routine. Their experiments include playing eighteen holes of golf, running several miles, or lying silently all day in bed. Many years ago, in Rome, a noted singing teacher, who taught many of the successful performers of the day, shared his viewpoint on what to do or not to do on a performance day. What follows is based on his advice.

The worst thing you can do is not sing a note until performance time. All day long you do not know your vocal condition. This causes unnecessary anxiety and is not a healthy procedure. On a performance day, having had a good night's sleep, get up in the morning at a reasonable hour and have breakfast. The act of chewing and swallowing is part of waking up your vocal instrument. Take a leisurely bath or shower, which is part of the physical warming-up process. (Many singers like tub baths because they are luxurious and indulgent.) Then, before noon (assuming you have an evening performance), sing through your entire voice in a *brief* warm-up on the exercises you make use of in the daily regimen. This should consist of perhaps twenty minutes of vocalization, with pauses beween the exercises. Don't do more, but be sure you do at least part of the daily regimen. After a few light physical exercises, begin with humming and with gentle onsets in lower-middle voice, adding some short agility exercises and some nonstrenuous resonance balancing and range extension vocalises, but include little sostenuto or *passaggio* work. Then don't sing again until just before performance time, and then only to run a few arpeggios or scales. Do not do continuous singing immediately before the performance.

If you are accustomed to an afternoon siesta, take it early enough so that you are up by at least four o'clock for an eight o'clock performance. Don't sleep more than half an hour. It is a mistake not to eat until after the performance. A singer needs the energy that food provides. Eat a light meal much earlier than normal, perhaps in mid-afternoon or after your nap. On performance days, be certain to avoid all salty or spicy foods, which make you feel dry or thirsty on stage. Don't wait to drink liquid until just before going on stage, or until the pauses. Be sure you drink a lot of water during the course of the performance day, because your body will lose liquid during performance. The vocal folds need to be well lubricated, not dry.

During the course of the day, take brief walks, if the weather permits, or read some non–music-related materials. But sometime during the course of the afternoon take an hour to look through your role or recital music without singing it, reminding yourself of what you want to do with it. Above all, avoid most talking. This includes telephone conversations.

Don't arrive at the hall just in time to perform. If you have a stage role to sing, get there in time so that the hairdresser and the makeup people can take care of you early. (Don't inhale any hair spray.) Best of all, learn to do your own makeup. If you do not have your own dresser for the role, get there in time so that you do not have to stand around and wait for assistance. (There may be only one dresser for several members of the cast.) Even if there is no costuming and if you are fortunate enough to use your own hair, get to the hall half an hour in advance of the performance. Rushing at the last minute is not conducive to quietude. Check the set to be sure all your props are in proper location; don't depend on anyone else for this. Especially as weather becomes severe in wintertime, arrive at the hall early to allow your body and your voice to become accustomed to changes in air and temperature. When scene changes make great stirrings of stage dust, insist on having the stage sprayed. It is a good idea to have some fruit in the dressing room, so that between acts, or groups, you can chew and swallow a few pieces. This is a way of "clearing" the throat. If the performance is a matinee, adjust the procedure.

Following the performance, be sure that you do not sit around in clothing damp with perspiration. As much as possible, avoid talking following a heavy performance. Singers are loquacious, and the adrenalin runs high in the performance ambience. You can do more harm to your instrument by loud talking and laughter than if you were to immediately do the role of Donna Anna all over again.

In general—not just before performance days—sleep is an absolute essential for the singer, because singing is an athletic event. Physical exercise is also important to the conditioning of the body. The more orderly the life you live, the better physical condition you will find yourself in on performance day.

Singers should avoid becoming entangled in preperformance rituals, because often the conditions of those rituals cannot be met. One of the reasons for having a performance day routine lies in the stability and tranquillity that it provides. A set performance routine provides an orderly process of performance readiness.

51

Warming Up the Voice

Listening to singers warm up can be amusing to the uninitiated bystander. What takes place during the warm-up process may be very diverse and of varying value. The technique of warming up the voice should be a major part of any systematic vocal pedagogy. It should not consist of dashing through an improvisatory sampling of vocalises. Most singers need to have an established warm-up procedure, probably spread out over twenty to thirty minutes. As vocal skill increases, warm-up time tends to diminish.

Because the vocal instrument is physical, a graduated program of warming up is as appropriate to singing as to any athletic occasion. To start off singing high-lying phrases, or phrases that traverse the entire range, is not advisable.

Before any vocal performance, including voice lessons, and prior to the vocal warm-up itself, it is wise to do a few minutes of light physical exercise that produces a feeling of elasticity and freedom throughout the body. Swinging the arms in windmill fashion, dropping head and arms downward and then returning to a standing position, and gently running in place may be part of the process of awakening the body. Heavy, prolonged physical exercise just before performance should be avoided.

The warm-up package ought to begin with gentle, brief onsets and offsets (attack-and-release technique) in a comfortable range of the voice. Humming in medium range and using syllables with nasals and vowel sequences are useful devices. Exercises that induce flexible tongue and jaw action form part of the warm-up sequence. Agility patterns, both ascending and descending, may gradually be added. After initial exercises of this sort, a few minutes of rest should be taken before turning to passages that deal with vowel definition and modification, and with moderate amounts of sostenuto. Registration and *passaggio* vocalises follow. The warm-up should conclude with rapid arpeggios of somewhat extensive range and rapidly moving scale passages. A warm-up process ought not to dwell on specific technical problems; treatment of problematic aspects of the voice should be reserved for the daily technical work, as should longer periods of sustained vocalization.

There is a danger in excessive warming up. Singing thirty minutes of heavy vocalises before performing an operatic role of demanding proportions, or an extensive recital, is illogical. So is singing through large parts of the role or the recital with your coach or accompanist before going out on stage. The old theater adage "Don't sing the bloom off your voice before the performance" continues to be a wise one.

Warming up on stage during act I, or during the first group of the recital, is generally disastrous. It is true that an indulgent critic will occasionally excuse the evidence of such "warming up," but the long-range effects on the singer can be detrimental. Diving immediately into heavy vocalization, which is often demanded at one's first vocal entrance, is not healthy practice. The same common-sense advice pertains to rehearsal preparation, of course. Walking in off the street and onto the set and beginning heavy phonation is a good way to bring on early vocal fatigue.

One of the advantages of a prearranged warm-up cycle comes from the information it gives the singer as to the status of his or her voice. There are times when physical condition requires a longer warm-up period. An established warm-up routine offers psychological as well as physical security to the singer. The singer who has little notion of how her or his voice will feel until hearing it on stage is bound to be a nervous performer. The warm-up routine assures the singer that the voice is capable of functioning well in the tasks that lie ahead.

Warming up is not only essential to the performance-day routine, it should be part of each day's initial vocal work. The singer is unwise to break the silence each day with some untried sequence of exercises. Before turning later in the day to more detailed technical work, the singing voice should have experienced the "daily regimen."

This "daily regimen" is of particular value to the singer/teacher who must use the instrument of performance itself in the process of teaching. A singer invites problems if he or she walks into the voice studio to do a day of teaching without first having sung. It is equally unthinkable for a choir director, who, one would presume, has vocal training, to approach the rehearsal without having made use of the singing voice. Even if the teacher or conductor does little vocal modeling, or is no longer an active performer, the speaking voice itself will have benefited from the warm-up procedure.

Except for those rare occasions when the singing teacher wants to hear the student's voice before that person has engaged in any singing, every singer should arrive at a voice lesson already warmed up. Otherwise time is lost, and teacher's opinion of the student's performance level is not enhanced. Some students, knowing that the studio teacher will probably begin the lesson with vocalization, falsely assume that such technical work during the lesson substitutes for warming up. As a result, the teacher may be unable to move ahead systematically with more vocalization. (There is an exception to this rule with the beginning student who still needs to learn a warm-up routine.)

Sometimes it is useful for the teacher to use a part of the lesson period to hear the student (even the artist student) go through the prearranged warm-up package, in order to see that there is agreement on how the exercises should be executed, and in what sequence. However, the singer should never become dependent upon the voice teacher for the warming-up process for public performance. Warming up is something one must learn to take care of on one's own.

Whenever possible, singers should be able to warm up alone without having to share space with other performers. In theaters and halls, where practice space is often at a premium, it is wise for the singer to arrive early enough to go through the warm-up routine privately. It is extremely disconcerting to share a warm-up room with a colleague who nervously improvises a series of vocalises, who sporadically breaks forth into unexpected vocal noises, or who repeats your every arpeggio.

The secure singer is the prepared singer. A large part of performance preparation has to do with knowing how to use a systematic warm-up procedure. Every singer and teacher of singing should develop a reliable routine for warming up the voice. This routine will vary from individual to individual, but it should remain consistent. Even those who have always assumed they do not need a warm-up generally become convinced of the benefits of systematic warming up as they begin to make use of it.

52

The Technique of Marking

"He told me just to mark the rehearsal. I tried, but it tires me more than if I sing out." Voice teachers with students cast in academic opera often hear that remark. For the moment, it is best to leave out of consideration the problem of excessive rehearsals in academic situations (often far more in number than those faced by a seasoned professional) and to look for ways to protect the young operatic singer. Marking is certainly one.

Markieren (marking) is an international theater term for the technique of sparing the voice during rehearsal. Volume is reduced, high pitches may be lowered an octave, and very low pitches raised an octave (a practice sometimes termed *punktieren,* or pointing). At times only the cues needed by one's colleagues or by the orchestra are sung, the remainder of the phrase being merely lightly indicated. In the male voice, pitches in upper range may be sung in falsetto in substitution for *voce piena* (full voice).

Caution must be exercised in both male and female voices that not everything be sung an octave lower, because this practice can be more harmful than singing the passage as written. In no event should any form of stage whisper or loud speaking above other voices or over the orchestra be part of the marking process.

Marking should be limited to those periods of rehearsal when saving vocal energies for other tasks is of primary concern, or when the singer is not in good vocal or physical condition. It is a mistake to adopt marking as a standard rehearsal procedure. One of the problems of advising a student to mark is that he or she may then wait until too near the performance date to have fully sung the role, and will have little notion of how best to pace it.

Many conscientious stage directors and choral and orchestral conductors want to spare the singer, but they also want as much rehearsal preparation as possible. Sometimes they request that the singer sing a role, or a strenuous choral work, at piano-dynamic level, without realizing they are requesting a feat that few seasoned artists could accomplish. Sustaining a role, or a choral line, that contains long phrases and high *tessitura* frequently demands more energy and technique at piano-dynamic level than at the printed dynamics.

As anyone who deals with opera casting in academia is aware, finding suitable material for young singers is not an easy task. Operatic roles are, in general, intended for mature vocal athletes. Young voices should not be forced into a league to which they do not yet belong. On the other hand, the opera program is a major performance outlet at almost every conservatory or department of music, and such performances can be of immense preprofessional value to the student who can handle them. The problem of combining young voices and opera can partially be solved by judicious choice of title and by double-casting roles. Marking technique can be an assist in managing problematic performance situations. Three questions surface: who, when, and how? We will deal briefly with each of them, in order.

Who? The soubrette, for whom quickly moving passages, scanty orchestration, and lightness of character portrayal are the rule, will not have the same need for marking as might the lyric soprano who has more sustained singing requirements, heavier orchestration, and a role demanding more dramatic and emotional intensity. It is clear that Zerlina may have fewer stamina problems during extensive rehearsals than will Donna Anna, yet Zerlinas also fall ill. Young (mid-twenties) male voices are frequently not at the same level of maturity as are their female counterparts, and may need to make greater use of the technique of marking.

When? Although indisposed singers should cancel whenever possible, there are occasions, especially in the professional world, when cancellation can be avoided if sufficient care is taken, and *marking* can be part of that process. However, constant marking for an ill voice is not advisable. Rest is. Assuming a well performer, let us work backward from the actual performance dates. Generally, in both the academic and the professional worlds, there are several dress rehearsals. It is to be hoped that at least the heavier roles will be double cast, permitting alternating rehearsals, so that a day of rest occurs for each cast between dress rehearsals and the days of performance. If each cast has two dress rehearsals, the first should be sung, the second marked. In no case should a single cast be asked to "sing out" in both dress rehearsals and in the forthcoming performance. In most instances, the dress rehearsals are preceded by the *Sitzprobe* (usually the last general orchestral rehearsal, sung without dramatic action). This is the time when balance between orchestra and singing voices, and ensemble balance among the singers, are established. Most conductors expect "full voice" at this rehearsal. If the singer has sung the *Sitzprobe* full voice, he or she should not follow it the next day with a fully sung dress rehearsal.

Moving backward from the performance period itself ("opera week" on many campuses), the singer is generally involved in several weeks of stage rehearsals. At some point during "run-throughs," the singer should negotiate the entire role in the hall in full voice, preferably several times during the preparatory weeks. At other times, part of the role can be sung, part of it marked; cautious marking during stage rehearsals is advisable. Other performance requirements should be reduced. Even a good vocal technique does not save the voice from overuse, a condition to which young voices are more prone than are mature voices.

How? As has already been indicated, some volume and pitch changes are crucial. Yet only changes that actually save the instrument should be incorporated into marking. Singing a large part of the role in the wrong octave is far more dangerous than singing most of it where it is written. In all cases, decisions as to when and where to mark should be made in advance and should not be spur of the moment searches for improvisatory pitch adjustments.

Before a singer marks a rehearsal, especially in professional circumstances, she or he should mention that fact to the stage director, the conductor, and the other singers. Or if, midrehearsal, a change to marking seems advisable, a statement should be made.

Sometimes an insecure singer will use marking as a shield against performance anxiety. In such cases, it becomes a detrimental device. Equally disturbing is the singer who always marks so that his or her colleagues never know what to expect in performance. It is patently unfair for a healthy singer to purposely avoid singing in rehearsals in the hope of gaining a performance advantage over the other singers.

A number of singers who are having long careers, it should be pointed out, almost never mark rehearsals; they always sing. When technique is solid, the vocal instrument healthy, and the role appropriate to the voice, singing a reasonable number of rehearsals is not a problem. However, even the professional who feels quite comfortable about using the voice at full energy level in rehearsals should alternately sing and mark dress rehearsals, as suggested earlier. If there are two orchestral dress rehearsals and only one cast, it is then favorable to sing the first half of the role in one rehearsal and to mark the second half, then to reverse the process the next day.

Marking, for the student singer, should be examined as a technique with the teacher before the singer attempts it in rehearsals. Teacher and student should identify the specific phrases and pitches at which marking is to occur. By using this approach the risk of the common experience of tiring the voice through incorrect marking, done in the hope of saving it, will be considerably reduced.

53

The Vocal Contestant and the Judges

One of the few doors that may swing open for the American singer hopeful of a professional performance career is to be found at the end of a sometimes murky corridor known as *the contest route*. Some contests offer the fortunate winner an important recital appearance with exposure to professional music criticism, an operatic appearance not otherwise available to a talented but unknown singing actor, or monetary awards that ensure voice lessons and literature coaching with prominent teachers. Voice teachers, especially those affiliated with professional organizations devoted to furthering the development of the performer, recognize the contest route as of major importance in the growth of students at all levels of accomplishment, and they try to locate for the student the competition most appropriate to the student's current performance achievement. Certainly nothing is more discouraging for the immature singer than to enter a contest intended for the accomplished young artist, and to receive a set of negative comments about her or his unpolished condition.

Judges for singing competitions who comment that the contestant has a wonderful instrument but the wrong technique, and that a new teacher should be found (a frequently heard report from all parts of the country by teachers who enter advanced students in major contests) are equally misguided. It is impossible for a judge to know how close the contestant comes to achieving the technical goals of the current teacher, or what progress has been made in areas that still may be problematic. People who make such unethical statements should not be permitted to judge contests.

Typically, a young singer's first competition is judged by teachers of singing who have been exposed to vocal sounds and to frequent contest adjudication throughout their professional lives. Early contests, however, may be the only ones in which the singer will be judged by persons who know the literature being sung and who are trained to evaluate singing voices. Increasingly, the teacher of singing faces a strange phenomenon lurking along the contest route on which he or she sends forth the talented young artist. Today, the qualifications of the judges who make decisions regarding the art of singing appear to be in inverse ratio to the importance of the contest. Indeed, some district and regional contests that lead to national finals of considerable consequence may be judged by persons (at times even a single person) who not only are not singers or teachers of singing but johnny-come-latelies to opera direction via the drama theater, or the newspaper music critic who has graduated from book reviews and antique shows to ballet and opera criticism, or the symphony conductor who rarely uses a vocalist in his programming, or the artist management representative who neither sings nor plays an instrument but who "knows what a star looks like."

Lest this seem like speculative comment, some specific examples may be in order. At a recent competition for the young singing artist, none of the three judges was a singer or a teacher of singing. Somewhat typically, one judge was the conductor of a modest civic symphony orchestra that presents five concerts a year, another the nonsinger chairperson of a modest music department at a nearby educational institution, and the third, the conductor of a modest civic chorus. In the audience were many National Association of Teachers of Singing members attending a regional meeting. When the contest results were announced, astonishment reigned among the persons professionally equipped to make judgments about singing and vocal performance. In another nationally acclaimed vocal competition that takes place annually in a major metropolitan area, members of the local music club (which offers quite substantial prize money) "weed out" all but a few performers, who then proceed to the final round, which is judged by outside guest professionals who are not members of the club. An interesting tale can be told of one such "weed," who, on winning a second and more major contest adjudicated by some of the same final professional judges, was told that she should have entered the contest sponsored by the above-mentioned metropolitan music club, because she was far superior to any of its finalists!

Let us cite another example. I recall judging a nationally advertised contest for musical artists, with substantial monetary prizes, open to a number of performance disciplines, at which professional pianists and noted teachers of piano judged the piano entrants, string professionals the string players, and wind professionals the winds; but the vocal division adjudication was in the hands of a committee composed of one voice teacher (myself), two pianists, one woodwind player, and a conductor whose instrument to this day remains a secret. When I questioned the arrangement, I was assured by the national competition chairman that whereas special knowledge is required to make judgments in the complex instrumental fields and in their literatures, all musicians can judge the singing voice.

Another hurdle for the contestant is the problem of adjudicators who decide to apply their own interpretation to the published contest rules. One thirty-year-old dramatic baritone, in a competition where the termination age is thirty-two, is clearly professionally ready with regard to his instrument, his training, and his communication, and without doubt the superior performer. The chairperson, in announcing the winner (an attractive soubrette aged twenty-three), tells the stunned audience that the committee decided they should look for young talent that although perhaps not yet professionally formed, shows potential. "The decision of the judges is final," say most contests, and probably with good reason, inasmuch as so many contest results are questionable.

The singing artist must have an exceptional native vocal endowment, and must possess a secure vocal technique. In addition, she or he must be carefully coached in the stylistic subtleties of vocal literature and in essential language precision. But frequently the vocal contestant is judged by persons who know neither the literature of the *Lied* nor of the *mélodie*. (Chances are that the judges have at least some familiarity with the more standard operatic aria repertory, although one of them may request from the submitted repertoire list "the aria with the high C", when none of the arias has a high C). The ability to properly pronounce and inflect languages foreign to a singer is a professional essential, yet there are some interesting aberrations. I was once told by a highly successful tenor of international repute that he had to make his American operatic debut in a major house, singing a role in French, a language in which he had not previously sung and with which he had tremendous problems in this initial essay. His debut, however, was highly successful with regard to critical acclaim. As he put it, "Of course, most of the critics, this particular conductor, and the management knew nothing about sung French. What's funny is that, of course, the chorus members and other cast members all were chuckling over my many mispronunciations." Such, at times, is the state of vocal art in high quarters! However, no singer should assume that contest judges, if they are true professionals, will ignore language distortion. Language accuracy and finesse are major parts of performance evaluation.

Perhaps one of the functions of professional organizations devoted to singers and to the teaching of singing might well be to approach the persons who organize and administer contests (they are seldom practicing musicians) with the request that singers be judged by knowledgeable adjudicators. Further, the questionable practice of having singers judged by preliminary judges whose aesthetic orientations and qualifications may be very different from those of the final judging panel should be discouraged. In the most respected and successful international contests, the same judging panel hears all rounds, even if it takes several weeks to do so. Above all, the contestant, while taking seriously comments from professional evaluators, should know in advance that, despite the wording of the brochure, contest judgments are in no way final. The singing world is populated with contest winners whose names you will never again hear mentioned, and with lots of Honorable Mentions whose careers have blossomed in stunning fashion! But do enter the right contest.

54

Twenty-one Proven Ways to Alienate Competition Judges

1. Arrive late for your appointed time, so that the judging panel must wait several minutes. (Each minute spent in waiting adds immeasurably to accumulated annoyance.)

2. Announce from the stage a program change, although the contest rules state any change must be made in advance in writing. (This will ensure confusion among jury members as to how to resolve the problem, and headaches for the people who have organized the contest.)

3. Provide your accompanist with a series of illegally photocopied sheets, preferably folded in half, which must be spread out over the entire piano rack, and which may buckle a few times or periodically spill over onto the keyboard.

4. Assume the demeanor of the world-famous artist. Bow regally to the empty hall before and following your performance. If the contest takes place during the daylight hours, wear formal concert attire. Females should wear huge orchid corsages; males, red carnation boutonnieres.

5. From the stage, identify some prominent member of the jury and call out that your teacher sends warmest greetings. (This works especially well in alienating the remaining members of the adjudication committee.)

6. Choreograph your aria with hand and torso gestures. Particularly effective for a negative evaluation is the hand continuously thrust forward as though patiently waiting for a dog on the leash. If you want to further lower the evaluation of your performance, prance around and *stage* your aria. Arms thrown upward and outward on the final high note will complete alienation of the judges.

7. Choose demanding material that you hope will knock over the judges, something you managed to get through a time or two in the prac-

tice room when you were in great form. If you are not sure of your *Fach,*
sing selections from several vocal categories. Further, choose a thirteen-
minute *scene,* or a long concert aria, when you have a total of ten minutes
allotted for performance.

8. Bring a glass of water with you as you enter the stage, place it on
the piano, sip from it before beginning to sing and between numbers.
Leave the glass on the piano as you exit. (As the contest progresses, its
presence will recall you to the jury.)

9. Inform the jury that you have a cold, that you didn't sleep well last
night, that you have traveled 400 miles today, and that you just this very
minute arrived at the hall.

10. If, in the interest of the time allotted to each contestant, the jury
chair interrupts your performance and asks you to proceed to a later section of the aria, or to another aria, show your annoyance by turning to
your accompanist and dramatically shrugging your shoulders.

11. If participating in a song contest, sing only strophic songs with long
piano interludes. Or use only literature written for orchestra and voice.

12. When initially sending in your contest registration form, don't
bother to time the items as requested. Or, even better, fool the contest
organizers by listing each item a few minutes short, in the hope of getting
to sing longer. Throw a fit when cut off mid-aria.

13. Be certain to include at least one "cute" number, going on the assumption that most members of the jury really don't know much about
singing anyway, and would prefer to be entertained.

14. If the audition is local and public, pack it with friends who will
yell "Bravo!" or "Bis!" after each selection. (This assumes that judges respond largely to popular judgment, and that it would never occur to them
that you brought your claque with you.)

15. If asked to cut the *da capo,* strenuously object and announce that
you have marvelously inventive embellishments the jury really must hear.

16. If contest rules are not specific, particularly in the first round, sing
everything in your favorite language with lots of melismas to show your
command of coloratura, or, conversely, sing only material with sustained
passages that show your endurance. You might also sing selections that
chiefly lie in that "new" part of your voice you are currently discovering.

17. In contests of several phases (as is usual in international competitions) ask to speak privately with several of the judges either before or
after each round. Telephone their hotel rooms just before dinnertime for
advice, or, better still, after 10 P.M.

18. Before your appearance in each round, hold the warm-up room for
yourself as long as you can, and make special demands on the volunteer
committee.

19. Treat the other contestants as though you had already won or were sure of winning, and the audience (among whom sits the jury) with a certain amount of haughtiness when you enter and leave the stage (great artists are special!)

20. Find someone to play for you who won't need to be paid (good sources are roommates, mothers, fathers, spouses, or voice teachers), on the assumption the jury is interested only in hearing your voice, not in the totality of the performance.

21. When you place third, demand to interview members of the jury to question why you were not first. Ask "What happened?" Remember, many times the same judges keep appearing on adjudication panels, and this combative tactic assures future alienation as well.

55

Beginning with Another Teacher

Singing the first time for another voice teacher may be difficult. Will, once again, everything learned in the past be wrong? Will the new teacher insist on starting from the beginning, on building from the ground up? Surely there is no other performance discipline in which such diametrically opposed techniques may face the student who changes teachers.

The beginning voice student has little reason to question suggestions and criticism from a teacher. The experienced singer, on the other hand, who for some reason seeks out a new pair of listening ears may encounter a completely different set of aesthetic and pedagogical ideals, and have to sort them out in the light of past experiences and logical thinking.

Not always is the new teacher sufficiently aware of what it means to a singer to put one's future into new hands. The first audition lesson is a special occasion for both teacher and singer. Ideally, the teacher will be both kind of heart and psychologically sensitive. Yet how many of us, upon changing teachers, have faced the dogmatic battering ram at the first encounter! This may stem from an unconscious desire on the part of the new teacher to convince the student that he or she is now in better hands. A question of ethics is involved. Necessary changes can be made with tact and with care. There is no need to denigrate what has already been accomplished.

Valid judgments about the student's previous instruction cannot be made in an informational vacuum. One cannot know exactly what the singer was doing technically when first in the hands of a former teacher, nor what his progress has been in those very areas that the new teacher finds deficient. Questions regarding past concepts are in order, but condemnation of past teaching may even serve to hinder future work on the same set of problems. From a purely practical standpoint, it is difficult to understand teachers who can never find anything good to say about pupils sent to them by another teacher.

Most singers are not fooled by the teacher who confines the new student to a limited range or repertoire, and who then, six weeks later, when the singer is allowed to negotiate the scale and sing a substantial portion of the repertoire, announces, "You see, I have given you a high C!" Even students who in general respect the new teacher laugh about the self-congratulatory claims of the "miracle worker" teacher. The former teacher who has prepared the student for advanced study with that teacher is seldom amused, and responds by sending other pupils elsewhere.

Singers are in search of quick solutions. The hope of finding the magic phonatory muscle is a common singer fantasy. Surely there must be a teacher out there who can put it all together for me! Someone is always willing to take advantage of that hope. Although the old saw "there are no good teachers, only good students" is a lopsided observation, there is little doubt that in the long run "putting it all together" must be accomplished by the individual singer, regardless of the merit of the teaching. No teacher has a right to claim sole credit for the success of any accomplished singer, particularly not that of an inherited one!

The artist singer who looks for a new teacher should be wary of the person who represents himself as the only source of technical or musical knowledge. If the new teacher is the only one who knows about the technique she teaches, the wise singer will go somewhere else. There are no secretly discovered inventions that can be applied to the singing voice.

Good teaching recognizes what is admirable. It encompasses enough imagination to acknowledge that the singer who stands in front of the new teacher has already traveled some distance down the vocal development road or the new teacher would not have accepted him or her.

56

Early and Late Bloomers

Chronological age is not a reliable indicator of vocal maturity. A widely held opinion is that the college-age singer is a very young singer, and that serious vocal development lies only in the future. College-age instruction is thus seen as a kind of holding operation until the voice "grows up." In actuality, a large number of professional careers were begun within this very age group. According to a survey of 500 famous singers of the present century, by C. Smith ("Parameter Analysis on a Large Quantity of Statistical Background Information Relating to Opera Singers," unpublished dissertation, 1976), most made their professional debuts between the ages of twenty and twenty-five. Despite that interesting statistic, caution is essential when dealing with the late-adolescent/young-adult voice. However, to encourage a singer to "mark time" during undergraduate years with regard to technical development, under the assumption that the voice is too young for serious study, is to abdicate teaching responsibilities.

"Protective teaching" is detrimental to true vocal development. There are many ways to produce bad vocalism and *undersinging* is one of them. A male of twenty-one should not sound like a fifteen-year-old youth, nor should a young female adult sound like a girl of fourteen. Such vocalization is actually not protective but debilitating. Almost as much harm can occur in undersinging (in which the young voice remains devoid of energy, often because of high levels of breath mixture) as by oversinging (pushing the young voice into false maturity).

The singing voice is an instrument that depends on proper airflow, subglottic pressure, and vocal-fold activity. Some of what passes for "relaxed" singing violates dynamic balance just as badly as does pressed phonation. "Whispering" while singing is as undesirable as "grunting." "Sighing" induces high levels of airflow not turned into tone. Today's vocal student tends to be influenced by the intimate sounds of electronically amplified performance, in which projection does not depend on coordination of breath and phonation. Popular vocal styles have made inroads into traditional classical singing techniques, often without being fully recognized.

Females are frequently early bloomers and males late bloomers, although there are exceptions among both. Following puberty, males may suddenly discover that the newly developed cartilages and folds of muscle located in the neck make them capable of producing sounds that impress people around them. This new vocal sound is a mark of transition from childhood to young manhood. A male with an interest in singing is almost always a "late bloomer" with regard to his physical instrument, which undergoes more radical mutation than does that of the female. Not knowing he was to become the possessor of a valuable musical instrument, the young man may never have had any type of musical training. His late blooming is therefore both physical and musical.

Another category of late male bloomer is the young man who has relatively sophisticated musical training because he has studied another instrument, or because he has had extensive treble choral experience. He brings musicality to his "new" instrument and applies some of the same basic techniques he used as a boy soprano or boy alto, but he does not yet have the finesse in his new literature that he had in the treble literature. He is musically ready to perform complex literature, but does not have a sufficiently developed vocal instrument, or, as a rule, the language skills needed to do so. These limitations may make it difficult to fit such a musician/singer into the curricular demands of academic performance majors, because he has been singing with the "new" voice a relatively short time, yet he must accomplish the performance-major requirements. The serious private voice student may be able to avoid the rigid time considerations placed on the student in an academic program, but his developmental problems are similar. How should the teacher approach the young late-blooming male voice?

First of all, it must be remembered that if an eighteen-year-old male singer has undergone change of voice at age fifteen, his new voice is only three years old. He cannot be expected to sing with the same skill as does his eighteen-year-old soprano friend. The early months of his voice study should be used to establish a free sound in the middle region of the singing range, never far removed from the speaking range. When several notes of good timbre and of easy production have been routined, exploration of pitches on either side should follow. It is not here assumed that the singer is incapable of making those additional pitches, because most young males can manage the range of an octave or a tenth by the time the voice has become relatively "settled." However, those additional pitches are often executed with tension (either without sufficient energy or with the wrong application of high energy levels). It is best to proceed gradually from a few solidly produced notes in lower-middle range (the speech area) half tone by half tone. Breath management, the onset of sound, vowel definition, vibrancy, and timbre consistency are early goals. These techniques can be acquired by working at them systematically.

Every singer should be allowed some literature as soon as vocal study begins. The making of music ought to occur in every lesson. Singing skills acquired through vocalises should soon be transferred to nondemanding vocal literature. (At all stages of development, there should be a crossing over from the literature to the vocal exercises.) Finding appropriate literature for the beginning male singer often taxes the ingenuity of the teacher. The task is made more difficult by the young male singer's realization that his female colleagues of the same age are performing more advanced literature, and by his awareness of the difference a few years' maturity makes in other male voices around him. Songs of limited range, transposed literature, and some of the easier exercises from vocalizing systems such as Vaccai, Panofka, Sieber, Garcia, and Lamperti may also serve as transition from individualized vocalizing to the song literature.

In contrast to the youngster just described is the male singer whose instrument changed and "settled" early, who is capable of making rather mature vocal sounds. He may even have easy access to pitches at both extremes of the vocal range. The problem is that he does not yet possess the size of instrument and the vocal stamina to manage the literature he will comfortably sing in the future. He has already studied most of the "twenty-four arias" in the standard *arie antiche* collection, and he longs to sing the operatic literature. He can pronounce Italian, but is not yet linguistically equipped to profit from studying *Lieder* or *mélodie*. What to do with him? English-language songs provide much of the answer, including some of the more modest Purcell, Arne, Handel, and Haydn arias in English. A number of excellent collections of early Italian arias, with limited range, are also now available.

The choice of literature, however, is not the most pressing task with the unusually vocally mature young male singer; the problem is how to convince him to wait until his body has caught up with the demands of the more extensive literature he has heard and that he longs to sing. This early bloomer must learn to conserve his instrument—to not use up his capital—and to patiently develop necessary nonvocal skills. He must be helped to understand that maturation in the male instrument is a lengthy process.

With young females, early or late blooming often depends on differences to be found between vocal categories. Even though the female does not experience pubertal changes to the same degree as the male, physical maturation plays a role. In general, the larger the female instrument, the more time it takes to harness it. Soubrettes and coloraturas often display rather remarkable technical prowess at an early age, whereas at a similar age the potential *soprano lirico spinto* voice remains unwieldy. Just as with the later-maturing male voice, the female with a sizable instrument should understand that her vocally lightweight female colleague can be expected to sing better at that age than she. It will comfort her to know that the more dramatic female voices often have a longer career expectancy, making up for the slower rate of maturation that discourages her as a young adult. In general, young female voices of more than soubrette size do not have the same easy access to upper range as do their lighter voiced friends. Although all human vocal instruments function by the same fundamental principles, the big soprano voice requires more time to learn to produce an even scale throughout the range. The history of professional singing is filled with early coloratura careers, for example, whereas the more dramatic voices seldom are among early starters.

A problem for the soprano with a sizable voice is the tendency for people with whom she works to assume that because she has "a short top" and a rich timbre she must therefore be a mezzo. A surprising number of lyric and dramatic voices have been falsely classified as mezzos because they did not early have the upper range facility of the lighter *soubrette/coloratura* category. One of the least productive approaches with a young sizable soprano is to make her begin with the soubrette or coloratura literature under the assumption that she will thereby lighten her voice. However, more usable literature is available for all ages and categories of young female singers than is the case for the young male.

The mezzo, it should be remembered, is a category of soprano. The young mezzo should not be asked to darken her voice in order to sound more like a mezzo (chances are she is a soprano anyway). She has a wide choice of middle-range literature; much of the *Lied* and *mélodie* repertory lies gratefully for her. In this regard, she has a distinct advantage over the young baritone, for whom much of the literature (particularly that designated in transposition as suitable for either mezzo or baritone) has a *tessitura* he cannot easily manage.

A frequent false judgment about the female voice comes from the belief that a robustly built woman, or one who is obese, is a mezzo. Although morphological considerations are pertinent in determining vocal categories, the notion that being overweight indicates a lower category of voice is not tenable. Weight does not add depth or richness to vocal sound any more than placing the green protective pad around the pianoforte increases its resonance.

The contralto voice is such a rarity that most teachers do not encounter singers of that category. A very real danger exists, however, in telling a young mezzo that she is a contralto and in allowing her to sing in only the lower half of her negotiable range. A logical viewpoint suggests that the contralto may not even exist as a practical performance vehicle in the young female, because the potential contralto sound needs years of maturity and growth. Asking a young woman to use heavy vocalis muscle activity ("chest") runs the risk of her never finding the proper graduated crico-arytenoidal coordinations in upper range. One of the most pernicious errors is to require a large soprano or mezzo-soprano voice to rely almost solely on "chest" voice in order to strengthen the alto part in choral music.

In both male and female voices of substantial size, it may be detrimental to demand too much subtlety too soon. The notion, for example, that all young singers who have reached an advanced enough technical level to sing aria material should start with Mozart, Bellini, Donizetti, or Rossini, may be disastrous for the potentially *spinto* voice. To ask every young female voice to attempt the *tessitura,* the extended phrases, the *sostenuto* and the agility demanded by those composers is a bit like asking an infant to attempt ballet leaps before learning to walk. Unfortunately, this idea is deeply rooted in American vocal pedagogy. (Some contests for very young singers demand a Mozart aria, as opposed to other aria material, for example.)

Other kinds of late blooming sometimes occur in both female and male voices. They are related to self image, to psychological factors, to late exposure to musical training, and to previous technical approaches. Some persons with potentially professional voices simply do not find their instruments until somewhat later in life than normally is the case. They may have always assumed their voices were limited; that they did not possess sufficient communicative skills to be effective, or that they were not good enough to compete in the professional arena. Sadly, they often have been hampered by well-meaning teachers who never allowed the true voice to emerge because of a lack of understanding as to how the application of energy can take place without pushing the instrument. A perturbing aspect of the pedagogical scene is the number of potentially fine voices that were never allowed to discover completeness *(voce completa)* during formative years when growth and experience are essential.

What of the person who suddenly discovers at age thirty that he or she seriously wishes to begin the study of singing? It should be pointed out that singing is an art dependent upon a number of factors, many of them having nothing to do with vocal sound. Previous musical background is of great importance. To begin late is to move the preparatory years into the years that should already be given over to professional activity. Acquiring vocal skill takes years. All late-starting singers should be reminded that vocal longevity is not geared to when one begins study.

Anyone who has a desire to sing should receive a serious response from anyone who teaches singing. The older student has as much right to learn to sing as does the late adolescent. However, it is also the ethical duty of the teacher to point out that the number of professional opportunities for singers is limited, and the indisputable fact is that people who hire professionals look for experienced singers whose physical circumstances fit the occasion. Regardless of how well she might sing, a forty-five-year-old Despina (unless already an established artist, with box-office appeal) will not get the job if a twenty-six-year-old is available. Career building should be well under way before the age of thirty. There has always been the rare exception, of course.

Another category of late bloomer is the male who, although actually a tenor, has always sung baritone, but with difficulty. A number of tenors, earlier classified and trained as baritones because they were unable to achieve the tenor *tessitura* with ease, discover in their late twenties that they are capable of making the necessary category change. They are fortunate if they have had good musical training and performance opportunities despite having suffered false voice classification. Such singers generally need at least a two-year period for the transition. Professional considerations make it difficult to accomplish such a change much beyond the age of thirty, although there have been some exceptions here as well.

Above all, it is not the prerogative of the teacher of singing to tell any talented singer still in the early stages of development that he or she will or will not have a singing career. The complex package of factors that leads to success as a singing performer is difficult to discern with certainty until growth and development have taken place. Singers mature at differing rates. Everyone has heard stories of famous singers who were rejected for admission at reputable schools of music, of the great Italian *spinto* tenor who was told by six of Italy's leading teachers to go back to the farm and forget it, of the singer who never sang even a minor role while in the university opera department but who ten years later has a contract at a leading European opera house. The admissions people, the *maestri,* and the opera director were not really mistaken; the singers simply did not early indicate much potential. Conversely, the early bloomer who could dazzle with high notes and astounding pyrotechnical agility during conservatory days may never again be heard from. The male that out-sized and outdistanced all of his contemporaries during college days may no longer enjoy that distinction as the later blooming voices mature. Normally, vocal development continues without arrest throughout the fourth decade of a singer's life.

It is a gratifying experience for the teacher to hear a young voice, to estimate its potential, and to watch it mature. Audition days at schools of music are always exciting events, not just for the candidates but for their judges. But it is equally interesting to later compare the entrance ratings of performance major candidates and to see where persons who received very different kinds of ratings end up after four or five years, at degree completion time. Early judgments regarding vocal potential often prove inexact; they should be cautiously made. The possibilities for a successful singing career cannot be precisely calculated in advance. Both teacher and student have to keep in mind that vocal maturation, chronological age, and professional potential do not always mesh. Some singers bloom early, some singers bloom late. The important thing is to make the most complete preparation possible in the hope that nature and circumstances will be kind.

57

Creative Practicing

Given the nature of today's popular culture, how does a young person get "turned on" to so-called classical vocal study? The choir director at school or church, an avuncular opera buff, the thrilling discovery of an operatic recording or the colorful video reproduction of an appealing opera may generate initial enthusiasm. Soon the realization of the physical joy of vocal performance and the satisfaction of artistic expression serve to propel the young singer to consider performance as a desirable vocation.

Early performance successes are heady experiences. One's peers show new respect. Persons who are considered experts begin to speak of "promising potential." "Talented" and "gifted" are expressions that fall pleasantly on the ear. With the help of a fine local teacher, acceptance into a performance program at a major school of music becomes possible.

It is probably at the point of entrance into a degree program that it dawns on the young singer that what was great fun for the talented high school amateur now requires new kinds of responsibility in preprofessional circumstances. Whereas there was never any doubt about being the uniquely qualified solo singer in high school, at the arts academy, at church or temple, or in one's own town or city, now there are numerous other singers with similar performance histories. It is something of a shock to discover that the new teacher at college or university is accustomed to dealing with unusual vocal talent. No longer is one unique.

Further, the new teacher seems to hear many more things that are in need of correction. Those areas of the voice that were never quite at the same level as the best parts of the instrument now take on a new importance. Technically detailed practicing, as opposed to singing because it is fun, is suddenly required. Even those favorite songs and arias that had previously met with great approval at service clubs and school musical reviews now appear to be in question as vehicles for public performance. Perhaps the Metropolitan Opera contract is not as close at hand as parents and the folks back home had been assuming! In short, preprofessional reality strikes.

The transition from talented amateur to serious preprofessional is problematic not only for the student but also for the new studio teacher. The new teacher faces the considerable task of making sure that the student retains an essentially good self-image, and of nurturing the initial curiosity that drew the student to the field of performance, while at the same time directing attention to the lack of certain skills and the need for greater discipline. How can the teacher redirect youthful energy and enthusiasm without diminishing valuable assets? This is a major pedagogical problem. There is, fortunately, an answer: *creative practicing*.

Problem solving in itself can be made a creative act shared by teacher and student. There must be an overall plan that outlines goals, with explicit instruction as to what should take place in the practice room when the student is working alone. Identification of a technical fault during the lesson without an accompanying solution is disheartening to the learner. Noncreative teaching consists of running the gamut of current pedagogical ideas without determining which ones are based on efficient action and which are purely subjective. Clearly, pedagogical trial and error does not substitute for specific information grounded on an understanding of the voice as a functioning instrument.

During the lesson there must be assessment of problems, prescriptions for their correction, and some indication of the probable time span required for results. Often it is unclear to a student that some problems are long-range, dependent upon a gradually developing coordination. The student may incorrectly assume that if the solution has not proved successful during this lesson, or this week, it may never work, and he or she abandons it too quickly.

Creative practicing does not mean just doing one's own thing; it means creatively using the information given during the lesson. Creative practicing can take place only if it is based on specifics, with an understanding as to what is to be accomplished. Each solution opens up the possibility for additional progress. Every practice session should build on the creative excitement of solutions previously offered in the studio.

Vocalises can be useful in "warming up" the voice, but their chief purpose should be to build the total technique of the singer. Only vocalises that have proved to produce specific coordination in singing are acceptable. They should be noncomplex, and they should induce desirable physiologic and acoustic function. But won't the student become bored with vocal exercises, and can't singing through songs and arias produce the same results? The answer in both cases is no.

It is often overlooked that vocal timbre is emotive, and that every vocalise should be treated as a musical expression, an emission of sound that in itself is communicative. A less-than-beautiful vocal sound communicates nothing of beauty. ("Vocal coloration" that produces ugly sound is neither musical nor expressive.)

An ingenuous viewpoint assumes that technical work involving vocal sound is basically noncreative, and that creativity can enter only when literary or dramatic ideas are expressed. Were that the case, approximately half the standard vocal literature from previous centuries would fail to qualify as performance-worthy, because much of its *raison d'être* is pure vocalization, frequently wedded to monotonously repeated, insipid texts.

Singing a rapid arpeggio over the span of a twelfth on a series of changing syllables can be as exhilarating an experience as singing the cadenza passages of a *cabaletta*, if it is approached with a creative attitude. The vocalise itself is more useful technically because it limits the area of skill to be routined. It concentrates more narrowly upon specifics. Of course, it is entirely possible to execute that same arpeggio in a nonemotive, mentally detached fashion, in which case its purpose is lost. Consistency of resonance throughout a sequence of changing vowels can be a joyous, creative experience, if a singer has the proper love for making vocal sound. Recognizing vowel modification so as to avoid openness or excessive "cover" in a mounting scale pattern can become an exciting adventure in timbre matching. Such work is highly creative.

There is seldom any value in practicing vocalises that do not have musical merit. A scale, a triad, an arpeggio has such merit. Vocal techniques that incorporate grunting, groaning, yawning, sighing, barking, or primitive calling—the list could be extended—are largely useless technically and aesthetically, in addition to being functionally detrimental to the vocal instrument. Every phrase, brief or long, fast or slow, loud or soft, must present a musical experience. True, not all attempts at beautiful sound will be equally successful. It is not possible to produce only aesthetically pleasing sounds while attempting to master technical skills, yet the ideal of tonal beauty should always prevail, both in private and public phonation. Nothing that sounds worse and feels worse can be an improvement, even in the short run.

The practice room does not serve as a laboratory remote from performance-ready sound, nor does the vocal studio itself. The ultimate goal of technical study remains, simply, the communication of beautiful sound and textual content. In the practice room, the student should sing series of vocalises as though performing before an audience. The physical joy of singing must always be present; the instrumental sound of the voice must be emotive. An imaginary audience accompanies creative practicing. One never sings, whether practicing or performing, for oneself.

Thus far in this consideration of creative practicing emphasis has been placed on using series of vocalises, because it is the vocalise that remains the chief vehicle for technical development of the vocal art. However, phrases from the vocal literature itself can be treated technically without loss of the creative spark. Even musical expression and textual communication need to be systematically *practiced*.

Student and teacher creatively share in analyzing and determining what remains lacking in technique and expression. Creative practicing is an extension of creative studio teaching. The practice room becomes a friendly and exciting place where vocal technique and artistry are united. It need not be simply the room in which one "warms up" the voice prior to tackling the literature. Creative teaching and creative practicing produce the creative singer.

58

A Stroll Past the Practice Rooms

Have you ever wondered why the young woman with the beautiful soprano voice sometimes comes to her lesson with a hazy sound in middle voice, although that opaque sound normally is not there? What about the young lyric tenor who has been making tremendous strides in his top range but who seems to be developing a raspy sound in upper-middle voice, especially in approaching the *secondo passaggio?* A cold? An upper respiratory infection? Allergies? Asthma? This condition seems mysteriously to come and go during the course of the semester.

Then you happen to stroll through the practice room unit, intending not to spy but to deliver a message. As you near the area you hear a loud cacophony of vocal sounds, polytonal in nature, coming out of not totally soundproof practice rooms. Vocal arpeggios up and down; a mixture of beginner and graduate singers. The singers are in competition with a trumpeter or two, and a noisy percussionist, located in nearby rooms. For security reasons, the doors all have little windows so that you glance in as you look for your voice student. What you see and hear may be shocking.

From a room down the hall you hear *Nessun dorma* sung by a voice that you almost recognize. But of course, it couldn't be your lyric tenor Daniel, because you would never assign such an aria to him. There isn't a voice teacher in the country who wouldn't agree that giving twenty-one-year-old Daniel such heavy material would be unethical. Whose student could that be?

Unfortunately it is Daniel, *your* student. If you can wait a minute before bursting in, you may also hear *Cielo e mar!* No need to be concerned about asthma, URIs, or allergies. The problem is Puccini and Ponchielli at the wrong time in the young tenor's life. As you are about to rap on the door, across the hall comes *Suicidio!*, an appropriate way of inducing an early career termination for the soprano to whom you have assigned Norina's aria. Now the reason for the off-and-on hazy middle voice of the young soprano is explained.

Young singers fall in love with exciting vocal literature, and there scarcely exists a teacher of singing who doesn't have to warn talented students against singing dramatic literature too early. Practice room areas are also competitive regions. If the baritone next door is displaying some problems in tackling Germont, why not show him how, through the adjoining wall? When singers hear other singers, something is triggered in the mind; an empathic kinesthetic response occurs. Like excited youngsters around the swimming pool, into the fray they dive. There is also the joy of singing through groups of arias for admiring friends, or for the new meaningful relationship whom the student would like to impress. Reining in ambitious students is part of responsible voice teaching. Students almost always feel they can tackle more advanced literature than they are able to handle. The vocal fatigue the student brings to the studio is often the result of having sung destructive vocal literature outside the lesson.

Teacher's practice-room promenade may also reveal why the vocalises that have been assigned in the studio are not producing the expected results. The teacher may hear a number of indiscriminate vocalizing patterns that, although they may not be harmful, are not a part of the assigned technical system, and are not appropriate to the student's current needs. It may, therefore, be salutary to have each student devote an occasional lesson to demonstrating exactly what his or her practice sessions are like. If there is no plan, no organization to the practicing, there will be little positive result.

There are times when advanced students can help monitor what goes on in those practice rooms that we teachers tend to avoid. Occasionally it is useful to have a first-year student and an experienced student observe each other's practice habits. No actual instruction takes place, but listening together can be useful.

It is not just the practice area that we should be concerned about, because there are other locales where students tend to fatigue their vocal instruments. Discos should be off limits to serious singers. When Peter sounds hoarse, check his hand to see if he is still wearing last night's disco entrance stamp. Or how many church jobs is Jennifer holding down? How much practice teaching is she doing this semester in her Music Education program? How many gigs is Brian singing with his band? In short, much of what contributes to vocal problems among today's singing students is beyond the control of the voice teacher. That is why every teacher of singing should warn each student about the negative effects of abuses and misuses of the voice. It is especially painful when a teacher discovers that abuse is taking place in the practice room itself.

59

What Technical Work Have You Done Today?

In looking back over the past several decades at opportunities available to the student singer, one is struck by two developments; first, the plethora of master classes given by noted performers, most of whom are not chiefly occupied as teachers of singing, and second, the proliferation of vocal competitions. Nearly every major city in Europe currently has such a competition. The catalogue listing international competitions, at one time restricted to little more than a dozen, grows annually. In addition, many local, regional, and national contests are available to today's singing student.

Competitions and public performance in master classes can be exciting occasions in which disciplined young singers are offered a forum for the display and the evaluation of their abilities. Both sources may be of great value to singers properly prepared to participate in them. They may prove to be occasions of frustration for participants, judges, and listeners if a singer lacks the technical skill expected in serious competitions for vocal honors.

Frequently, in competition and master-class situations, the preparatory musical and dramatic coaching clearly has been of the finest. The singer exhibits a warm and charming personality, yet the competition judge or the master teacher wonders what happened to tonal ideals in the process. Everything except stabilized timbre resulting from solid technique is present.

Public teaching sessions with well-known coaches and prominent performing artists may provide musical and textual assistance to a technically strong performance that is in need of polish. More often, they consist of entertainments devoid of lasting instructional value. When the "master class," is over, a typical response from a talented singer may be "I didn't think anything was really wrong with what I was doing," or "I didn't understand the criticisms," but equally typical is the realization on the part of the singer that basic vocal problems that inhibit artistic performance have not been addressed.

Yet many of these same singers have been through a number of major voice studios in several metropolitan centers, studying briefly with teachers who have excellent records in building successful careers—without, however, having discovered vocal security. In such cases it is easy for a singer to erect a protective shield and to blame former instruction for results that depend not on past teaching but on oneself.

It is a telling thing to ask some singers who have been "around" for a while and who for years have shown "promise" the following question: "How much do you work on vocal technique each day?" Expect this kind of answer: "Well I always warm up before singing through the standard audition arias. I also try to add a role or a song group to my repertoire each year." The sequel question, of course, is "Yes, but what *technical* work do you do on your instrument each day?" The answer is often a blank stare.

Having been through the hands of a great artist in a several-week-long summer course, a semester or two with a noted teacher, and a few weekend master classes with some others, surely one must then have the right prescription for achieving successful performance. Unfortunately, such opportunities may lull the singer into believing that the technical basis of singing is acquired by artistic osmosis. In addition, persons sufficiently advanced as singers to be accepted into major voice studios or as participants in important competitions already do many good things that will find approval from teachers and judges. Why, then, are they not winners or on the road to professional engagements? It is generally the remaining technical problems that stand in the way, problems that are avoided rather than solved.

Were the question "What technical work have you done today on your instrument?" put to a string player, a pianist, a clarinetist, or to any other instrumental musician, the questioner might well receive detailed information as to what specific exercises, patterns, and technical systems are in daily use. Yet some singers honestly believe that, following a brief warm-up, singing through a few repertory items is all the daily "practice" necessary. In some cases, such "practice" takes place only several times a week, not daily.

On the contrary, what is needed is a daily routine that will lead to the acquisition of technical skills required by the instrument in any kind of appropriate literature. Tito Gobbi once mentioned that in the early 1950s he felt his vocalism had become somewhat problematic; he realized that he had stopped working "technically," having assumed that performance alone would keep him in proper vocal shape. Only by returning to technical work did he feel he regained his former security.

A sad fact is that many young singers today, very few of whom are congenitally lazy, believe that vocal talent itself is sufficient for the demands of performance. How very different that viewpoint is from those found in autobiographical accounts of legendary singers of the past who conscientiously devoted portions of each day solely to technical work. This new attitude comes, in part, from the easy success of some performers in the popular arts, and in part from the less-than-honest current autobiographical musings of some few established singers who wish to have it believed that they arrived as full-blown artists without effort or outside assistance.

Any young singer who wants to become a professional should identify those aspects of technique that are not consistently secure. Then such simple procedures as getting up at a decent hour every day to begin a regimen of vocalization with specific technical goals in mind should be adopted. (It must not be just a quick "warm-up" so that you won't kill yourself on the big arias.) Any day devoid of technical work, aside from those days when illness strikes or during some predetermined annual vacation period, will diminish the chances of ultimate success. Technical problems are not solved by singing for Maestro X or Madame Y at the next "master class" held in your area, although those "master" teachers may give some limited technical as well as interpretative advice. Technique does not result from entering yet one more contest for "experience."

Singing is a serious discipline requiring as much technical knowledge as does the playing of any other instrument, if not more. Language skills, musicianship, imagination, and artistry are all essential to the singer but none of them will be of much value if the technical problems of the singing instrument are not resolved. If such inner discipline is too demanding, a professional singing career may not be the best vocational goal.

Have you worked technically today?

60

The Lonely Soccer Player

He might have been fourteen years old, or perhaps he was a bit tall for his age. He was alone on the playground, hurrying along in his peer-designated running suit and appropriate shoes, carrying his soccer ball as though it were a sacred object. He would throw the ball high into the air, run under it and deliver a smashing upward blow with his head. Then he would dash toward it as it fell and give it a tremendous kick with his foot. After each success he would dramatically throw himself to the ground, then stand up and make a long, low bow to an imaginary audience.

At age fourteen, Pierre had devised a systematic technique for acquiring a skill highly prized in his cultural environment. He wanted to make the team. He was practicing—making permanent—a particular group of maneuvers. He understood that an athletic skill is something that has to be acquired, and he was prepared to take the time and effort to learn it. He also wanted to be appreciated.

There are singers who dream of bowing in acknowledgment before an audience that appreciates skillful vocalism. In many cases, however, they are unwilling to undertake the drilling tasks that would ensure consistency in performance such as the lonely adolescent soccer player exhibits. It is very easy to become bored by the unimaginative activity involved in developing the freedom required of the torso muscles for good breath management, and by the woodshedding work on agility, vowel definition, resonance balancing, smooth registration, sustaining ability, dynamic control, and range extension. Performance skills can be built only if the singer, like the young soccer player, is willing to monitor performance. It is not enough to "have something to say" if the channels for saying it have not been established. Artistic insight and intuition cannot be realized if the technical tools for their expression are lacking.

The aspiring singer, like the youthful soccer player, must be willing to practice certain coordinations that will then become reflex actions. No singer can hope to exhibit artistry until the basic rules of the craft have been mastered. That craft is acquired only as part of a total discipline.

Such a discipline is not easy, although it is founded upon the ease that emerges from all efficient function. As in all of art, that which is most beautiful in the singing voice results from the skillful treatment of the

189

physical properties characteristic of the specific art form, not from some rare individualistic, imaginative spark. The painter must know how to mix colors and differentiate brush strokes, and must understand the laws of perspective before he or she can artistically vary them to arrive at his or her own individualism. All of art, including the art of singing, begins with disciplined behavior.

Perhaps the most difficult person to teach is that singer who is convinced that innate artistry and expressive power are unique personal possessions, and that emotion and feeling equal communication. The world is full of unrecognized sensitive singers who must sing only for limited audiences. The truth of the matter is that unless the voice is technically free as an instrument, there is little chance for it to be used artistically.

Anyone who works to acquire a performance skill has in mind the satisfaction of exhibiting that skill before an admiring public. The fourteen-year-old soccer player bows to an imaginary audience after each successful technical maneuver. The singer in the practice room should similarly practice before an invisible audience, and perhaps even indulge in a few secret dramatic bows. The singer who assumes that art exists independently of discipline, who wants to stand up and emote without routine technical habits, lacks the insight of the adolescent soccer player, who knows that his future place on the team depends on his ability to deliver specific techniques required by the game he is playing.

61

How to Really Bomb a Master Class

Part I: Instructions for the Student

1. Although the advance materials mention that all music to be performed in the public master class is to be memorized, come onto the stage carrying a copy of the music you are to sing, something you've looked at only recently.

2. Announce to the master teacher that you have chosen to sing an item full of technical problems that you would like to have solved during the twenty minutes allotted to you.

3. Don't warm up in advance.

4. Mention that you are in the midst of changing techniques, and that you want to demonstrate the two ways you can sing, to find out which one is right.

5. When the master teacher points out things in need of improvement, insist that you never make those mistakes except when you are nervous.

6. Choose an eight-minute aria that will take up one-third of your time. Look indignant if you are interrupted.

7. If, in the interest of time, you are requested to cut the *da capo,* plead to be allowed to sing it because you have embellished it.

8. Choose something in a language you have difficulty pronouncing.

9. Begin by using up the time to explain to the master teacher and the audience the character and the dramatic situation. Make it funny.

10. Announce that (a) you are just getting a cold, or (b) you are just getting over one.

11. The first time you are corrected, cry.

12. If male, wear red suspenders and no jacket; if female, wear unaccustomed high heels and a tight-waisted dress that looks great but is uncomfortable for singing, or

13. Regardless of what your teacher may have advised, wear sneakers, jeans, and a sloppy sweater.

14. Have friends whistle and cheer when you finish.

15. Although a professional accompanist has been provided, use your mother.

16. Enact the aria.

17. Before you begin to sing, mention all of the shows you have been in and the contests you have won.

18. Refuse to do any of the vocalizing patterns suggested.

19. Always justify what you do: "I did that because ———." Disagree with the master teacher on matters of technique and on interpretative suggestions.

20. Be hesitant to admit that any of the technical suggestions are helpful. Refuse to recognize any differences in sound or sensation.

21. Request to go later than scheduled, because you can't sing before a certain hour of the day.

22. Choose a Broadway tune when you know the master teacher is a *Lieder* specialist. Or, to avoid any silly diction corrections, sing something in Russian, Swedish, or Czech that you have learned phonetically, although neither the master teacher nor you knows the language.

23. Publicly explain that you have always had very bad teachers, so that your faults are not your own responsibility.

24. Near the close of your twenty-minute session (perhaps in the eigh-

teenth minute), be sure to ask a complicated technical question that would take an additional twenty minutes to answer.

Part II: Suggestions for the Master Teacher

1. Begin by being anecdotal, recalling your own impressive performance career. Recount having been embraced on stage by Bernstein, and what Ormandy said about your artistry; mention how many times you have sung each of your major roles, and in which houses.
2. Follow this with an account of how you selflessly gave up a major career to devote yourself to teaching.
3. Sit at a desk or table, just out of range of the singer's vision, and while smiling and swaying to the music, conduct with your pencil.
4. Sit in a chair next to the piano and conduct the accompanist. Then spend a large part of the twenty minutes in instructing the pianist as to how the piece should be played.
5. When working in a large hall, insist that your speaking voice has wonderful projection, and refuse to use a microphone.
6. Interrupt the singer after the first eight bars.
7. Convey your suggestions privately to the singer so that the audience members (who have paid a registration fee) cannot hear the comments.
8. Begin immediately to point out what is wrong and avoid mentioning anything positive about either the voice or the performance.
9. Claim to teach *bel canto*.
10. Make several quite minor suggestions and ask the singer to sing the entire piece over again. (This will fill much of the time if you are at a loss as to what to do.)
11. With a sorrowful shake of the head, say that the technique is totally wrong and that a teacher change is necessary.
12. With another shake of the head, mention that the assigned repertoire is totally wrong.
13. Make constant running comments to the student as he or she is singing.
14. Sing along with the student, especially if you yourself have sung the aria.
15. Avoid all technical suggestions for fear of offending the people who invited you.

16. Tell the singer he or she has no talent and should not continue studying.
17. Insist on accepting only *your* tempo, interpretation, embellishments, and cadential figures.
18. Spend a lot of additional time with the singer you most enjoy; cut short the sessions with the others, particularly if they are not especially gifted.
19. Keep looking at your watch or the clock on the wall.
20. As the singer performs, stare intently at a copy of the music with your head buried in it, then lecture the singer on how best to communicate the text to the audience.
21. Make the same suggestion to everyone, regardless of the individual problem.
22. Give a mini-lecture of eight to ten minutes about the composer's intent.
23. Describe the circumstances under which the poem was created; include details of the poet's life, especially if they are a bit bizarre.
24. Above all, be artistically grand and speak from Mount Olympus.

62

Developing Independence in the Student

Because of the highly personal nature of the art of singing, the rapport between the teacher and the singing student is one that exceeds that of most teacher-student relationships. This condition can produce gratifying personal and professional rewards, but it also may tend to encourage an undesirable dependency of the student singer on the voice teacher. Currently, as throughout the history of the solo singing voice, mature singers are to be found who remain dependent on their teachers for all of their performance needs. In many cases, such dependency is fostered by the teacher/guru, whose hold over the successful singer is fruitful both financially and psychologically.

Ethical problems aside, building such dependency represents incomplete pedagogy. It is not the teacher's privilege to treat the talented singer as a piece of marble to be sculpted and displayed as the product of his or her own creation. The test of a successful pedagogy should be the ability to provide the learning tools with which the singer constructs his or her own art.

Professional singers are imaginative people; otherwise they would not have entered a field that requires communication of musical and dramatic ideas. Still, they universally need to be given the technical principles that permit them to find freedom for using their instruments in a creative way. For this assistance, every singer needs a teacher. But the singer who remains a creature of his or her teacher is seriously disadvantaged.

It is not the case that making a student dependent on oneself is always intentional. Some systems of voice teaching are veiled in mystery. The teacher seems to have secret solutions, magically dispensed, while the principles upon which the solutions are based remain a private domain. Teacher offers the student a continuing pedagogical womb, and the umbilical cord is never severed.

At times well-meaning teachers seem themselves to believe that they are the sources of unique powers that are summoned up on the spur of the moment for each technical need. They imaginatively *invent* in response to problems. Such solutions are often highly compensatory in nature. By frantically sorting through a repertory of quick nostrums, vocal cracks are momentarily plastered over, technical holes are partially plugged, and interpretative Band-Aids are applied. No factual diagnosis has been made, and no prescriptions for dealing with the vocal faults have been offered. The singer may be provided a momentary psychological lift, but continues to limp onward without having had basic problems solved.

One is reminded of the ancient tale that appears in several folk literatures of the well-intentioned noble who provides a hungry beggar with an elegantly prepared fish, while a wise old commoner gives the hungry man a set of fishing tools and instructions for catching and preparing fish.

The occasional phenomenon of the established professional singer who must travel with the voice teacher is a testimony to the wrong kind of instruction and to the wrong kind of personal relationship. There are other established singers who must be "warmed up" by the teacher before each public performance. Such practices attest to the failure of the teacher's vocal pedagogy, not to its success. Good voice teaching should *free* the singer from dependence on the teacher. The well-prepared, secure singer will from time to time happily check back with the person from whom he has received a set of performance tools.

Proper boundaries should be established early. Young people are malleable and often in search of heroes and heroines. No instruction in the entire field of music offers greater possibility for the invasion of another human psyche than does the teaching of singing. This relationship between singer and teacher can ethically be an intimate one, but distinct professional boundaries should be established early. If the voice teacher takes on the duties of mother, father, lover, confessor, guru, or spiritual director, the essential professional boundaries have been violated. Mutual affection and respect are essential between teacher and student, but calculated power over another person (the desire for power is perhaps the last of the vices to be laid to rest) should play no role in vocal pedagogy.

An example of the abuse of power is that of the teacher of singing who erects a high tower of ego from which small streams of nourishment are funneled downward. (There is even the case of the prominent voice teacher who assures his students that he is "the Rolls-Royce" of voice teachers, perhaps an American adaptation of the Mount Olympus ideal!) Fortunately, most persons who choose to help others in finding the joys of performance do so out of a conviction of service. We should nevertheless consciously resist being placed, or placing ourselves, in positions in which students become dependent upon us for their personal and professional lives. The good teacher develops the independent singing artist.

63

Is There a Cure for Performance Anxiety?

Much has been written recently about performance anxiety—what used to be less elegantly termed "stage fright." Workshop sessions and journal articles discuss techniques for reducing fear of public performance, and medical science has been exploring substances that block feelings of stage disquietude, although opinion remains divided on the wisdom of their use.

Certainly there is cause for apprehension about an upcoming public performance if one is ill. No singer should be faulted for developing a case of nerves when hoarseness, congestion, or upset stomach strikes. Personal crises can also take a serious toll on psychological balance. No other musical performer is so at the mercy of physical and mental condition as the singer.

The technology of our age permits a number of shortcut strategies for a variety of activities and skills. The pocket calculator allows me to dispense with my lifelong struggle with the multiplication tables; if I wish, I may do my writing seated at a machine that will correct my faulty spelling; I am not required to shift gears as I absentmindedly drive along; I can have a complete dinner ready in five minutes, despite my limited culinary talents; advocates of the auditory approach to language study tell me that I no longer need to memorize tedious grammar rules; and, with the aid of a machine, exercising my body need take only a brief period each day. Modern invention, alas, has found no such shortcut for the acquisition of a dependable vocal technique. The requirements of time, hard work, and discipline are the same today as they were in past centuries.

A singer who has never managed to successfully sing a recital in the studio or a role during stage rehearsals would be foolish to trust to deus ex machina assistance during public performance of the same material. No one can expect reliable coordination in performance if it has rarely occurred in the practice room or the voice studio. To assume that because it happened once or twice out of a number of practice tries it will be there in public is to invite grave performance anxieties. If satisfactory results have appeared only intermittently, or without the singer's knowing exactly how they came about, it is illogical to hope for ease of mind when facing an audience. If, on the other hand, the singer is consistently able to perform well in rehearsals, there is no logic to performance anxiety. A singer in good vocal and mental health may look forward to performance with pleasure, because the mind and body have been routined to produce a predictable outcome.

Last-minute attention to remaining technical problems in the literature to be performed, or late memorization of complex and difficult texts, especially in languages only marginally known to the singer, often contribute to "nervousness" that spills over into other aspects of the performance.

It is easy for performers to assume that technical problems that existed when the literature was initially chosen will disappear during the forthcoming six months of practice, only to realize a week before the scheduled recital that one was too optimistic. It is wiser to cut from the program any item that still presents an occasional technical hurdle than to worry about it so much that insecurity infects the group or the entire recital. However, procrastination in recital preparation often excludes the option of substituting some other *Lied* or *mélodie* for the scary one.

Inevitably, there are passages in any stage role that lie less well for the singer than does the rest of the role. If the problems they present are not solved in acceptable fashion long prior to performance time, the singer should try to cut the passage, to make alternate decisions regarding phrasing, to make text or translation changes—or even to reconsider his or her appropriateness to the role.

One of the most maddening experiences for a singer is to be coerced by a conductor or coach (or voice teacher) into taking that exceedingly long and difficult phrase in one breath, the way Bjoerling or Milanov did it, even though timbre, intonation, and stamina suffer greatly, when respectable vocal sounds would be possible if a little compromising about such standards were to take place. The same goes for achieving the exact dynamic level requested by the composer; if trying to manage the *pianissimo* (or the *fortissimo*) results in unstable or ugly sound, the composer's intent has not been realized. If the singer has to sing the role, he or she should not be placed in a state of anxiety over a nuance of some particular passage. This is especially pertinent in academic opera productions. If young singers are required to take on professional tasks, those who cast them should be prepared to make compromises.

Both technical and artistic security can be developed through performance experience. Modest public appearances should be part of preprofessional experience. Young singers should have opportunities to try out performance technique on a regular basis, for example, in studio class, departmental recitals, or opera scenes programs.

Often overlooked is the fact that experiencing performance anxiety harks back to a lack of both technical security and performance routining. Technique, after all, is the ability to consistently repeat the same patterns of coordination, whether they occur in playing tennis or in singing. To rely chiefly on the emotional high of the performance moment for success is usually to court disaster.

Even in the presence of technical security, two common psychological factors may still contribute to "stage nerves." The first of these lies in miscalculating the expectation level of one's performance. Not infrequently, a young singer approaching professional capabilities will score success in a particular stage work, competition, or recital, exceeding everyone's expectations, including his or her own. The singer then tends to imagine that the surrounding world has now placed him or her on an artistic pedestal that in reality does not exist. It is easy for a performer to assume that an audience has a higher opinion of one's abilities than is actually the case. Unnecessary pressure can be avoided by objectively assessing expected levels of performance accomplishment. It is the teacher's task to help keep that in mind.

An illustration may be in order. A young tenor, with a few recent, fine early-professional successes, reports to his teacher that singing in public is getting more difficult. "Why am I getting nervous?" he asks. "Because," says his teacher (to the singer's great surprise), "you have become conceited." "But," protests the tenor, "exactly the opposite is true!" He insists his anxiety stems from modesty, out of fear that he is not good enough. "Not at all," says his teacher. "You are afraid they are not going to think as highly of you as you want them to think, or as you regard yourself. That is a form of conceit."

His teacher explains that this singer deserves to have a very good self-image because he possesses excellent vocal material, shows increasing technical proficiency, and, as an emerging young artist, is growing in his ability to communicate as he performs. That is exactly the performance level currently expected of him. To regard that level as finished artistry is to indulge in conceit and to place oneself under enormous performance pressure. Teacher indicates several levels of a hypothetical pedestal, and continues: "You have placed yourself at this height, which is a position appropriate to the accomplished professional, when in actuality you are at this very fine, more median level. Always set current performance expectations realistically, while working toward future goals, and you will be a much happier performer."

In part, unrealistic expectations on the part of the advanced student result from high-level instruction itself, in which student and teacher (or demanding coach) maintain high goals and search for excellence. However, an experienced performer soon learns that there is no such thing as performance perfection—that it is not possible always to deliver 100 percent. In fact, an established artist often exhibits greater freedom in performance after the first "mistake" of the evening has occurred. Perfection is not a realistic performance goal. Reliable performance is.

A second, perhaps more subtle and even more debilitating psychological drain comes to the performer who uses his or her critical powers as ammunition against other singers. Singing is a highly competitive field. Comparisons are constantly made among singers about other singers; relative abilities are weighed and judgments delivered. Good singers listen critically to each other, because that is one of the ways they learn. However, critical listening is not the same as destructive knifing. This issue is at the heart of successful performance psychology.

The more generous a performer can be when listening to fine performances, the greater will be the ease reflected in his or her own performance. This is because one associates one's own responses as an audience member with those of every audience at large. If a singer writhes inwardly at beautiful sound from a singer in his or her *Fach*, or gleefully notes what has not gone well for a colleague on stage, that same singer is likely to perceive the audience as enemy when he or she is the performer. It behooves performers to develop an attitude of generous (though critical) listening, because, in the performance world, as in any other, bread cast upon the waters has a way of returning to one.

Performance is an act of sharing, not one of self-aggrandizement. The compelling recitalist acts as a mediator between the vocal literature being performed and the listening audience, like the person who shakes the beautiful paperweight so that others may look in at the miniature scene of falling snow. The singer presents a world that connects performer and audience, and thereby avoids the uncomfortable feeling of being an isolated object to which the audience directs its attention. Singer and audience share experiences, and self is transcended. This performance quality is largely what separates the true artist from the mere showman.

Establishing a generous attitude toward the performance art itself, whether that of others or one's own, comes about through conscious development. It is as much a part of the discipline of performance as is technical and musical preparation, and should be developed early in the voice studio itself. Even when the craft of singing is in hand, one should make certain that one's own performance expectations coincide with one's current performance ability. When performance becomes an act of communication, rather than of personal display or of public confrontation, performance anxiety greatly diminishes.

The best cure for performance anxiety, then, is to direct attention away from oneself through the acquisition of a highly reliable vocal technique, excellent musical and textual preparation, systematic rehearsal procedures, frequent performance outlets, a realistic attitude toward one's own abilities, and generosity of heart toward one's colleagues and one's audience.

64

Please Tell Me My *Fach*

Preprofessional singers, such as those enrolled in performance degree programs or preparing for careers through private study, often want to know to what specific vocal category they belong. They have heard about the German-theater *Fach* system, and they have a sense of urgency in determining where their own voices may fit into it.

The word *Fach* refers to any specialized work or skill. A *Facharzt* is a medical doctor with specialization that goes beyond the training of the primary care physician. *Fachausbildung* is professional training in any specific area. In the German-language theater, *Fach* refers to a specialized category of opera role, such as dramatic soprano, soubrette, *Heldentenor*, lyric tenor, Verdi baritone, bass-baritone, and so on, within one of the chief vocal categories. A light lyric soprano is not expected to sing roles in the dramatic or *Zwischenfach* categories, and a lyric baritone is not required to sing Verdian roles. In the professional world, *Fach* designation is a device for the contractual protection of the singer so that he or she will not be forced to sing roles that require unhealthy modes of phonation to accomplish.

It is quite another matter to burden the college age student with *Fach* exactitude. Maturation of the singing voice follows a developmental continuum. It is rarely possible for a teacher of singing or a vocal coach precisely to pinpoint a singer's *Fach* during the early years of vocal training. Emphasis on *Fach* determination can become a pedagogical fixation serving little purpose in preprofessional training. Most students of singing are not ready for the subclassification of vocal categories that make up the *Fach* system, because most are not at a point in their development that permits experts to arrive at such decisions.

Besides, much of the vocal literature does not require *Fach* categorization. The preponderance of the literature of the *Lied*, the *mélodie*, and the art song lies in appropriate range and *tessitura* for voices of all *Fächer*. There are exceptions, of course; one does not assign *Prometheus* (all major settings of the poem are included here) to a young lyric baritone, nor does one give *Die Allmacht*, *Gretchen am Spinnrade*, or *Ariettes Oubliées* to the young soubrette.

With regard to operatic literature, most young singers should not be plowing through arias. Raising *Fach* to a central instructional position during the undergraduate years amounts to unnecessary pedagogical obfuscation. Accurate vocal categorization within the overall, major divisions will emerge as both technical security and age move forward. Too often, *Fach* becomes a voice-teacher fetish—part of the "I know what you don't know" syndrome of voice teaching—and is mysteriously waved before the young singer as though it were a rare gem of professional information. Making the early determination of *Fach* a central part of pedagogy may serve to create an aura of authority around the teacher but contributes little to the welfare of the student singer.

With considerable frequency, student singers who participate in so-called master classes buttonhole the visiting teacher to ask, "What is my *Fach*, and what roles should I be working on?" when student's mastery of basic vocal technique is not yet sufficiently secure to make such a judgment possible. A more disturbing situation is to hear, "My teacher says I should be able to sing this aria because it is in my *Fach*." Although it is plausible to determine relatively early the general category to which a talented singer belongs, it is approaching the foolhardy to try to determine subcategories before the vocal instrument itself has become free to function in the technical areas essential to all good singing, and until the singer has arrived at some level of maturity.

Even relatively general categorization may be difficult in the case of the young male whose *passaggi* events appear to lie slightly above those of the lyric baritone and slightly below the traditional *passaggi* of the lyric tenor. A similar dilemma may exist for the young female singer with a sizable vocal instrument. Because she has more depth of quality than most of her soprano peers, she is told by some that she is a mezzo-soprano, while other authorities insist she is a soprano. Her problem is that the young soprano with an ample instrument often has not yet established sufficient ease in the upper range to manage the higher lying soprano literature. She is currently a "short" soprano who may early be falsely classified as a mezzo. In these cases, both female and male singers must wait for the development of sufficient technical skill, which will reveal the proper *Fach*.

The complexities of the professional *Fach* system go far beyond simple classifications of soprano, mezzo, contralto, tenor, baritone, or bass. Utilization of the *Fach* system requires consideration of the orchestral writing that underlies operatic roles, of the *sostenuto* and *tessitura* demands, and of the extent of velocity skill expected; it must also take into account the morphology of the individual performer. Seldom is the undergraduate or young graduate student at a point where clear demarcation of *Fächer* is called for. The *Fach* system exists, it should be recalled, largely for determining assignments in the opera house.

Fortunately, the North American singer is generally in far less danger of excessive *Fach* speculation from his or her teacher than are some European-trained students, for a quite specific reason. American professional singers have long been accustomed to performing a broad range of vocal literatures, including *Lieder, mélodie,* art song, oratorio, musical comedy, and opera—a vast amount of material that crosses many of the barriers that separate literature designations in the German-theater *Fach* system. The American vocal pedagogue who has a serious addiction to early *Fach* designations, thus relying on a European system, suffers from a pedagogical disease against which the student should be on guard.

65

The Aging Singer

The title of this brief discussion is not "The Aging *Voice*" but the "The Aging *Singer*." There is a reason for that distinction. Our interest is not in examining the effects of the ravages of time, the quality of laryngeal tissue among the aged, or the extent of ossification in the larynx. It is how the aging singer can beat the odds by keeping at it.

What is written about the normal physical change that occurs in the body as it ages is enough to make any singer over thirty consider a career change. Reading geriatric studies that detail the decline of "the aging voice" can take the wind out of anybody's sails. None of us doubts that the body eventually runs down, but some second thoughts about the professional voice user who is growing older are worth considering.

The professional singer is not the normal voice user. Like all athletic prowess, the vocal skills of the professional singer have been highly developed, honed, and maintained. The average seventy-year-old woman can't perform complex, agile dance movements, but Martha Graham could because she had learned how to dance and she had never stopped dancing. The typical male in his sixties may show considerable deterioration in his medical vocal profile, audible in the loss of speaking-voice vitality. Yet Beniamino Gigli, performing in large concert halls well into his sixties, was able to sing recital programs consisting of seventeen arias, concluding with the *Aïda* final duet with daughter Renata, and then come back on stage to sing six aria encores, all in beautiful voice. Why? Because he knew how to sing and he had never stopped singing.

Based on average predictable trends in behavior patterns for the aging voice, there is a certain expectation of diminution of vocal condition from at least the fiftieth year onward. This expectation spills over onto the most advanced of all professional voice users, the singer. It produces a psychological weight that bears down hard on aging singers. How easy it is for us to think, "Well, I'm now at that age where the voice begins to show the wear and tear of all those years," when it is exactly the well-trained professional who has *avoided* the wear and tear that causes the aging pattern in the "normal" voice. Because muscle tonus is kept at a level far beyond what average patterns indicate, average conditions do not prevail in the larynx that has kept going.

The problem is largely one of courage and energy. It takes a certain aplomb to keep on singing when one hears, "You mean you are still at it?" or "Aren't you at retirement age?" One gets the impression that there is something unseemly about continuing to sing beyond a certain age, a kind of lawless flouting of the geriatric rules. This is why a number of people stop singing before they should. Society expects it of them.

Please do not misunderstand. Professional singers should not place themselves in public performance circumstances when they can no longer cut the performance literature. This writer has on occasion lamented the lack of good judgment on the part of some well-known artists who insist on holding management to their long-term contracts after the voice has ceased to function well. Knowing when to quit *public* performance is a sign of good judgment. There is, however, such a thing as a gradual reduction of literature demands. Someone who has had a great career singing highly exposed literature should not continue to do so if the exposure is painful to those who listen. More modest literature also exists. Nor will a singer who loves the vocal art stop practicing just because public performance has ceased.

Keeping the vocal instrument alive and vital is particularly important to the teacher of singing, who often does his or her best teaching in the final teaching decade. The ability to use one's own instrument as a tool in teaching is invaluable. It is not necessary to be able to sing all the roles one once could, or sing all one's former song cycles without taking a pause. But it is still quite necessary to demonstrate good vocal sounds in the studio. This can only be done if the teacher of singing allows no day of normal health to go by without exercising the vocal instrument. (Vacations are allowed!) It is much harder for an older voice to recover good tonus after long periods of silence than it is for a younger instrument. Therefore, it's best to keep going. The worst thing is to stop and then to make occasional tries at former levels of vocalism.

The aging singer often has a problem that is more psychological than physiological. There may not be the same sheen on the voice; there may be the loss of a few notes at the top of the range or at the very bottom; but if the voice is kept functioning, its rate of physical deterioration will be retarded. It must be kept in good shape by doing daily series of systematic vocalises, including onsets, agility patterns, vowel-defining exercises, sostenuto, resonance balancing, and range extension vocalises (although the range may perhaps now be more limited than formerly). Don't quit; keep going, although not necessarily publicly. Do not allow the vocal deterioration of the average speaker or amateur singer to spill over onto your professionally trained instrument. Numerous female and male singers who have some time ago celebrated their sixtieth birthdays still maintain their vocal instruments in good condition. They do so by following the example of Martha Graham: they don't stop dancing (or, in this case, singing).

66

The Wisdom of the Body in Singing

The perfect singer would not need to bother with the details of vocal technique. Such an amazing creature would already possess the necessary physical coordination. In actual practice, it is difficult to recall ever having met such a person. At least, such remarkable phenomena do not present themselves at the studio door. Excellent vocal talent never arrives fully formed, like Minerva from the head of Jupiter. Even the highly talented singer of university age who shows wonderful professional potential generally is much in need of the four or five years of projected study. It is only after this period of work has taken place that polishing and perfecting can become major concerns. Achieving vocal perfection is not a realizable goal in early study years; learning proper coordination that will allow freedom *is*. But for some singers this becomes a lifetime search.

Much of what goes on in the voice studio might strike the casual visitor as unimaginative, routine work, far removed from a final artistic product. Artistic singing is a unified act. Only the acquisition of skillful technical detail makes such unification possible. Although it is not possible, at any level, to long separate technique from artistic concerns, reaching the goal of efficiency requires technical work that at times must be separated from final artistic goals. The voice teacher is the person who holds the key to unlocking the door to such freedom. However, it is the singing instrument itself—that person who stands in front of the voice teacher—who finally determines to what uses technical information may be put.

The singing population is a highly diverse one. There are those persons who have what appears to be innate sensitivity to music and poetry, while others seem to experience the act of singing chiefly as a physical activity involving kinesthetic and visceral responses that produce exciting vocal sound. The rare singing talent has some of both in proper proportions, yet most people are stronger in one of these areas than in the other. In addition, the ability to progress vocally requires an understanding of technical goals and of the instruction being offered to reach them. Yet musical sensitivity, native intelligence, and the physical love of singing, even when placed in the hands of a skilled teacher, may not produce a fine singer. Enter the wisdom of the body.

The singing instrument—the body—must be able to respond to the technical information it receives. There is a wonderfully expressive term from the old German lyric theater that describes the ability of a singer to turn technical information into physical function: *Sängerischesgefühl,* the singer's *feel* for the act of singing. Like any athlete, the singer must be able to translate technical ideas into specific physical coordinations. The body itself already possesses the wisdom to accomplish that end, and it will do so if it is not hindered by unnecessary instructional baggage.

This wisdom of the body has been accumulated throughout the personal history of each individual. It begins with crawling, with early speech sounds, with learning to get mashed potatoes into the mouth rather than on the tip of the nose, with the first lurching steps. It will continue to exercise its function during a lifetime of activity if we do not cut it off through psychological and cultural inhibition, or violate it through wrong physical behavior. Such wisdom is part of the shared reservoir of human experience.

Were the child to be taught that in walking one must curl the toes under, or that to speak the tongue must be held in a retroflex posture or the lips fixated, or that the head must be thrown upward and backward as a means of locomotion, the wisdom of the body would be nullified. Yet the singing student is constantly confronted with erroneous techniques that diminish the natural processes of body function in the hope of achieving controls that actually upset natural coordination. Sometimes, in the process of detailing corrective devices, every teacher of singing runs the peril of ignoring the totality of the singing instrument—the wisdom of the body.

The body in which our imaginative and communicative persons are housed lets us know when it is functioning freely, if we will listen to its advice. This does not mean that a passive physical state is appropriate in order to accomplish free singing. Indeed, dynamic muscle balance—proper tonus among muscle groups—is essential to any vital activity. Many problems faced by singers result from attempts to relax parts of the body that should be activated; to remove essential energy under the impression that the least amount of physical involvement, the better. Other problems are induced by excessive energization and by unproductive controls exercised over the systems of breathing and resonation.

It should be the goal of good vocal pedagogy to avoid contributing to either hyperfunction or hypofunction among cooperating muscle groups. The wisdom of the body must be permitted to make repeatable those coordinations that produce freedom in singing. Technique is not a set of confining rules but a liberating force. When the body is free, spiritual and artistic expression can be realized through the singing voice. The wisdom of the body, channeled through techniques that permit freedom, is a reliable guide for the singer.

67

Studio Procedures

Actual teaching sometimes suffers in competition with the myriad things a voice teacher is expected to do. There is the off-campus professional performance schedule that must be kept going, not just for our own satisfaction, but because we want to provide a model of activity for our students, and because the administration expects it of us. There is new music to be learned for the annual faculty recital, preparation for the course that has to be taught, committee duties to worry about, working up an important audition, prodding the agent who always needs to be nudged, and, with it all, giving one hundred percent to a full-time teaching schedule. How can one keep on top of it all? Organized studio procedures can help relieve the overwhelmed feeling.

In order to save time, some teachers hand out sets of generalized vocalises. These exercises are run through by the student in a somewhat routine manner, if at all, because the vocalises are not tailored to the student's current needs. Indeed, asking all students to do the same exercises in the same sequence is not advisable.

Because no one who works with fifteen to twenty performance majors each week can possibly remember all the details of their individualized instruction, a practical solution is to require each student to keep a small bound book that will accommodate a permanent record of the vocalises and repertoire assigned them. Every week, the teacher should add a few new vocalises to each of the categories that compose a systematic approach to voice building. One student may already be capable of agility but lack good vowel definition; another may have fewer problems in tracking vowels but have register difficulties; yet another may be in need of breath management and onset exercises. Passing out to all students a few sheets of the standard studio vocal exercises is not the answer.

One of the advantages of having the student keep a record book, which is brought to each lesson, is that the teacher then knows exactly when and what technical work has taken place during lessons, and which particular exercises were proposed. Doctors keep records of patient diagnoses and what therapy was prescribed; so should voice teachers. Let's call this permanent record the Technique Book—a blank, paginated laboratory book in which the teacher indexes categories of exercises involved in systematic technique; each area is then expanded weekly as study progresses. These books become a permanent part of the singer's professional gear, now and in future years, when they will be referred to for both teaching and performing information.

One section of the individual Technique Book should concern repertoire assignments. If it is not possible to have a relatively large collection of vocal literature permanently at hand in the studio, then a method for cataloguing possible repertoire for each vocal type should be in place. As soon as the teacher knows a voice, the semester's repertoire planning should begin. It ought to comprise a balanced diet of material. The student and teacher then plan well in advance what songs or arias will be worked on in lessons during the coming weeks. It is disconcerting for a student to come for a lesson and be asked, "What are you going to sing today?" Check the Technique Book to see what has been assigned as this week's repertory goal.

Another section of the Technique Book should contain the student's own log of practice and performance experiences. The teacher should know what the student is practicing and for how long. The student should identify which literature is going well, which vocalises are most efficacious and which of them are difficult to execute. Periodically, the log should be jointly examined by teacher and student.

Time moves very quickly in the voice studio; there is much to do. Each lesson following the earliest encounters should be equally divided between technique and the application of technique to the repertoire. Inasmuch as vocal technique does not exist in a vacuum, every lesson must have a performance character about it. If possible, the lesson should be recorded, preferably on video, so that the student may profit many times from a single lesson experience. The student is responsible for providing video- or audiocassette tapes. Only insecure teachers refuse to have lessons recorded.

Because time is precious, and because (whether in the private or the academic studio) the student is paying dearly for lessons, personal reminiscences should be eschewed. Talking away a lesson is very expensive socializing. Perhaps the most annoying experience for a student is to pay a substantial fee for a voice lesson and have the teacher be on the telephone for a third of it. A young Canadian soprano went, at considerable personal expense, to New York to take a series of lessons with a noted teacher whose fee those days was $90 an hour. During one lesson, the phone rang with a call from a conductor who wanted to engage the teacher for the coming season, and who suggested various programs and rehearsal and performance schedules, for a total of twenty minutes. The voice lesson then continued, and at its close the young Canadian handed the teacher $60, rather than $90. The teacher/telephonist was incensed. Any reasonable person is on the side of the student. The best procedure is to receive no phone calls in the studio during teaching hours; have them transferred to a number from which contact with the caller can later be made.

An active performer who teaches is ethically bound to make up missed lessons. Giving students to a studio assistant at the same lesson cost is not conscionable. What about lessons missed by the student? This is a pressing problem for the private teacher who has reserved lesson time that could have been assigned to other students, but is now lost. Studio policy should be for the student to arrange a lesson exchange with another student in the studio (this is easier to accomplish in an academic situation), or to pay the lesson fee. There is no other way the private teacher can be protected.

Another protection must be against the caller or letter-writer who wants to arrange an "audition" or a "career evaluation," which means at least half an hour of your time during which you give a voice lesson as part of your evaluation. (Who is auditioning whom?) Such "auditions" should be at the normal lesson price. A request for evaluations of audiocassette or videotaped performances is similar in nature. It is wise to have an established policy of doing "evaluations" only in live lesson situations.

In the academic community, dress rehearsals for required student performances can add up to an extra week or two of teaching time each semester. Students should be encouraged to arrange hall rehearsals at their regular lesson times, and realize that the comments made during the "dress" (which is often a learning session of great merit) constitute a lesson. This is particularly the case when the teacher must cancel other lessons in order to attend the dress rehearsal.

Every lesson should end on time, even if the student arrives late. It is not fair to make others wait, or to slice off five minutes from each of the remaining lessons during the course of the afternoon, to make up for the time lost because of a tardy person. Students whose lessons are brief because they were late soon realize that punctuality is part of professionalism.

The content of the instruction offered is, of course, what the student is paying for. However, studio organization will save time and effort, and will permit better delivery of the pedagogy. One's own energies and concentration will be more focused. Even first-rate teaching can be effective only if there is a structure through which it is channeled.

68

Truth in Advertising (A Critical Look)

A viable professional singing career is, almost without exception, hard-earned. Any singer who can point to a number of years during which the wolf has been kept away from the door through financial return received exclusively from singing engagements deserves special recognition as a successful "pro." Given the exigencies of the performance world (it was not easier thirty years ago, despite what our younger colleagues may like to assume), singers who have been hired to perform leading roles in professional opera companies, in either North America or Europe, have arrived at a level of professional accomplishment that merits admiration.

That makes it all the more difficult to accept some of the inflated public relations material that otherwise truthful and responsible people circulate under the assumption that "professional" imaging must be enhanced through huckster techniques. In so doing, they diminish the value of actual performance histories of other singers, and they do so at the risk of losing their colleagues' respect. There certainly is no shame in having spent one's performance years singing chiefly minor roles in regional opera companies. Nor is activity with this or that professional chorale or in a symphonic chorus professionally insignificant, but is it not deceptive for a bass to list in his credits that he sang *Boris* (or some other title role) with the New York Philharmonic under Bernstein when he was actually a member of the chorus? Is that being fair to the person who actually sang the role or to the other principal singers? More than one Kate Pinkerton has listed performances of *Madama Butterfly* in her PR materials without an exact role designation having been indicated.

A professional colleague who has made a substantial career in the German opera theater recently made a plaintive comparison of his own publicity materials with those of a "friend" who had spent a similar decade studying and auditioning in Europe. During that period, the "friend" had appeared in a single recital of American music on a regional European radio broadcast, given several privately sponsored recitals, had entered two major European competitions without advancing beyond the second (or third) of four rounds, and had sung in the chorus of a provincial opera house for a single season. The brochures of both singers report ten years of professional engagement in the European theater.

Another frequently encountered PR device is to present oneself as "winner" of the you-name-it competition when in receipt of the third prize or "honorable mention" award, although someone else actually won. "Top American winner" in international contests where no such designation exists shows considerable PR ingenuity. So does "highest rated mezzo." What is wrong with mentioning a second prize award, a bronze or silver medal? Call yourself a semifinalist, and keep your integrity.

In academic circles a number of institutions are surprised to learn that a member of the Voice Department has been announced to the world as "Artist-in-Residence." Less pernicious but no less amusing is the person who is *currently* teaching at his or her place of employment. The reader is to assume, perhaps, that said institution is a temporary way station en route to more interesting career engagements. Academic biographies that elevate the presenter of a one-time, private master class in a major European city to international pedagogue status should also be corrected.

To continue this admittedly hard view of the way some of us present our professional profiles to the world, a look should be given to the soprano who performed a leading role in *Così fan tutte* in the student production at a New York music school (or one in Boston, Philadelphia, Cincinnati, Chicago, Oberlin, Ann Arbor, Bloomington, Rochester, Austin, Tallahassee, or Baltimore) and who later informs her readers that she has "frequently appeared in opera" but fails to mention that those performances were at student, not professional, level.

How many times have students told us that their teachers have sung at the Metropolitan or La Scala because they saw posters of those opera houses on the studio walls of their teachers? A closer examination should also be made of statements that indirectly suggest the singer has had a career at the Metropolitan Opera House. How many times have we seen the two or three annual *Messiah* performances and the yearly faculty recital end up in publicity materials as "frequent oratorio and recital appearances"? Indeed, sometimes they are reported as having been "coast to coast" or "throughout America."

Perhaps the prize for ultimate fuzziness in advertising should go to the American soprano who, having participated in a small privately organized opera workshop (enrollment of six singers) near Salzburg, now lists *Salzburg Opera* among her professional credits. Is there some hope that the hurriedly scanning eye will take in "Salzburg" and "Opera" and assume the singer has sung at the internationally prestigious Salzburg Festival? A runner-up for the PR aplomb prize should be awarded to the mezzo who, on the basis of a college choir tour a number of years ago, now lists "concert performances throughout Europe and America."

Some singers who scrupulously follow ethical behavior in all other areas of life appear to lose that perspective when it comes to their "billing." They would not think of stealing from the purse of a colleague, but they steal from them something far more valuable: earned performance credentials. This ethical blindness may well be because of the exaggerated claims made by professional managements for some of today's well-known and not-so-well-known singers. (How many "one of the outstanding artists of the day" can there be in one year?)

Administrators and others who examine professional credentials ought to look carefully at documents submitted by applicants for teaching positions. Broad claims to extensive careers need to be investigated. So should the listing of prominent teachers, many of whom heard the applicant but one time in a master class years ago. To present oneself as having had career experiences and professional training not actually encountered is a form of professional robbery. As responsible members of the teaching/performing profession, we should examine the PR materials that go out under our names and make certain that they correspond to reality. We ought not to blame the publicity agency or the college information service for putting out misinformation. We should correct it. Members of professional organizations should lead the way in urging the avoidance of extravagant performance claims, and in establishing truth in advertising in a profession that is badly in need of it.

69

The Practicality of Creativity

We live in a society in which the value of work is measured by its practicality. The artist's role in today's world is not what it was in previous centuries. Recall that for nearly one hundred years the chief labor at Salisbury was the building of a cathedral. Remember how the *botteghe* of Florence were the center of a great city's commercial life.

We Americans compete for better housing, food, and clothing, as well as material benefits that go beyond the necessities of life. By so doing, we contribute to an order that constantly monitors how much or how little one possesses of available worldly goods. From infancy, appetites are whetted by hucksters who seek to pressure us into possessing as many things as we can afford to accumulate. Most of the hours of our existence are spent in acquiring the means to accumulate more things.

There is an alternate viewpoint to consider. Wordsworth expressed it this way: "Getting and spending, we lay waste our powers." These "powers" are the resources hidden within each of us that transcend the world of getting and spending. These springs of creativity, present in every individual, regardless of native intelligence, talent, social status, or age, permit us to go beyond the narrow physical world, to enter the artistic/spiritual core of human existence.

The urge to be creative is so central to some persons that all other things become secondary. We become poets, novelists, painters, dancers, actors, and musicians. Our imaginative powers have responded to the creative environment provided us by home and school.

The home has increasingly lost the central influence it once exerted on a child's cultural and social life. With the disintegration of home life, the school has become chiefly responsible for the formation of the individual, including the creative spirit. But in today's schools, artistic pursuits tend to be considered impractical frills. Music training is on the decline in both home and school. There is a danger that it will continue to lose ground, especially when money is in short supply. How can young people nurture their spiritual and artistic natures if they are early deprived of an environment that could alert them to Wordsworth's "powers"? If children, after school hours, are fed a daily diet of televised entertainment devoid of artistic nourishment, and if the school offers them none, how is the reservoir of national artistic and spiritual heritage to be preserved or replenished? If there is to be little or no music and art in her homes and schools, how can America consider herself a spiritual and artistic world leader?

This is an age in which an immense volume of information can be stored and retrieved. How much of it is devoted to the enrichment of the human spirit? Young people today are buffeted about by a popular culture that they themselves did not create. Much of what passes for entertainment aimed at the young has no link with artistic and literary heritages that convey civilizing elements to the individual. Schools at all levels should not passively acquiesce in the current cultural truncation by succumbing to the performance fads of the moment. For professional musicians, there will be no future audiences if no opportunity exists to build musical interests among children and young people.

The community at large can no longer, as in preindustrial centuries, expend its energies on the erection of a cathedral or temple, on the musical and graphic pageantry celebrating the liturgical year, or on ornate decoration of a civic building. Current society is faced with determining how to provide health and prosperity for as many as possible. We are all cogs in this relentless productive machine.

The amount of information essential to the pursuit of most professions can now be scarcely crowded into the few preparatory years available or affordable. How does one justify the arts as being essential to this societal pattern? There is no doubt that academic test scores offer some measure of a student's ability to assume responsibility in the adult world, but if the wells of creativity remain untapped, the individual cannot live a full and rewarding life. The capacity to cope, in any work or profession, is partly dependent on a recognition that the good life goes beyond meat and potatoes.

There is an urgent need for teaching the science of creativity. Daily encounters between players in all walks of life require insightful, creative interaction. The failure of personal and public relationships results largely from a lack of creative response to life. A society composed of persons whose ability to respond to creative stimuli has been reduced is a society in serious decline.

Nor can the creative impulse develop solely through personal experience. It requires immersion in the historical sweep of creativity. Without some awareness of how the poet, the novelist, the dramatist, the painter, and the musician have shaped thought and perception, of what real value are speed-reading and computerized learning techniques? Do not the culturally blind and deaf form a major percentage of America's handicapped? Does not society in general also suffer from their loss?

It is shortsighted to assume that music and art programs in schools and colleges are expendable whenever budgets need to be trimmed. American education is now reaping what was sown in recent decades when it began to replace the liberally educated person with the technically proficient person. Many high school and college graduates leave school without having learned to modify creatively the mundane duties that constitute much of life. Feeding, clothing, and housing the body do not satisfy all human needs. Men and women cannot live by bread alone.

The performing arts are not simply frosting on the educational cake. They are, in actuality, the very substance of education. *What* one knows is far less important than *how* one knows to put that information to creative use. Practical creativity can best be fostered by disciplines that may, at first blush, appear impractical in a world in which practicality demands the dominant role. The discipline of music is remarkable in its ability to release "powers" that lie dormant. Music-making deserves high priority as a means to awakening the complete person.

For the largest number of people, the human voice is the most accessible of all the expressive media. Those of us who work with singers should actively join the ongoing battle taking place in today's society and give strong support to the preservation of the musical heritage so vital to the welfare of our children and grandchildren.

IV

On the Singing Voice and Vocal Function

70

The Singing Teacher in the Age of Voice Science

What should a responsible voice teacher be teaching in a scientific age? In principle, what a responsible voice teacher does in this scientific age is not appreciably different from what responsible voice teachers have been doing for several centuries, most of which have been replete with teachers who considered themselves enlightened and scientific. That is why it is particularly important, in this final decade of the twentieth century, and will increasingly be the case in the coming century, for singing teachers to be cognizant of developments in related fields, and to understand their potential for enhancing teaching.

There is a prevalent opinion that in past centuries singers had little interest in science. That viewpoint is not supported by historical review. Consider, for example, the following description of respiration in singing:

> [T]he ribs raise outwardly, and . . . the diaphragm . . . descends and compresses the abdomen. . . . For good expiration . . . air must be made to leave with more or less force, with more or less volume, according to the character of the song.

Those words were written not by Bouhuys in the 1970s, nor by Hixon in the 1980s, but by Jean-Baptiste Berard in 1775.

Similarly, current interest in the study of supraglottic effects on laryngeal sound was preceded by generations of voice teachers interested in the acoustic adjustment of the resonator tract, as expressed by Mancini in 1774:

> If the harmony of . . . the mouth and fauces is perfect, then the voice will be clear and harmonious. But if these organs act discordantly, the voice will be defective, and consequently the singing spoiled.

Manuel Garcia, inventor of the laryngeal mirror and a renowned singing teacher, clearly appreciated the importance of scientific knowledge about the voice. His comments of 1847 could have been written today:

> The capacity of the vocal cords to vibrate, the dimensions of the larynx, the thorax, the lungs, the pharyngeal, buccal and nasal cavities, the disposition of these cavities to resonate, constitute the absolute power of the voice of an individual. . . . The singer, in order to dominate the material [physiological] difficulties of his art must have a thorough knowledge of the mechanism of all these pieces to the point of isolating or combining their action according to the need.

A case could be made that teachers of singing have always wanted to know how the vocal instrument functions. Rather than being a new idea, such interest in the available factual information characterizes the mainstream of historic vocal pedagogy. Today's teacher of singing participates in a long tradition.

We should not fool ourselves, however, into believing that what generally takes place today in vocal studios in America or elsewhere is based on acquaintance with the current literature of vocal science. Many teachers of singing give a nod of approval to the helpful scientist, and exhibit tolerance and indulgence toward colleagues who have an interest in the subject, but deep in their hearts they know that "singing and teaching are matters of instinct and artistry." There is no possibility of improving on what Madame X handed down to Maestro Y, who in turn gave it unadulterated to "my teacher." Comparative vocal pedagogy reveals stratified systems of both fact and nonsense existing side by side.

What should today's voice teacher be doing in the studio? In any age, the main duties of a teacher of singing, with regard to technique, have always been chiefly two: (1) to analyze vocal problems, and (2) to design proper solutions for them. It is a pleasure to have students who exhibit few technical problems, but the teaching of such pupils is not really voice teaching as much as it is sophisticated coaching and performance preparation. The teacher who helps the less well coordinated singer to establish a solid vocal technique is the real singing teacher. The potential of the student must be discovered, and technical means offered for rectifying problems impeding fine performance. How can this be done?

One choice is to teach by modeling, that is, the teacher sings the passage or exercise for the student. If a teacher can demonstrate a beautifully free vocal sound, the student may gain some insight into how it is produced. If the teacher has been a great singer, an astute student may glean certain subtle aspects of style and even a little technique. However, if the teacher is an over-the-hill opera diva or divo, the student may pick up some tendencies it might be better not to have picked up. If a teacher has never gotten his or her own instrument sufficiently mastered to be professionally useful, the student may be in real trouble when attempting to imitate the teacher's voice.

It is important for the teacher to have a basic knowledge of physical function and vocal acoustics, and to be able to explain what the student is doing wrong, and why, in language that speaks to the individual student. The main prerequisite for the teaching of singing is none of the following: a fabulous ear, excellent musicianship, highly refined taste, a bubbling personality, good will, or a successful singing career (although all of these are vital assets). The chief requisite is to be able to recognize malfunction in a singing voice and to know how to correct it. If one does not know how the vocal machine operates, it is foolhardy to think one can reach a wise and consistently accurate assessment and resolution of vocal problems.

How much scientific information does the voice teacher need? As much as she or he can get. There is a growing body of information to help the voice teacher understand what is really happening in a singer's voice, and how vocalises can be used to induce the sounds that imprecise imagery intended. Such information provides the teacher with a new language for today's students, the majority of whom do not readily comprehend traditional imagery. A battery of helpful instrumentation exists that provides exact information on aspects of vocal timbre that occupy so much of vocal pedagogy. Included are a number of electronic devices that display the sung spectrum and tell us much about what singers call "resonance balance." The fiberscope/stroboscope and the electroglottograph also provide information [Titze 1983]. Many of these devices are available on North American campuses and in vocal care clinics accessible to teachers of singing.

Nevertheless, unlike the car mechanic, the singing teacher does not deal simply with a mechanically complex instrument. Knowing how the voice functions has never yet produced a great teacher of singing. The fine vocal pedagogue must combine mechanistic information with psychological and aesthetic understanding.

The teacher of singing must accept the enormous responsibility for the health of a student's voice. To rely entirely on imagery is to be saddled with a serious handicap in teaching healthy vocalism. The teacher and student *may* finally arrive at what teacher wants by hit and miss. Persons using divining rods have also been known to locate groundwater.

Although foremost teachers of singing of the past concerned themselves with the factual information available to them, today's singing teacher has access to a greater body of solid information and rational tools than ever before. We owe it to our students to take advantage of not only what was known two hundred years ago, but also what is known today. The advice of Bartholomew, a pioneer in the study of the acoustics of the singing voice, still is appropriate:

> Imagery should be used merely to suggest indirectly through its psychological effects a certain muscular setting which is awkward for the beginner. The teacher, though using it, should bear in mind at all times the true facts. . . . Furthermore, since imagery is largely individual and thus variable, when it is trusted as a physical explanation, the so-called "True Method" becomes as variable as the individual temperament, instead of as stable as Truth is usually expected to be.

Discovering new and interesting techniques for teaching the art of singing is not the reason for assimilating information about the function of the vocal instrument.The singing teacher in a scientific age is now able, through current analysis, to interpret vocal traditions so that viable vocal techniques can be communicated in a systematic way; the teacher has the means of sorting through what is offered, at both the historical and current vocal pedagogy smorgasbord, and of choosing rationally what is most nutritious and discarding the extraneous.

How can emerging information for use in the studio be expanded? Singers of stature should be willing to cooperate in noninvasive investigations of the singing voice. To make such information useful, all major schools and techniques of singing should be identified in research reports. In published accounts, participants of varying performance backgrounds should not be indiscriminately lumped together as "professional singers." The subtle individual properties that set one voice apart from another should not be averaged out. In order for scientific research to be valid and to have practical value in the voice studio, teachers of singing must be involved in the research design and in its accomplishment.

Unless it is recognized that a number of separate singing techniques exist, conclusions reached in studies about singers need to be read cautiously. Singing teachers readily hear timbre differences; they need to know what kinds of singing produces them.

Much of what goes on in the vocal studio is extraneous, or even counterproductive. This is true in the teaching of all athletic skills (of which singing is one). In discussing sports biomechanics in 1984, Abraham reported:

> Analysis of high-speed films of elite performers has led to many interesting observations. Baseball pitchers, for instance, have been apparently wasting much time in the past strengthening their wrist flexor muscles to improve speed of their pitches. Research at the University of Arizona has revealed

that the wrist "snap," which does contribute heavily to the speed of the pitched ball, is actually caused by the sudden deceleration of the forearm and occurs so fast the wrist flexor muscles cannot even keep up, much less contribute to the motion.

Many exercises thought to strengthen or relax the musculature of the singing voice may have no more relationship to actual function than do the exercises of the major-league pitcher. Learning to "relax" or to "strengthen" certain muscles of the face, neck, and torso may contribute little to singing, yet some vocal instruction is largely directed toward such activities.

One main goal of teaching in this and any age should be to do no harm. Every aspect of vocal technique must be in agreement with what is known about healthy vocal function. No one can know it all, but we all must be willing to modify what we do know as our information expands. Demythologizing the language of vocal pedagogy is part of that process; consultation with experts through reading in related disciplines is another.

As teachers of singing in a scientific age, we must ask ourselves how much we really know about the subject matter in which we are dealing. Do we have knowledge based on fact, or do we rely on anecdotal opinions? Do we know the literature of our own field as well as that of related fields?

We live in an advantageous age in which the traditions of the past and the information of the present can be combined in exciting ways. The responsibility, excitement, and rewards of our profession lie in our rising to new challenges to make the present and future of voice teaching even greater than its history.

References

Abraham, L. "Sports Biomechanics: Application of High Tech to Olympic Engineering." *Texas Professional Engineer,* 1984: July-August, 16–19.

Bartholomew, W. T. "The Role of Imagery in Voice Teaching." *Proceedings of the Music Teachers National Association,* 1935.

Berard, J. B. (1775). *L'Art du Chant,* trans. and ed. S. Murray (1969). Milwaukee: Pro Musica Press.

Garcia, M. (1847). *A Complete Treatise on the Art of Singing,* Part One, trans. D. V. Paschke (1983). New York: Da Capo Press.

Mancini, G. (1774). *Practical Reflections on Figured Singing,* trans. E. Foreman (1967). Champaign: Pro Musica Press.

Titze, I. "Instrumentation for Voice Research." *The NATS Bulletin,* 1983: 38 (5) 29.

71

On the Invasion of Vocal Pedagogy by Science

At times it is lamented that science recently has made undesirable inroads into the domain of the voice teacher. The argument runs like this:

Why should the voice teacher be concerned with physical and acoustic matters? After all, in the golden *bel canto* period singers didn't bother themselves with scientific fact. The artists of the second Golden Age that bridged the nineteenth and twentieth centuries knew nothing about either physiology or acoustics. Those were the days of the great teachers—Garcia, Stockhausen, Bassini, F. Lamperti, G. B. Lamperti, Behnke, de Reszke, Marchesi, Fillebrown, Kofler, Shakespeare, Greene, and Cotogni. Physiology and vocal function are topics that belong in the realm of medicine and are not the province of artists. Investigative studies of a mechanical or medical sort should be reserved for medical and scientific journals. Journals devoted to vocal pedagogy and performance should deal with singing. Teachers of singing are not scientists.

However, when the historic literature of vocal pedagogy is examined, one discovers that much of it did consider the scientific viewpoints of the time. The careful reader cannot help being struck by the realization that "the old Italians" and later pedagogical writers of note based their precepts of vocal technique on then-current physiological assumptions. No one questions that Manuel Garcia was both *the* voice scientist and *the* maestro of vocal technique during his long life. Garcia's conclusions (not always correct, of course) were based on early direct observation of vocal fold behavior. Garcia the singing teacher brought to prominence the laryngoscope, with which otolaryngologists still examine the vocal folds. Garcia was not alone among nineteenth-century and early twentieth-century pedagogues in showing preoccupation with the physiological aspects of singing.

In our own century, Marchesi, Shakespeare, Lehman, Bachner, Klein, Mills, Curtis, Bartholomew, Greene, Witherspoon, F. Miller, Clippinger, Martienssen-Lohman, Stanley, and Husler (the list could be greatly extended) often dealt with specific scientific aspects of singing. Current pedagogy is influenced by the writings of singers who in the near past and the present make use of scientific information regarding the singing voice, including such names as Vennard, Appelman, Coffin, Proctor, and Large. Some current scientists, notably Titze and Sundberg, direct much of their interest to the singing voice. The number of physicians who have concerned themselves with the singing art is considerable, and many of them work (or worked) closely with the professional voice community, including such Americans as Gould, Lawrence, and Sataloff.

Nevertheless, avoidance of information regarding the physical aspect of singing is still the hallmark of some outmoded teaching. For example, a voice-teacher friend recently remarked that he feels no need for such information because his "ear" provides him with all the information he needs for the teaching of singing. Certainly he saves himself much time and energy by disregarding the by now vast literature on vocal function, although there may be a suspicion that he wastes a great deal of teaching time in trying to find appropriate pedagogical solutions to problems. There is also no reason to believe that factual information would be detrimental to his "ear." In fact, others who teach at the same institution as he tell me that their "ears" are tuned to quite different aesthetic values than is his "ear." Whose "ear" then shall we trust? His, theirs, yours, mine? The tonal concept that lodges in the "ear" of the teacher should be examined in the light of verifiable physiological information.

There is no doubt that people sing professionally by a variety of techniques. However, this does not mean that a successful singing technique can be based on breath management, laryngeal action, and resonation that run patently contrary to the known facts of function. The teacher of singing needs to know the literature on vocal function and on the acoustics of the singing voice just as assuredly as the medical doctor needs to know the literature of diagnosis and treatment.

72

The Invisible Instrument?

The finger of the pianist can be placed in exactly the desired position on the keyboard, the proper angle of the wrist can be demonstrated, and the posture of the elbow as it relates to the body and to the forearm can be manually adjusted. Physical aspects of string playing can be monitored visually. Lips and fingers of the wind player are readily observed. Other instruments, it is thought, are visible, while the voice remains unseen.

In general, what cannot be seen is not easily understood. Although pedagogical uniformity toward any instrument does not exist, keyboard, string, and wind instruments probably are beset by fewer pedagogical mythologies than is the vocal instrument. The descriptive language of vocal pedagogy frequently becomes subjective and mystical. How hidden, actually, is the vocal instrument?

Unless subjected to mechanical examination such as that provided by laryngoscopic, fiberoptic, and stroboscopic means, the vocal folds cannot be directly viewed. Nevertheless, a great deal of information about laryngeal function in response to total body coordination is available through surface observation. Lack of freedom within the phonatory system is often indicated by the external musculature of the neck. While it is true that the complete resonator tube is not accessible to external viewing, a large percentage of the vocal tract is visible. Certainly the position of the apex and of at least part of the dorsum of the tongue, the position of the mandible, and the shape of the lips reveal much about the configuration of the vocal tract and about vocal-tract response to laryngeally generated sound. Subglottic pressure and airflow rate are not externally visible phenomena, but information regarding breath management can be gained by watching the chest, the rib cage, and the movements (or lack thereof) of the antero-lateral abdominal wall musculature during the breath cycle. Stance and posture are visible.

External observation, coupled with information about physical function and a knowledge of vocal acoustics, can assist in raising the teaching of singing beyond subjective speculation and reliance on mythological language. Perhaps the excellent *eye* of the singing teacher is as necessary as is the excellent *ear* in dealing with the "unseen" vocal instrument.

73

Have You Read the Literature?

We live in an age of rapidly expanding knowledge in most disciplines. The surgeon must keep abreast of new developments, the psychologist must be aware of current techniques, the social scientist has new information to digest from ongoing studies, the lawyer must regularly renew his sources, and—the singing teacher? Why should the teacher of singing need any new information? After all, great singers have existed for hundreds of years, and the vocal instrument has not undergone any major change.

Tolerance of diverse ideas in any field implies awareness of the existence of varying viewpoints. There have been, as everyone is aware, conflicting hypotheses about such basic matters as the origin of the universe, the nature of the cosmos, divergent theories regarding continental drift and solutions of ecological problems, and opposing predictions regarding the ultimate fate of the planet. These ideas are based on a reading of the data, and are extended or abandoned as new information becomes available. To contend seriously for the respect of informed minds, they must be based on factual, although perhaps as yet incomplete, information.

With regard to singing, it is recognized that not all teachers operate under the same set of hypotheses, nor do they all advocate the same techniques. Although tolerance is a commendable attribute (especially among voice teachers!), blind acceptance of nonfunctional procedures is not. It is improbable that the particular technique that chance and circumstance have dictated to a singer is the only complete or even most efficient approach to vocalism. Saying "It works. Why should I look elsewhere?" is no more appropriate for the teaching of singing than for other disciplines. Probably in no other field is it possible to find with such frequency the simplistic viewpoint that "What I have been taught is the right way!"

The teacher of any subject should read the developing information of that discipline. The reservoir of factual knowledge regarding voicing is extensive. Within the past decade, vocal investigation has produced considerable literature as to how the voice functions. Not all the answers are in, nor will they be for many years to come. Yet this expanding knowledge is available to persons who deal professionally with the voice.

No longer does the teacher of singing have to guess how the vocal folds respond to airflow, what breathy or pressed phonations look like at the level of the larynx or as measured by instrumentation, what the contributing sources of resonance may be, what the spectra from a "resonant" voice look like, how vowel tracking relates to vocal timbre, the causes of nasality, and what factors produce the "ring" of the voice. No teacher of singing can attempt private research into all of these pedagogical areas, just as no single physician can be directly involved in research in all medical fields. However, the vocal research literature is there to be read, and it is as important to vocal pedagogy as are comparable literatures to other fields.

There is an attempt at times to divide the voice-teaching profession into "scientific" teachers and "empirical" teachers. This is a false dichotomy, because the singer uses a physical instrument in an empirical way. Could it be that "empirical" language prevails with a teacher because he or she has not taken time to investigate the literature of function?

That such a situation may be the case is suggested by two incidents that occurred at an international conference of teachers of singing. A noted voice scientist had presented several sessions that dealt with the acoustic properties of the vocal tract and their relationship to the laryngeally generated sound. Suddenly an angry voice rang out. "You keep talking about the 'vocal tract.' I have been teaching voice for twenty years and I have never heard of the vocal tract!" Dismissed by that comment was the vast sum of information accumulated on vocal acoustics. Unwittingly revealed was the fact that none of the literature in his field from the past twenty years had been read by that teacher.

At still another recent international conference, much information was presented by an American acoustician on formants in general and on the phenomenon of the singer's formant in particular. At the pause, one voice teacher was heard to remark to another, "These American scientists don't even know the English language. There is no such word as *formant*. The word is *format!*" So much for science! A strong chance exists, however, that the colleague who doubts the existence of the "singer's formant" even as an expression to be found in the English language will have his or her curiosity sufficiently aroused to check into the matter and to discover eventually what he or she was looking for in all those years of searching for "placement" imagery. Everyone must make a beginning somewhere, and most of us will have to confess some original hostility toward ideas that today are old hat to us. Tolerance must include toleration of the intolerant.

Teachers of singing deal in vocal sound. Vocal sound is the result of physical action and acoustic properties. Is there any question that a teacher of singing should know as much as possible about the substance in which she or he deals? Surely it is not wise to dismiss a body of information that one has not yet investigated.

In fairness, we should ask, What about the very real problem of acquiring the vocabulary to read the literature? A language teacher who refused to learn the rules of grammar (although fluent in the spoken language) would not gain much respect among linguists. A teacher of singing who today refuses to find out what the terms "vocal tract" and "singer's formant" may mean surely is not in a more favorable position with either colleagues or students than the limited language teacher.

Admittedly, it is hard for all of us to find time to read the literature. Teaching singing is very hard work, and knowing the literature is part of that task. The extent to which a teacher directly refers to the physiology and acoustics of singing must be a personal pedagogical decision. There surely is no question that the teacher should know the current functional literature of the subject being taught. It will not turn him or her into a scientist but into a teacher who can support "empirical" findings with fact, and thereby avoid delivering embarrassing and harmful misinformation.

74

Taming the Terrible Triplets of the Vocal Tract: Tongue/Hyoid Bone/Larynx

Small children find the tongue an expressive instrument for communicating negative sentiments to their playmates face to face and about parents and teachers behind their backs. Sticking out the tongue, vigorously indulged in at any age, has distinct sociological and psychological implications that extend quite literally beyond the tongue's biologic functions. Although tongue distention beyond the lip bastion can be a liberating action, its acceptability is restricted to the first decade of life; its practice is not considered appropriate conduct in faculty meetings, courts of law, sessions of the United States Congress, or stockholder meetings, where it might be far more useful than what usually is expressed by words. However, even when not protruded in an antisocial way, the tongue can get its owner into innumerable communication difficulties during the course of a day.

The tongue can disrupt the singing voice just as disastrously as it can upset social relationships but for very different reasons. Much of the vocal tract is occupied by the tongue. The tongue, which is composed of a bundle of muscles, is attached to the hyoid bone, from which the larynx is suspended by a membrane. When the hyoid bone is fixed, the mylohyoid depresses the mandible (lower jaw). The mylohyoid muscle can elevate the hyoid bone and the base of the tongue, and raise the floor of the mouth. A group of laryngeal elevators (supra-hyoid muscles) are attached to the mandible, to the mastoid area, and to the tongue. A set of laryngeal depressors (infra-hyoid muscles) attach to the hyoid bone, to the sternum, or to the upper ribs. The positions of the larynx and the tongue are partly dependent on relationships among these related groups of muscles. This can be clearly seen by watching movements of the larynx when the tongue is moved about in the mouth. Even by observing speech in another person, or by watching oneself in a mirror while speaking, it becomes apparent that the tongue/hyoid bone/larynx complex is actually a functional unit. When not properly tamed, these three instruments can become the terrible triplets of the vocal tract and cause problems in the singing voice.

As is well recognized in vocal pedagogy circles these days, the human phonation machine is composed of a motor source (the breath mechanism), a vibrator (the larynx), and a resonator system (the larynx, the mouth, the pharynx, sometimes the nose, and, at times, some limited, fixed subglottic resonance). What is not always fully recognized is the extent to which the tongue controls events of the resonator tube (vocal tract) and the tongue's effect on laryngeal efficiency. This is because the tongue is the ringleader in determining resonator-tube shapes, and because it is something of a bully, lording it over the rest of the hyoidal and laryngeal-positioning mechanism. Much of what goes wrong in the singing voice can be blamed on the lack of cooperation among these three siblings of the vocal tract. Like bad children, they often have opposing ideas as to what they wish to accomplish, and this obstreperous behavior causes innumerable technical headaches for the singer/parent.

The timbre of the singing voice is chiefly determined by three factors: how the motor source delivers air, what happens at the level of the larynx, and how sound is modified as it passes from the larynx through the resonator tube. Many imaginative theories of tone production have been proposed, but there is little doubt that phonation is the result of myoelastic (muscular) and aerodynamic (moving air) events involving subglottic pressure, airflow, and vocal-fold approximation. The sound initiated at the level of the larynx is filtered by the resonator tube, and the distinctive quality of individual phonation (the timbre) results. The accepted phonetic theory of speech recognition is founded on this assumption. It is, clearly, equally applicable to the sounds of singing.

How much direct control can be exercised over this sound-producing machine? Systems of singing offer various solutions. Many are based on superficial deductions that fail to take into account actual function. For example, each vowel has its own particular configuration, both at the level of the larynx and in the resonator tube filtering process. The definition of vowels, without which there would be no intelligibility in language communication, is dependent to a large extent on a proper match between laryngeal vowel formation and vocal tract shape. (Of course, the role of consonants, both voiced and unvoiced, is equally vital.) Some techniques of singing ignore phonetic information and attempt to maintain a single posture of the vocal tract for the formation of all vowels, in all ranges of the voice.

Each vowel has recognizable predominant formants (acoustic energy peaking) that distinguish it from other vowels; that characteristic gives each vowel a unique spectral appearance, independent of the spoken or sung fundamental (pitch). Although there is some degree of independence between the laryngeally generated origin of sound and the filtering effects of the vocal tract, *interdependence* between larynx and resonator tube is required if the vowel is to be recognizable and if vowel distortion is to be avoided. In the singing voice there must be a match between vibrator and resonator tract.

Any static setting of resonator shapes will disturb the interrelated actions of the tripartite mechanism of tongue, hyoid bone, and larynx, which are an anatomical unit. Normal nonpathological speech patterns permit freedom of tongue, hyoid bone, and laryngeal action. This does not mean that the resonator tube and the larynx never alter from the speech mode to the singing mode. Rather, it means that the tongue, in speech and singing, must be free to undertake the articulatory motions of either activity.

In large measure, singing technique is directed toward "taming" unruly behavior on the part of members of the "terrible trio" through establishing smoothly functioning cooperation among them. The more limited requirements of spoken phonation are in general met automatically. Assuming speech habits free of pathologies, the postures of the resonator tube normally adjust to permit configurations that produce vowels and consonants. The singing voice, with its extended *tessitura* and intensity levels, must undergo additional disciplining. The natural cooperation that occurs in spoken phonation must be more highly tuned for the demands of artistic singing.

It is chiefly in responding to extended fundamental frequency, to greater amplitude, and to expanded demands for beautiful timbre that singing goes beyond the requirements of speech. The voice remains the same instrument, whether in speech or in song, but the tasks have changed. In the heightened action of singing, the need for technical control is augmented.

Although in amateur singing the larynx may rise and fall with the change of pitch, the alternate shortening and lengthening of the vocal tract that is so much a part of popular idioms and of some ethnic vocal literatures has no place in "classical" singing. Laryngeal elevation and depression (and corresponding muscular adjustments) in amateur singing produce timbre alterations not considered acceptable in cultivated singing. Studies conducted with performing artists indicate that a stabilized laryngeal position, neither visibly elevating nor falling in response to pitch change throughout the vocal scale, is a universal mark of good singing.

The tongue, the domineering member of the vocal tract, is capable of extensive distention and retraction. Upward or forward movements of the tongue will cause a marked response in elevation of the hyoid bone and the laryngeal mechanism. Although we cannot see the internal action of the complex muscle bundle that forms the base of the tongue, we are able to see the apex and body of the tongue, and to learn from this observation to reduce tension in singing by keeping the apex of the tongue in contact with the inner surface of the lower front teeth, on all vowels. In repose (no phonation), when standing or sitting, with persons free of orthodontic problems, the apex of the tongue should rest at the lower front teeth. This is the acoustic at-rest posture readily located by saying "hm!" or by pronouncing the neutral vowel, the *schwa,* as in the "uh" said when one is thinking aloud. With the front (lateral) vowels, the anterior portion of the tongue is "closer" (raised toward the hard palate), while with the back (rounded) vowels the tongue is lower in front and somewhat elevated in back. The neutral vowels find the tongue near the at-rest posture. Many singers, however, in attempting to produce an enriched vocal timbre or hoping to maintain an "ideal" learned posture (a mold) through which all vowels are then sung, often experience tongue tensions that do not permit the normal shaping of the vocal tract that is demanded for clean vowel differentiation and free vocal timbre.

There are several frequently encountered inexact tongue postures for singing.

1. *Placing the tongue too low, at the roots of the lower front teeth rather than in contact with the inner surface of the teeth, and thereby humping the body of the tongue upward.* If the tongue lowers to the roots of the teeth, forcing the body of the tongue to elevate, the space between the hard palate and the tongue will narrow. Space between the back portion of the tongue and the velum will also diminish. The resultant loss of upper partials is perceived by the listening ear as a "dulling" of the sound, and often as a lowering of intonation.

2. *Pulling the tip (apex) of the tongue upward and backward.* When the tip of the tongue is curled upward toward the hard palate, the vowel becomes distorted and the timbre loses its clarity. The resonator shape does not match the intended vowel formation.

3. *Retracting the tongue into the mouth.* Pulling the tongue directly backward (retroflex posture) from the acoustic at-rest position during singing tends to force the larynx (via the hyoid bone) to assume an excessively low position. This accounts for much of the "heavy,

dark" production often perceived by a singer as providing a bigger, richer voice. Clean diction and clarity of timbre are not possible.

4. *Elevating the tongue by pressing it upward against the molars*. Raising the tongue to maintain near contact with the upper molars tends to retain the lateral acoustic posture of the vowel [i] ("ee") and exaggerates brilliance, producing harshness of timbre (through augmentation of upper harmonic partials associated with the [i] vowel), while at the same time inducing a relatively high laryngeal position, which serves to shorten the vocal tract and remove depth (lower harmonic strength) from the sound.

5. *Excessively grooved tongue for all vowels*. Attempting to form a constant groove in the tongue (tongue depression) places extreme pressure on the base of the tongue, forces the larynx downward, and induces tensions in the pharyngeal wall.

6. *One side of the tongue held higher than the other*. Unequal postures of left or right side of the tongue are due to severe tensions among muscles of the tongue bundle. Tension is transferred to the larynx via muscles attached to the hyoid bone, from which the larynx is suspended.

Although each of the first five malfunctions indicated above are advocated in some pedagogical sources as a means for improving vocal timbre, the sixth one is not. It may result, however, from resonator-tract tensions induced by the other five maladroit maneuvers.

In addition to the effects of undesirable tongue postures per se, attempts to spread the pharyngeal wall have a direct bearing on the position of the tongue, because the palatoglossal and palatopharyngeal muscles, as well as the glossopharyngeal muscles, are placed in sustained tension. The timbre is "throaty" (pharyngeal in character), resulting in a *Knödel* (a "dumpling" in the throat).

There is increasing but incomplete evidence that in good resonance balance (in which the singer's formant is present) the ventricles of the larynx (sinuses of Morgagni, which lie between the true and false vocal folds) are enlarged. The false folds retract, and the vestibule of the larynx and the pyriform sinuses appear to become more spacious. These desirable conditions for the singing voice, although still possible at times, cannot exist as favorably within the raised laryngeal configuration.

Natural vocal-tract shapes occur when the breath is taken with a sense of "openness," that is, without conscious adjustments of space in mouth or pharynx. Coordination between the initial "deep breath" and simultaneous complete vocal-fold abduction (glottal opening), without altering the neutral tongue position, permits the tongue and therefore the entire vocal tract to move to the subsequent natural posture demanded by a specific vowel.

The complete adduction of the vocal folds (closure of the glottis) that then follows produces both the clean onset and the fully resonant, unmanufactured vowel. In infancy, the tongue, unless disturbed by pathologies, learns to produce the phonetic articulation demanded by speech and by heightened emotive expressions such as laughing and crying. During phonation, any time the tongue assumes sustained positions contrary to phonetic articulation, encumbrance must occur somewhere within the vocal tract.

Most undisciplined behavior on the part of the tongue can be observed in the hand mirror. Such errors can be corrected through using phonemes that place the tongue close to the acoustic at-rest posture, as with [v], [f], [b], [p], [k], [g], [m], [s], and [z]. When the subsequent vowel is sung, the apex of the tongue still must remain in contact with the inner surface of the lower teeth.

In singing, as in most of art, what is the least complex and most direct is best and most beautiful. Techniques of singing based on tongue configurations not to be found in the phonetic definition of vowels and consonants, or built on exaggerated laryngeal depression or elevation, are harmful. The "terrible triplets" (tongue, hyoid bone, and larynx) have then been forced into actions that produce either hypofunction or hyperfunction in some part of the phonatory mechanism. Interestingly enough, schools of singing that refuse to look at the physiology and acoustics of the singing voice often invent highly complex systems out of the conviction that it is too difficult to learn how the voice actually works, or even out of fear that factual information will lead to "unnatural" production! The viewpoint that the speaking voice and the singing voice are completely different instruments, and that therefore phonetic acoustic rules do not apply to singing, is seldom afforded validity in serious vocal pedagogy circles these days.

An aim of vocal pedagogy should be to avoid complex conscious maneuvers that must be learned by the throat, tongue, and mouth. Rather, the participants of the vocal tract should be allowed to cooperate in accordance with the laws of nature. Only then will the "terrible triplets of the vocal tract" behave properly.

75

The Three Musketeers of Tension:
Tongue/Neck/Jaw

They stick together. It's one for all and all for one with these three characters who want to control your life as a singer. Problems of breath management aside (and the three musketeers can even induce problems in that area), the major sources of tension in singers tend to be located in the tongue, in the musculature of the neck, and in the region of the jaw (the mandible).

Because the tongue occupies much of the vocal tract, and because of its construction as a muscle bundle free anteriorly, laterally, and dorsally (although attached to the floor of the mouth and to the hyoid bone), the possibilities for tongue tension are considerable. The tongue is also the chief agent for changing the spatial arrangements of the buccopharyngeal (mouth-pharynx) cavity, which is the chief resonance chamber of the voice. Whatever maneuvers one makes with the tongue can influence laryngeal position, often unfavorably.

The neck, in which the chief instrument of phonation is housed, is a complex of muscular systems attaching to the head and to the torso. The external frame support of the larynx is dependent on the musculature of the neck. Laryngeal musculature is both internal and external, and what one does with the nuchal muscles (back of the neck) and muscles of the submandibular area (below the jaw) influences laryngeal function.

The jaw itself is the third member of this unholy trinity of actors, and, because it is capable of both lateral and perpendicular movements, it is not adverse to taking control and trying to run the entire phonatory operation.

The physiologic functions of each of these three important parts of the singer's anatomy have been extensively examined by experts, and that information is available to persons interested in knowing how these systems work. Here the concern is not with their mechanical function but with some practical pedagogical devices for bringing these three militant brigands to heel. They are banded together in a permanent relationship, but sometimes operate independently of each other in causing tension.

There are a number of specific pedagogical devices for inducing freedom in tongue, neck, and jaw described elsewhere, but here the aim is to give

233

an overview of the most direct corrective measures involved in all of those devices. These comments are based on the premise that fixation (the maintenance of a static, set condition) in one or more of the three areas is tension inducing. The way to avoid a rigid physical position is to move something. Therefore, a simple antidotal recommendation for eliminating tension in tongue, jaw, or neck is to have the offensive member undergo movement. Do not tackle all three musketeers at once. Isolate each of them, then mount a freedom-inducing attack on each one.

Let us say that Tongue assumes one of his favorite recalcitrant positions; rather than remaining with the apex in contact with the lower teeth for all vowel definition and for a great deal of consonant formation, he insists on taking up postures that prohibit such phonetic formations. While making him stay where he belongs, that is, close to the acoustic at-rest posture, move him gently but quickly back and forth against the inner surface of the lower teeth, while singing a vowel, or a series of vowels on a single pitch. Do this without moving either the neck or the jaw. Then stop the movement, and retain the same sensation of relaxation in the body of the tongue that was achieved during the rapid movement.

Or, perhaps it is his close companion, Jaw, who wants to play the rigidity game, often in conjunction with laryngeal elevation or depression. While singing a pitch, apply the same corrective principle to him: move the jaw quickly in a lateral action related to chewing (without exaggeration), then stop the movement but retain the same jaw flexibility that the momentary movement established. Don't consciously move either the tongue or the neck while doing the jaw maneuver. Flexibility cannot be there in correct degree if the jaw is hung in a regurgitory posture, or positioned in a fixed smile.

Now give that third militant musketeer, Neck, a good licking by making the same quick lateral movement with the head. Give the head a rapid small sideways shake while phonating on a single pitch, then continue the phonation following the head-shake with the same looseness in the musculature of the neck. Of course, in order for benefit to accrue, the head must be in an axial position, not forward, downward, or upward. (Clearly there are times during singing in which the head will not be in an entirely axial position, as demanded by the drama, but non-axial head position should not be a part of basic vocal production.)

These three evil accomplices do not like being literally shaken out of their positions of control. First give them this treatment of mobility, which sets them running, in lower medium or speech-inflection ranges, and later at higher points in the mounting scale. It may take a number of attempts to achieve the full benefit of these simple exercises, but they are repeatedly successful in eliminating tongue, neck, and jaw tensions. Don't accept enslavement to malfunction because of earlier having given in to the aggressive trio. You can conquer them if you try! Just give them the shakes, and they will turn tail.

76

Gorillas, Giraffes, Lions, and Gazelles

A trip to the zoo should be an annual requirement for every teacher of singing. Although among our fellow vertebrates it may be the larynx of the lion that produces the most impressive sound, the laryngeal structures of other creatures remind us of the wonderful diversity within the animal kingdom. They allow us to observe how structural peculiarities contribute to the variety of sounds that emanate from assorted larynges. The graceful gazelle and the nearly voiceless giraffe seldom express themselves orally, whereas the gorilla can produce more than twenty kinds of vocalization, including whimpering, screaming, grumbling, and roaring while drumming aggressively on the chest.

If a trip to the zoo is out, make a survey of small and large dogs in the neighborhood. Compare pitch ranges and vocal timbres. You will notice that you cannot determine the sex of a dog from listening to it bark or howl. Most big dogs with large larynges and large thoraxes have resounding voices; little dogs tend to yap and squeak. If dogs could be taught to sing opera roles, we might have the interesting phenomenon of a male miniature schnauzer singing the role of Norina, while a female Newfoundland could be cast as Don Pasquale. Most house cats, clearly, are soubrettes, regardless of gender, and would be unable to cover all the role categories.

It would be preposterous to compare students who enter the studio door to inmates of the zoo or to a pack of neighborhood dogs or a gaggle of serenading cats, yet the long-necked soprano, the short-necked tenor, the thickly built baritone, the gangly bass, the robust mezzo, and the lithe, willowy male or female of slight physique all present diversities of the singing instrument.

Some technical faults in singing can be directly traced to misunderstanding the physical type of the singer. Too often we try to make all of our singers take on identical external appearances. A singer with a thick chest, or who is heavy breasted, may appear to have the sternum sufficiently high while actually standing with sloppy, slouched posture; a flat-chested student may never be able to achieve the appearance of what the teacher considers to be a noble stance. Some singers exhibit broad, full-moon faces; others display high cheekbones and "foxy" facial structures. The mouth may be cut fully across the face, or it may occupy a relatively small area of the visage. During phonation, teeth may be exceedingly visible in some specimens, while being completely hidden by the lips in others. Jaw excursion (the extent of the mouth opening) may be slight in some singers and extensive in others. To demand identical appearances may be asking them to commit a violation of nature.

In some singers, especially males, there is very little space between the chin and the larynx. In these no-neck individuals, laryngeal position may well be less of a technical problem than it is in the long-necked, skinny fellow with an expanse between chin and sternoclavicular joint. The larynx can more readily bob up and down in the long neck, potentially causing greater problems with laryngeal stability.

In contrast to some of the roaming dogs in your neighborhood, however, a large robust human body may not necessarily house a correspondingly large larynx. Occasionally career tragedies occur in the performance world because the 5'2" bass-baritone would never convince as King Philip, nor will the 6'1" soprano who can beautifully sing *Un bel dì* be successfully carried across the delicate Japanese threshold by a 5'5" tenor. We accept miniature collies, but we do not countenance miniature basses. No matter how lovable, lhasa apsos who grow too large should not be entered in competition. Fortunately, there are other things to do in this life besides singing on opera stages and entering canine beauty contests.

Most successful singing careers happen in conjunction with successes in the lyric theater. It is difficult—nearly impossible—to become solely a professionally functioning "concert singer" or "*Lieder* singer." Moreover, not all voices and physiques are properly operatic. Nor can the nonoperatic voice be turned into an operatic instrument in the voice studio, any more than the zookeeper can turn gazelles and giraffes into lions and gorillas. Particularly when the teacher performs actively and models, she or he must be on guard not to require the student to return an exact physical mirror image.

The human vocal mechanism freely functions only when its several parts are in proper relationship to each other. Good singing starts from the way in which the instrument is positioned. Whether the singer is tall or short, thin or thick, male or female, structural alignment must pertain. The external frame function of the musculature of head and neck, the position of the rib cage, the relationship of the muscles of the torso to the rib cage and to the sternum, and the balance of the body—dynamic muscle equilibrium—are principles that pertain for all singers. Problems emerge if we expect all physical types to look the same during the accomplishment of essential conditions. Vowel definition, vowel modification (so much a part of "covering"), mouth opening for the accommodation of ascending pitch, and facial expressions for the conveyance of common emotions should follow uniform technical principles, but individuals will not look the same.

Although the vocal sounds we hear in the studio may not always be as freely functioning as those to be heard in almost any corner of the zoo, most of us would still prefer to stick with our assorted sopranos, mezzos, contraltos, tenors, baritones, bass-baritones, and basses. However, we must remind ourselves that even within the singing species, a great variety of physical structure is to be expected and to be taken into account as we work technically.

77

Male and Female Created He Them

Equality is a matter of concern to fair-minded persons. How best to go about correcting historical inequities that stem from gender differences has become a major social consideration. Varying viewpoints have assumed political stances, both of the right and of the left.

The history of singing is not without its own forms of gender discrimination. Whether in the lyric theater, the church, or even poetic sources from which much of the song literature is drawn, equality of the sexes is not readily demonstrated. The appropriateness of the liturgical tradition of men-and-boy choirs is itself being currently questioned. Some of our female students return *Frauenliebe und -leben* to us with the explanation that they find it difficult to relate to such sentiments as "Ich will ihm dienen, ihm angehören ganz." "Nur in Demut ihn betrachten" is not how they view a desirable relationship between the sexes.

No matter how these imbalances eventually may be corrected, there remains one factor of discrimination in the art of singing that no social advance will ever eliminate: the young male singer is physiologically disadvantaged vis-à-vis his female contemporary until his post-adolescent years are over. (The question of early training while the young male voice is still undergoing radical change from treble—a topic still capable of initiating heated debate among teachers of singing—is excluded from this consideration.)

Teachers of singing who deal with the late adolescent male voice may be aware of the frustration some young male singers experience as they hear their female studiomates of the same age group perform with a degree of finesse and ease beyond the male capacity. The light soprano instrument may show technical accomplishments at age eighteen that rival the seasoned artist, whereas the eighteen-year-old bass may produce with comfort no more than a few hesitant pitches above the bass staff. Even at the graduation recital of a four-year performance degree program, the male may not yet have complete ease in his *zona di passaggio*. The reason is that the young adult male voice may be only six, seven, or eight years old at the time the bachelor of music degree is awarded. However, the twenty-year-old or twenty-two-year-old baritone or tenor must perform his junior and senior recitals with the same performance expectations from the world at large as does his soprano friend of the same chronological age.

Ingo Titze points out that an examination of laryngeal differences with regard to gender reveals that vocal fold length is significantly greater in the pubertal male than in the pubertal female. The vocal folds of the adult male are approximately 30 percent larger than those of the adult female (Ingo Titze, "Fundamental Frequency Scaling and Voice Classification," *The NATS Bulletin,* September/October, 1980). Small wonder that the young male singer who undergoes this remarkable laryngeal growth is unable to parallel the technical accomplishments of his female counterpart at the same chronological age. With the exception of some few practical editions, most of them edited by singing teachers who have understood the *tessitura* problems of the youthful male voice, many published transpositions for "low" voice are more appropriate to the mature male voice (or the mezzo-soprano) than to the college-age baritone, and much of the material published for "high" voice is simply not accessible for the young tenor.

If one accepts the premise that the male voice experiences a later maturation than does the female, one may feel inclined to argue for delaying vocal study for the young male. However, the American academic world is not structured to accommodate that possibility. One finishes high school at about age eighteen and one goes off to college—in this case, to music school. In the competitive music world, a delay of several years in general musical studies is not advisable.

Fortunately, a number of voice competitions for youthful performers take into account the maturation differences between the sexes via the literatures recommended and different age limits for participants in the male and female vocal categories. Despite that favorable situation, one hears at contests for the young singing artist the general lament, "Where are the male singers?" Part of the answer to that question must be that the instrument of the college and university male singer, in contrast to that of the female, is not yet sufficiently mature to compete. (Of course, many exceptions can be cited.)

There is, however, no cause for despair! As the years pass for these individuals, the balance of inequalities may shift: the soubrette/coloratura who began so beautifully with her display of *fioriture* and controlled *sostenuto* at age seventeen may discover that not many years beyond the age of forty it becomes more difficult to continue singing that literature with the same ease, while her baritone companion may continue to perform his repertory for an additional decade or two. The longevity of vocal types of either gender may indeed be related to the schedule of laryngeal maturation; numerous examples of dramatic voices that have matured late and shown astounding longevity come to mind. In any event, it would appear that vocal equality among the sexes is not temporally synchronized. Performance capabilities at both extremes of the performing years may be related partly to the fact that larynges are created male and female. Vocal pedagogy must take this into account.

78

In Search of the Tenth Rib

A major part of vocal pedagogy is directed toward the coordination of breath with laryngeal action. Not all techniques of singing are in agreement as to how best to accomplish that coordination. Varying systems of "breath support" may offer completely opposing views on how to manage the breath for the tasks of singing. Still others avoid the whole controversy by ignoring how airflow rates affect phonation.

Two prevalent techniques of breath management are the "down and out" and the "up and in" approaches, in which specific kinds of abdominal actions are recommended. Perhaps the most prominent and efficient approach to breath coordination in singing is yet another system, the centuries-old *appoggio* technique, in which the singer learns to establish and maintain a dynamic balance among muscles of the abdomen and the torso. By so doing, the rate of breath emission for energized phonation is evenly regulated, shunning either breathy or pressed phonation. There is an increase in the ability to sustain long phrases, and to renew the breath efficiently and silently for subsequent phrases.

In *appoggio* technique, during the inspiratory gesture of the breath cycle the singer is aware that expansion takes place in the lateral and anterior (side and front) abdominal wall, just below the rib cage, that is, below the tenth rib. Expansion is also experienced in the lower dorsal (back) region, where the eleventh and twelfth ribs are located. The extent of this expansion is largely dependent on muscle development and coordination in those regions. The accomplished singer/teacher has, in all probability, been making use of these muscle groups for years and is more muscularly developed in that region than is the student singer. A young singer with limited expansion capability should be assured that, with time and persistence, through the use of onset exercises, muscle development will occur.

It is easy, however, to overlook individual morphology—the topography of the body. Teacher and singer may have different types of physique, particularly with regard to torso length and rib cage structure. Some singers have short rib cages, with considerable space between the bottom of the cage and the crest of the ilium (hip bone). Other singers have long cages that extend nearly to the iliac region.

Although an acquired muscle coordination is essential to any singer who uses the *appoggio* system, there is danger that the teacher may look for muscular expansion too high or too low in the student's body. For example, many tenors and a number of baritones have shorter rib cages than do most bass-baritones and basses. The short-ribbed teacher may demonstrate muscular expansion on his own body and look for it to take place in what he mistakenly assumes to be a comparable anatomical area of his long-caged pupil. In trying to match teacher's model, the student may attempt excessive action directly at mid-rib level. The long-caged teacher, male or female, may unwittingly be inducing expansion for the short-caged singer too low in the abdominal wall.

As a rule, females have longer rib cages in proportion to their torsos than do males; they tend to have less space between the bottom of the cage and the top of the hip bone than do most men. In some cases, especially with compactly built female singers, the ribcage sits almost directly on the crest of the ilium. This sometimes gives the impression that abdominal action occurs at a lower point in the torso of the female than in that of the male. However, women do not breathe for singing in a fashion different from men. The process and the results are the same: longer duration in retaining expansion (the position of inspiration) of the abdominal wall.

It is not only the intercostals and the diaphragm (the chief muscles of respiration) that participate in the movements of the respiratory cycle. Although the organs of respiration are not in the lower part of the torso, the abdominal musculature, together with the positioning muscles of the upper torso, play a major role in retarding the inward collapse of the rib cage, and they delay the ascent rate of the diaphragm. The axial alignment of the body, a primary requirement for the development of *appoggio* technique, permits these coordinated muscular systems of the torso to assist in managing the breath for singing.

Before describing abdominal muscle activities to the student or employing the historic onset exercises, it is wise to locate exactly the bottom of the rib cage on the singer's body. Using only one's own physique as model may be misleading. Search for the tenth rib!

79

Teaching Voices of the Opposite Gender

Some female teachers of singing are most comfortable teaching only females, and there are male teachers who feel most successful teaching male voices. Yet most people who make their livelihood as singing teachers must deal with both female and male singers. Is it possible to be equally successful with both sexes?

There can be no argument that each vocal category requires its own particular set of technical nuances. But there are overriding physiologic and acoustic functions involved in singing that are more common among all voices than are the differences dependent solely on vocal category.

For example, although the events of registration and the problems they often present are not identical between males and females (even within the large *Fach* divisions of both genders), the principles of vocal registration are applicable to all voices. Similarly, although vowel modification occurs at differing points in the scale, the need for vowel migration while retaining vowel recognition remains essential to all. An even scale is an even scale whatever the vocal category, and the teacher of singing should understand what technical means may be brought to bear in its accomplishment. These principles transcend gender.

Admittedly, modeling, which plays an important role in the teaching of any instrument, may temporarily prove problematic if the student who stands before you is not of your own vocal type or gender. The tenor teacher of baritones has to learn how to model principles while avoiding the inducement of imitation of his own sound, as must the bass or baritone teacher of tenors. The mezzo-soprano teacher is in a similar situation with her soprano students, and the soprano with her mezzos. However, the problem of *Fach* difference is exaggerated to such an extent that some teachers avoid modeling entirely, under the false assumption that the student will "imitate" the teacher's timbre. This notion is particularly fallacious when it comes to male teachers modeling for females, and female teachers for males. The teacher who sings well, models well. He or she is able to show with his or her own instrument degrees of efficiency in the production of vocal sound. The student imitates the principle being modeled, not the voice of the teacher. Each voice will find its individuality through the application of common principles, not through the imposition of one uniform studio sound. If the students who study with a teacher all have the same identifiable sound, the teaching is faulty. Such "studio" sound is as frequently present with the nonmodeling teacher as with the teacher who models. Modeling is not its cause, the teaching itself is.

With regard to the teaching of female students by males, some aspects of vocal sound may be usefully demonstrated in *falsetto,* because falsetto (which by no means is the same as the so-called "head voice" of historic, traditional vocal pedagogy) is the sound imitative of the female voice, of which most male singers are fully capable. Falsetto is particularly useful in demonstrating vowel differentiation and vowel tracking, vibrancy, and aspects of phrase shaping. The varying energy levels between males and females is often best imitated for female students by the male in falsetto voice. It is also the case that many female singers have success demonstrating so-called chest voice for their male singers, although out of regard for the teacher's own vocal health caution must be exercised. An occasional demonstration by a female teacher of the kind of energy and timbre she uses in chest or chest mixtures can be useful (although not absolutely necessary) in teaching the young male singer.

It is, of course, possible to teach singing without modeling; some of the greatest vocal pedagogues were themselves not remarkable singers. A female teacher who knows how to convey solid principles through specific language can be just as successful teaching a male student as she is in teaching her females; the informed male teacher can be equally efficacious in teaching both sexes, if he commands clear pedagogical language. To avoid modeling simply because the student is of a different gender is to cut oneself off from a major pedagogical tool.

There does come a time for most students of singing when technique may be further enhanced through study with a person of the same sex. This may also apply by extension to vocal categories within the gender. However, many premier singers have never studied with a teacher of their own sex or *Fach*. Yet there are many cases of teachers who have more success with one category of singer than with another. This most often happens when teacher and singer are of the same gender and vocal category. One recalls the dramatic soprano who is unsuccessful in teaching *soubrette* voices, and the *leggiero* tenor teacher whose baritones sound emasculated or excessively bright.

Because the principles of good technical training deal universally with breath management, laryngeal freedom, and resonance balancing, regardless of gender or of vocal category, the good teacher of singing should be equally confident in teaching both male and female students. If instructions are conveyed through nonspecific language, the difficulty in teaching a person of either sex is increased. Students are ill-advised to think they must study only with a person of their own vocal category.

The teacher who understands the workings of the vocal instrument, who possesses the ability to diagnose problems and to offer prescriptions for their correction, and who can do so in communicable, precise language will happily teach singers of both genders and all vocal categories.

80

Instinctive, Artistic Singing

The long morning had been spent in considering rudimentary information on the acoustics of the singing voice. The singer's formant had been presented and explanations given as to how its presence throughout the vocal range, regardless of the fundamental being sung, could produce the timbre so desired by most performers of serious vocal music. Through the recognition of the "ring" associated with the singer's formant, a number of participating singers gave evidence of improvement in the general character and ease of the sounds they produced. Great excitement had been generated over the spectacular improvement in vocal quality among several singers as a result of new understanding about the manner in which vocal timbre is filtered by the appropriate configurations of the vocal tract.

At the break for lunch, one teacher/observer, who had earlier expressed undisguised horror at the presence of an overhead projector and a slide machine used to illustrate vowel formants and the singer's formant, made the following comment:

> That was all very interesting and I don't deny that it shows the lecturer has a lot of knowledge, but of course it has absolutely nothing to do with singing, because singing is instinctive and artistic.

At which point a babble of voices in several languages broke forth in protest against such a limited view.

The hypothesis that singing is an instinctive and artistic activity that should not be influenced by factual information regarding the acoustics of the singing voice, although rapidly losing ground, is still held in some quarters. It contains, on one level, elements of indisputable truth: artistry and the instinct for singing are present in the performance of any fine singer. The sharper analysis of the argument, however, concerns whether artistry and instinct can find ready expression when technical impediments remain.

It is not always possible to have a comfortable dialogue with people who resist information on the underlying physiology and the acoustic properties of the singing voice. The reason is that some teachers may unconsciously fear that new information will upset long-held concepts about singing. They resemble all doctrinaire thinkers who do not wish to reconsider their opinions in the face of new discoveries; they are not unlike persons who hesitate to explore intellectual horizons for fear such activity might lead to a modification or abandonment of cherished opinions.

Any such hesitancy to become informed as to the function of the singing instrument is particularly deplorable because much of the physiological and acoustic information now available through the means of scientific instrumentation strongly verifies many of the empirical notions found in historic vocal pedagogy. One would, however, be less than candid not to comment that the same scientific instrumentation often proves a number of pedagogical concepts to have only limited bases in fact, which is, of course, what makes some teachers afraid to explore factual information.

The argument against the use of acoustic, physiological, and even medical examination is often made because it is assumed that artistic, instinctive singing and factual information are irreconcilable. In the conversation that resulted from the incident described above, it became clear that the teacher/observer honestly believed that factual information tends to vitiate artistic imagination.

A danger exists in all pedagogy that a singer may fail to progress beyond thinking technically during performances. Whether founded in fact or in myth, technique should never become the paramount factor in performance. Even if it unintentionally does, accurate information about function will probably inhibit artistry less than will *myths* regarding function.

Openness of mind to varying aesthetics of the singing voice is highly commendable and should be promoted. There simply is no *one* way to sing; no teacher, no method, and no school holds exclusive rights to excellence in singing. Although it may be true that there have been a few teachers of singing of the past who had no idea whether the vocal folds are placed vertically or horizontally, that is hardly license for the rest of us to avoid learning about the physical action of the vocal folds during phonation. Some successful medicine was practiced before the discovery of the circulation of the blood, but one would hardly recommend being treated today by a doctor who is unaware of that important physical phenomenon. Why then should the teacher of singing, who deals daily with acoustics, be afraid of knowing how the voice works acoustically? I personally have never experienced a single voice lesson, among the nearly thousand voice lessons I have observed during pedagogical studies, in which the teacher did not deal extensively in acoustics and physiology. As soon as a student is told anything about breath management ("support") or resonation ("timbre"), the teacher is dealing in physiology and acoustics. Why deal in bad physiology and incorrect acoustics when fact is available?

Anthropological studies inform us that as humankind adapted to a changing environment, we came to depend less on instinct and to rely more on our inventive faculties in solving new problems. As a result, our instinctual responses are far less sharp than those of other creatures whose survival continues to lie chiefly in instinct, not intellect. (Most higher religions see this rational and adaptive facility as separating humankind from fellow creatures, and as bringing the human personality into a unique relationship with spiritual forces.) An infant deprived of speech sounds will not learn to speak. Communicative phonation must be learned through contact and does not result purely from instinct. Through imitating the behavior of other persons, the mother in particular, each newborn infant learns about the world around her or him. On the other hand, many animals enjoy a fair degree of self-sufficiency from an early age (how beautiful the birth of the giraffe or the pony, and their ability to almost immediately cope with movement!) but lack extensive ability for continued intellectual and personal growth.

A uniquely human component is *artistry,* which takes the means of nature and elevates them to a new dimension. Certainly, to communicate the poetry and drama of civilization through the medium of vocal sound, as does the cultivated singing voice, is one of the highest achievements of the human personality. Yet such communication can take place only through the means of the physical instrument of the singer. How can it then logically be maintained that ignorance of how that instrument works can produce artistic capability when artistry can only be as good as function?

One can be sympathetic to the kind of mind that wishes to be solely expressive and entirely instinctive. Sometimes teachers of singing themselves come out of very successful performance careers in which skills in handling the problems of their own singing instruments were established by empirical means. Certain facets of vocalism are of little concern to them, because those aspects were always under control or because charismatic performance abilities masked a number of remaining technical faults. Then comes the transition from stage to studio, where not every student has so easily acquired that particular kind of coordination or performance charisma. The instinctive habits that successfully propelled the artist-now-turned-teacher through technical difficulties do not rub off onto the less instinctive student. The student singer needs to understand the underlying causes of poor function and how such function can be improved. A student's violation of acoustics may be of a nature that never occurred to the teacher as performer. All the artistry and instinct in the world will not suffice to assist in the solution of such vocal problems. While in some instances the viewpoint that factual information is detrimental to artistry may produce only minimal pedagogical loss, there are other cases in which the teacher may unwittingly be hanging an albatross around the neck of the unsuspecting student.

The argument against the use of available scientific information is that voice teachers should leave acoustics to the acoustician and questions regarding physiological function and health to scientists and doctors. "Voice teachers should be teaching singing, not science," runs that refrain. There can be no disagreement with that statement, but it does not logically follow that the teacher of singing should remain in ignorance about important basic facets of his or her professional work.

This dichotomy in vocal pedagogy—science versus artistry—is not as old as one might presume. Most of the historic treatises that are called upon today in support of empirical teaching were written by the forerunners of voice science. It is difficult to find a major treatise on singing from the past that does not deal in the then-current information regarding physiology and acoustics. Perhaps the time has come for the teacher who believes that such information has "nothing to do with singing" to reassess the underlying reasons for such a viewpoint. If it turns out, as one hears at times, "that it just takes too much time to get into all of that," or that it is "too complex," one is tempted to suggest that perhaps the teacher should reconsider the extent of commitment demanded by the teaching of singing. Artistry is not just instinctive. It is also acquired.

81

Let's Build a Straw Man! (The Technique-versus-Artistry Debate)

The increasing interest in functional aspects of the singing voice may be expected to cause a degree of apprehension among teachers who have not yet had an opportunity to acquaint themselves with the developing body of literature on the use and care of the professional voice. This comes largely because of an understandable concern that some long-held assumptions may be called into question. Such anxiety has led, in some quarters, to the setting up of a pedagogical "straw man," an easily toppled caricature of functional vocal instruction.

This straw-man construction consists of the notion that vocal technique based on physiology and acoustics is to be mastered before any attention is turned to musical and artistic factors. When this flimsy and unreal figure is erected on a hypothetical pedagogical pole, he is, of course, easily assailed and deposed. One is then freed from the troublesome matter of acquiring factual information and from submitting to the discipline of learning what has happened in the voice teaching profession over the past few decades with regard to research into professional voice training and usage. A publication for teachers of singing recently posed the question, Should vocal technique be taught independently of artistry? Whatever its intent, the question served as a ready target for those who wish to portray precise technical study as being detrimental to artistry.

No musician in any field could support the assumption that mechanical technique must be mastered before attention can be directed to music-making. To treat the question as a serious pedagogical premise is to hide behind a straw-man argument and to predetermine the answers. Such a question interjects an artificial dichotomy into vocal performance pedagogy. If there exists anyone who would answer such a question affirmatively, he or she remains to be identified.

The creators of the straw man forget that most persons involved in both past and current voice research have themselves been serious artists and performers. However, the straw-man vocal pedagogue is made to resemble the mad scientist of the arcane laboratory who searches for alchemistic solutions to vocal problems. He or she is generally charged with searching for a "new way" to sing. Mainly as a result of the developing cooperation among persons who work with vocal professionals, today's teacher of singing has a number of means for verifying or modifying concepts that in the past often divided vocal pedagogy into opposing camps. A new way to sing is not his or her goal.

There is no logical reason to erect artificial walls between artistry and the elements of skill that together make up that art. The "either technique or art" syndrome raises such barriers and is detrimental to the furtherance of vocal pedagogy. To hold the position that one should deal only with artistry while ignoring the voice as a functioning instrument upon which artistry is built is equally untenable. Nonetheless, one hears the straw-man argument answered with the viewpoint that, through imaginative treatment of text and music, all technical problems in singing will disappear. That is, of course, patently nonsensical.

As soon as any aspect of vocal sound is discussed with a student, the teacher is dealing in physiology and acoustics, often of an inventive nature. When any teacher of singing comments on posture, diction, vowels, breath, agility, *sostenuto,* or dynamic levels, that teacher is dealing directly with physical materials. The straw-man creators prefer to ignore what is factually known about the voice as an instrument, and to offer solutions that seldom stand the scrutiny of reality.

Surely no one can believe in good faith that in today's highly competitive performance world there exist numbers of voice teachers who train professional singers by means of barren techniques devoid of artistic consideration. What is increasingly clear is that teachers of singing who avail themselves of information in all areas, including the psychology of performance, musical style, linguistic accuracy, and vocal function, are producing young professionals ready to enter the real performance world. (Many of these teachers and singers are North Americans, it must be noted.) Today's wise teachers avail themselves of *all* these tools, as did the major teachers of the past. One should entertain skepticism as to the actual intent of the person who actively campaigns against the dissemination of factual information and who hides behind the "I only teach what is musical" mantle. Musicality is precisely what vocal technique examined in the light of vocal function can facilitate.

It is time to forgo the foolish partisanship that comes from trying to divide vocal pedagogy into two opposing worlds labeled "science" and "art." It simply is not the case that current vocal pedagogy is becoming "scientific to the detriment of artistry." The only reason for any form of technical vocal study is to be able to sing in an artistic and communicative manner. Function and art cannot be long separated at any phase of development.

The next time you meet a teacher of singing at an international professional meeting who expends great energy setting up the straw-man technique/artistry pedagogical dichotomy, and who at every turn expresses disdain for those who labor to further the accomplishment of artistry through examination of the voice as an instrument, ask yourself what motivates that teacher.

82

The Misuses of "Scientific Information" in the Teaching of Singing

A common theme from this writer has been a plea for the removal of vocal pedagogy from dependency on mythological and imaginative speculation regarding vocal function. He often has remarked on the vacuity of vocal techniques that are not based on verifiable information regarding the singing voice as a physical and an acoustic instrument. The reason for this crusade is that anyone who has made a comparative study of pedagogical systems (some with large numbers of adherents) is amazed at the number of pedagogical systems that are based on inaccurate information as to anatomical structures of the head, neck, and torso, and on ignorance of the basic rules of acoustics.

This is not an innocuous situation, because singers tend to try to make the body work the way they have been told it operates. Certain singing techniques produce results in direct opposition to normal modes of physiological behavior, even to the extent of inducing vocal pathologies. Then the rest of the vocal pedagogy community has to try "recovery pedagogy" to help those singers regain normal function. The victims of misguided pedagogies suffer loss of time and money, and, above all, lack of success in their chosen field.

It might then be assumed that the answer for the teacher in search of functional information would be to turn to those manuals that purport to justify a particular vocal pedagogy through the application of scientific information. Unfortunately, such a route is not necessarily free of some serious pitfalls.

An example of such perils can be identified in a publication released by a major publishing house: *Voice and Song,* by Sine Butenschøn and Hans M. Borchgrevink (Cambridge University Press: Cambridge, England, 1982). In the preface to this volume, the reader is informed that scientific explanations are to be presented side by side with pedagogical accounts of a vocal technique termed "the dorsal method." The authors put forward the appealing viewpoint that knowledge and understanding of the physiological processes of singing, based on objective scientific data regarding anatomy, physiology, and phonetics, will verify the superiority of this vocal technique. So far, so good.

Then we read on and discover that the excellent anatomical figures throughout the book correspond only minimally to the recommended pedagogy. The volume falls neatly into an identifiable (though by no means chief) branch of the Northern European School. It advocates some of the commonly encountered technical devices dictated by the aesthetic demands of that school. But the application of science to pedagogy is difficult to discern in this book, although it announces its intent is just that.

For example, we are informed that the ventral muscles of the head *(longus capitis)* and the neck *(longus colli)* expand the thorax when unstressed vowels are sung, and that during the singing of staccato this portion of the musculature "snatches the tone." We are advised, without scientific verification, that

> [f]or [ɑ] the entire vertebral column is stretched as a single unit, whereas for [i] the pull on the vertebral column starts at the topmost joint (the 'nodding joint'), and the column is stretched from that point. In this way the [i] can be yawned 'further in and higher up' in the resonance cavity (don't forget about the jaw 'giving way.'). (p. 25)

It is also explained that the dorsal method of singing aims at tone production through a reflex mechanism comparable to retching, which "involves a tremendous expansion of the back and a violent jerk in the abdominal wall that normally causes emptying of the stomach in response to reflexes from the lower pharynx." (p. 24)

With regard to the conduction of frequencies, we are later assured (although no supporting documentation is given) that "in Caruso's case vibrations were registered right down to his fingertips." (Dare one ask when and under what conditions such vibrations in Caruso's fingertips were measured?) Further, the reader will be intrigued to learn that "in collapsed falsetto the tone is supported above the navel," that in an ascending scale the thorax becomes progressively broader and flatter, and that in a descending sequence of notes the thorax naturally becomes less flattened. During proper singing, we are instructed, the sternum (breastbone) recedes.

Perhaps most typically, concentration on pelvic contraction appears to play an important role in this particular Nordic/Germanic school:

> Rather suddenly the iliopsoas [the muscle of the loins; the great flexor muscle of the hips, constituting the iliac and the great psoas muscles] becomes the dominant muscle system. This sudden change takes place at a pitch 'area' known as das *Loch der Frauenstimme,* literally 'the hole in a woman's voice.' If sufficient support is not forthcoming here, the singer will suddenly be left without breath. The crisis may occur on f_1 as well as d_1 or c_1. If, however, one allows the iliopsoas to take the lead in the stretch, whilst leaving the cervical muscular activity unchanged, the support will adjust to the note. The result will be no *Loch* and no difficulty in breath control (the name 'hole' in a woman's voice may be explained by the characteristic shape of the female pelvis, deeper and broader than that of the male) and the compensatory greater curvatures in the lumbar vertebrae, which influences the direction of force and thus the action of the iliopsoas in women. (p. 34)

In "scientific" support of these assumptions, the book offers an excellent illustration of the iliopsoas and abdominal muscles! This volume, which bears the dedication "To James F. Bosma, who showed that the vowel is formed in the upper pharynx, thus explaining the basic physiology of the dorsal method of singing," is not an isolated case of the misapplication of "science" in attempting a justification for some traditionally recognizable methodology. A number of other books in the comparative vocal pedagogy library, some highly touted, quote respectable medical sources and offer excellent charts and drawings that depict normal physiological function. In some cases, the charts and anatomical illustrations have little or no relationship to the pedagogical portions of the text. Others show imaginative drawings of the supposed routes the "column of air" follows in the singing voice, pharynges and sinuses in sizes and shapes unrecognized by anatomists, and "resonance" charts that have no relationship to what is known about vocal acoustics. The best advice to the reader of such publications is *caveat emptor!* Perhaps the "floating cloud" and "hovering bird" pedagogue can actually be matched for imaginativeness and invention by the pseudo-scientific teacher!

Does this mean that as teachers of singing we are then excused from examining the physical aspects of the art of singing? Of course not. As in any area of information, one must be on guard against anyone's favorite hypothesis (including one's own) that is supported by less than accurately measurable (or by totally inaccurate) "scientific fact."

83

Relax and Sing?

As do all fields of endeavor, vocal pedagogy has its trends of the moment. Certain notions about singing come to the fore and occupy center stage for a period of time, then gradually drift into the background. There will be a rash of articles on a particular pedagogical topic, and several innovative master-class teachers will center their instructional method on it. Such notions are usually related to prevalent ideas that surface from the surrounding culture. They tend to follow a cyclical existence, rising and falling.

For example, with the surge of interest in physical exercise for body conditioning, strenuous physical warm-up exercises for the singing voice moved into prominence (with the added virtue of being not directly related to any special vocal technique, thereby mostly avoiding controversy). As some let-up in health-faddism ensued, fewer singers were intrigued by running, jumping, and leaping about, or by lifting objects while singing. When yoga began to take on popular cultural appeal, some voice teachers were quick to find correlations between breath-management for singing and yoga exercises. Right and left nostril breathing for singers has, however, lost favor with the passage of time. Devices for controlling the breath cycle that pertain to meditation have proven less adequate for the visceral activities of the singing voice; such techniques appear headed for the wings.

Stress and its resulting physical tension are at the moment a favorite topic of the popular psychology, so it is not at all surprising that there is currently an increasing interest in techniques of relaxation as they may relate to the singing voice. The singer, it is reasoned, must learn to relax in order to overcome whatever tension may be present. No one can deny that tension is a major problem for some singers, and that a singer who appears to be tense, or is suffering from performance anxiety, quickly diminishes the effectiveness of his or her efforts.

Well and good. Some consideration, however, needs to be given to the opposite side of this pedagogical coin. Although some singers do suffer from excessive tension, perhaps an equal or greater number of them exhibit an undesirable lack of energization, and insufficient muscular engagement in one or more parts of the coordinated singing instrument (the body!). Any time phonation takes place, muscular action occurs. Functional efficiency of the intrinsic laryngeal musculature is in part dependent on the dynamic balances of the supportive musculature of the neck and torso. Good vocal-fold occlusion and freedom of action within the larynx involve a constant shifting of muscular balances, all below the level of conscious control. The many configurations of the laryngeal muscles necessitated by changes of vowel, pitch, dynamic level, and vocal coloration can occur with freedom only when well-balanced muscular action (the avoidance of hyperfunction in some muscles and hypofunction in others) responds to appropriate subglottic pressure and airflow rate.

The quality of voicing is dependent on what happens at the larynx (the vibrator), subglottically (below the larynx) with regard to pressure and airflow (the motor), and within the supraglottic vocal tract filter (the resonator). No static relationship should exist among these contributors, nor do the necessary changes among them occur in a state of muscular relaxation. A dynamic muscle balance ensures flexibility, and is dependent on an alert ready-for-action condition in the body.

In all physical activity requiring an unusual degree of energy beyond the passive at-rest condition—singing certainly is a prime example—there must be a keying-up of mental and physical resources, a sense of body alertness, a psychological preparation for action. Such flexible muscular fine-tuning prior to action is evident throughout the animal kingdom as well. Notice the play of tension and freedom in the subconsciously controlled movements of your cat stalking an unsuspecting bird.

It simply is not the case that the body is in a state of relaxation at such moments. Why should the singer or voice teacher pretend that it is?

Some of the least impressive examples of singing result from overly cautious teaching in which any application of power or of energy is considered "pushing." Often unrecognized is the fact that poor vocal-fold occlusion, during which escaping breath is audible, is extremely unhealthy. In trying to find the right dynamic muscle balance for the singing voice, the habitually underenergized singer may well do more damage to the vocal instrument than does the person who occasionally experiences some unwanted degree of resistance at the glottis (too great a sphincteral response by the larynx). While "pushing" the voice is to be strenuously avoided, so should flaccid vocalization that is lacking in energy and vitality. Young voices must be handled with care, and should not be set tasks that go beyond the capabilities of the instrument at that particular time. Yet many voices fail to develop to their fullest capacity because those singers have been constantly advised to feel relaxed during singing.

One of the chief sources of tension for the singer comes from erroneous concepts of breath management. Tensions induced in the hypogastric and umbilical/epigastric regions of the torso, under the assumption that they "support the voice," are not constructive. The principle of muscular involvement, expressed through agility, flexibility, and suppleness, as these factors pertain in any coordinated athletic activity, should be present as well in singing; they do not occur through induced tensions. A good "breath support" technique should permit a singer to move freely during singing, to bend, dance, twist, crawl, kneel, sit, lie down, or stand quietly without motion throughout most of the singing range. No part of the body should be in a state of perceivable tension during the act of singing, but tonicity must be present.

When singing, one should be in a state of "relaxation" roughly equivalent to that experienced by a confident player on the tennis court, the skilled contestant at a swimming match, the Olympic figure skater, or the child about to take off on the hundred yard dash on the grammar school playground, waiting for the count of three. Ready for action, not "relaxed."

False assumptions about relaxing while singing often have unfortunate effects on communication during performance. When one has something of importance to share with others, one is eager to do so. The deadpan inward-retreat of the "relaxed" singer is seldom enjoyable either to watch or to hear. Vitality and dynamic presence are attributes of the artistic personality.

An occasional admonition to relax may be appropriate in assisting a singer to avoid hyperfunction in some muscle group. Any singer who experiences tension (as opposed to physical involvement) is not singing well. Frequently the problem is not one of tension, but of inertia; a lack of vitality induces dysfunction. General suggestions about relaxation for singing often exacerbate the very lack of dynamic coordination that causes tension and performance anxiety. Joyous singing is vital singing!

84

Easily, Not Lazily (Tonicity in the Singing Instrument)

Voice teachers are right to guard against "pushing" voices. "Pushing" (pressed phonation) results from an excessively long closure phase of the vocal folds in response to high airflow and elevated rates of subglottic pressure. In attempting to sufficiently energize the body to meet the demands of long phrases and high-lying *tessitura* and intensity (volume) levels, some singers induce too much laryngeal resistance to airflow. The most basic consideration in vocal pedagogy is how to teach proper balance between freedom and energization.

Although the vocal instrument may be viewed in several ways, one of the most convenient points of departure is to consider it an aerodynamic/myoelastic instrument, as Janwillem van den Berg of Groningen University Hospital, Netherlands, advised several decades ago. That is, the muscular vocal mechanism functions in response to air pressures. There must be fine coordination between the power source (the breath—the aerodynamic motor) and the vibrating source (the larynx—the myoelastic instrument). Much of pedagogical language addresses itself to a search for achieving the most efficient way to combine these two factors. (Their relationship with the supraglottic resonator system—an equally important part of the total mechanism—is not part of this brief discussion.)

"Pressed phonation" describes excessive laryngeal closure in response to excessive airflow. "Flow phonation" (also sometimes termed "free flow phonation") describes the proper supply of breath for the needs of the phonatory tasks. Certainly, the wise teacher of singing should search for free-flowing phonation and work against pressed, forced phonation.

It is exactly at this point in vocal pedagogy that some counterproductive factors stemming from excellent intentions may enter. Some teachers, in the hope of reducing valvular tension in the larynx, induce too high an airflow rate. They mistakenly assume that the extent of the closure phase of the rapidly adducting and abducting glottis is identical to that in the far-less-energized speech mode. They fail to take into account the parameters of *tessitura,* range, intensity, and duration of the breath cycle required by the singing voice. Excess air passing over the vocal folds is not conducive to either stable vocal timbre or to healthy phonation.

If the laryngeal valve is too tightly occluded, with an excessive glottal closure phase, it is possible to induce "flow phonation" by momentarily requesting a sigh (which results in rapid airflow), or even through suggesting a "relaxing" yawn. However, both devices, being associated with physical weariness, carry the peril of substituting breathy phonation for the proper balance between airflow and laryngeal response. The same distortions that are audible in "sighing speech" and in "yawning speech" are then even more marked in the sung vocal timbre. A momentary yawn, in fact, may be part of the body's preparation for a subsequent action, but yawning should not be extended into the activity itself.

A far more useful technique is to achieve the exactitude of vocal fold approximation and airflow through the discipline of the precise onset (the "attack") and the release. The latter is not only the termination of the phonation but also the renewal of the energizing source. The tonicity of the singing instrument is thereby maintained. One can apply energy with ease, but one cannot sing lazily and expect good results.

85

The Effect of Tongue Position on Spectra in Singing

For every kind of beasts, and of birds, and of serpents, and of things in the sea, is tamed, and hath been tamed of mankind.

But the tongue can no man tame; it is an unruly evil full of deadly poison.

(JAMES 3: 7, 8)

Although St. James's charge against the tongue was leveled on the moral plane, James has earned hagiolatrous appreciation from succeeding genera-

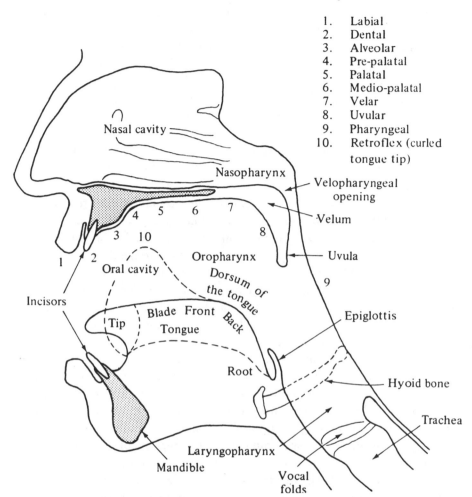

Some places of articulation

1. Labial
2. Dental
3. Alveolar
4. Pre-palatal
5. Palatal
6. Medio-palatal
7. Velar
8. Uvular
9. Pharyngeal
10. Retroflex (curled tongue tip)

Figure 1. A schematic view of the articulators, vocal tract cavities, and places of articulation. From *Normal Aspects of Speech, Hearing, and Language.* © 1973 by Allyn and Bacon. Reprinted by permission.

tions of singers and teachers of singing who must deal physically with that "unruly evil" during singing.

Attached to the hyoid bone, the tongue extends forward to the lips, thus occupying nearly the entire vocal tract (chief resonating system). The tongue is the most important of the articulators, and the shape it assumes and the space it occupies in the resonator tube help to determine the acoustic and phonetic aspects of any phonatory event (Kantner and West 1960).

The tongue may be hypothetically divided into regions (Figure 1). The tip (foremost edge) of the dorsum of the tongue (the upper surface of the tongue) is nearest the edge of the lower front teeth; the blade, or front part of the tongue (the tip included) is located below the upper alveolar ridge; the front area of the dorsum lies beneath the hard palate; the back area of the tongue lies beneath the soft palate; the root of the tongue (the most posterior area) is fastened to the hyoid bone, to the soft palate, and to the pharynx (Daniloff 1973). The under-surface of the tongue is connected to the mandible (the jaw). The tongue is free anteriorly, laterally, and dorsally (Zemlin 1968).

Hardcastle (1976) identifies seven articulatory parameters for the specification of tongue movement and tongue configuration during phonation: (1) horizontal and (2) vertical movements of the body of the tongue; (3) horizontal and (4) vertical movements of the tip-blade of the tongue; (5) convex-concave configurations of the tongue body in relation to the palate; (6) central grooving throughout the entire length of the tongue; and (7) spreading or tapering of the dorsum of the tongue.

According to Malmberg (1963), articulation may be classified with regard to the extent of tongue engagement at the teeth (dental), at the upper gum ridge (alveolar), at the front of the hard palate (pre-palatal), at the highest part of the palate (medio-palatal), at the junction of hard and soft palates (post-palatal), and at the uvula (velar).

The changing relationships of the buccal and pharyngeal resonators, which are necessary to vowel definition, are largely determined by the changing positions of the mobile tongue within the resonator tube. In the vowel [i], the elevated frontal tongue posture diminishes the volume of the mouth, thereby increasing pharyngeal volume. As a result, the formant in the upper portion of the spectrum rises. (The regions of the spectrum in which frequency components are relatively stronger are known as formants [Ladefoged 1962].) Contrariwise, when the back of the tongue rises toward the velum, as in the vowel [ʊ], and pharyngeal volume is decreased and mouth volume increases, the lower formant is strengthened. Ladefoged (1962) has illustrated this relationship of tongue posture both to vowel definition and to the spectral envelope (Figure 2).

Laryngeally generated sound may be distorted by improper tongue position in relation to vocal fold adjustment. For example, if the tongue assumes the position for [i] when the vowel [ɔ] is required, acoustic conflict and vowel distortion occur. Elsewhere in the vocal tract, additional adjustment must be made to compensate acoustically for the "wrong" tongue position. This may result in an alteration of the singer's formant or in extraneous muscle tension, and may even exert influence on the perception of pitch accuracy. Any such adjustment violates efficient function and demands additional effort at the level of the larynx.

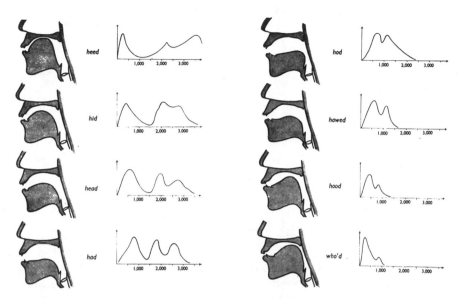

Figure 2. Based on data obtained from X-ray photographs of the vocal tract during phonation of various vowels. Reprinted from *Elements of Acoustic Phonetics*, by Peter Ladefoged, © 1962. Used by permission of the University of Chicago Press. All rights reserved. Tenth Impression, 1974.

During the production of a number of speech sounds (including all vowels and a number of consonants in most Western languages) the entire front portion of the tongue lies behind and in contact with the inner surface of the lower teeth, as in the posture for the production of the neutral vowel [ə]. During phonetic alteration, in those instances, the dorsum of the tongue assumes varying degrees of flattening or of elevation, but the anterior rim of the tongue remains engaged with the lower teeth, as when one says "m-hm!"

Spectrograms may be used to indicate the influence that varying tongue positions produce on the nature of vocal timbre. Spectrograms in this study were obtained through the use of a Ubiquitous Spectrum Analyzer, Type UA-6B (Federal Scientific). The nominal frequency resolution was positioned 30 cm from the singer's mouth. The designated tone was produced by the singer under normal (as opposed to non-echoic) acoustical conditions; a hold circuit was activated, and the spectrograms were recorded on an X-Y recording device.

Figure 3 indicates the spectral analysis of the vowel [ɔ] at approximately C_4 (262 Hz), sung by a professional tenor. The tongue is here in contact with the inner surface of the lower front teeth (not at their roots), inducing proper vocal-tract configuration for the selected vowel. In the spectrogram

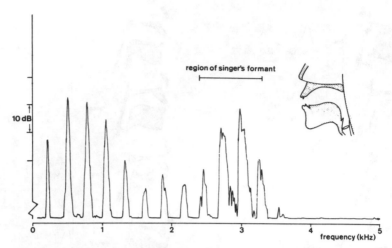

Figure 3. The vowel [ɔ] (as in "hawed") sung at approximately 262 Hz (C$_4$), with proper tongue posture. The spectral envelope indicates desirable vowel definition and singer's formant. (Note the favorable balance in sound energy between the region of vowel definition and that of the singer's formant.)

(Figure 3), the regions defining the area of the first formant of the singing voice (left part of the spectrogram), which ensures the "depth" and "warmth" of the voice, and those (right of the spectrogram) that correspond to the singer's formant or "the ring of the voice," are readily distinguishable. Between these two regions are found the partials that define the vowel. Partials of the sung tone are damped out, because the rounded vowel [ɔ] should properly show a valley at that point in the spectrum; if this valley were not present, a different vowel would be in definition, or the vocal quality would be "open" and "spread." Had the vowel [i] been selected, the middle portion of the spectrum would have shown higher intensity, because this is the acoustic property in this region of the spectrum that defines the laterally produced vowel [i]. Because of the relationships among these three regions of the spectrum (Figure 3), considerable acoustic strength is to be found among partials between 0 and about 1200 Hz; much less activity occurs between 1500 Hz to 2300 Hz, and considerable acoustic energy is displayed at about 2400 Hz to 3300 Hz. Because of similar intensity levels between the lower and upper regions of the spectrum, one sees clearly exhibited the *chiaroscuro* (light/dark) timbre of the resonant "classically trained" singing voice.

The same subject who recorded the spectrogram of Figure 3 also recorded three additional spectrograms at similar pitch, vowel and intensity levels, with the tongue, however, now in postures frequently considered to be faulty for singing: The tip of the tongue is positioned *below* the roots of the lower teeth (Figure 4); the tip of the tongue is curled backward into

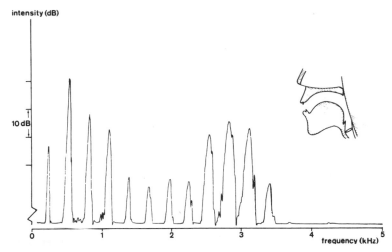

Figure 4. The vowel [ɔ] (as in "hawed") sung at approximately 277 Hz (C♯₄), with tongue below roots of the lower teeth and somewhat elevated in the middle. (Although the singer's formant remains intact, some vowel distortion occurs. A strong second partial is evident.)

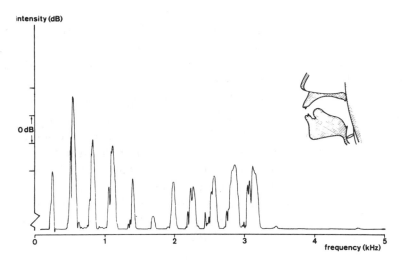

Figure 5. The vowel [ɔ] (as in "hawed") sung at approximately 277 Hz (C♯₄), with tongue curled backward into buccal cavity. In relation to the region of vowel definition, there is much less energy in the region of the singer's formant. The vowel distortion is about the same degree as that found in Figure 4.

the buccal cavity (Figure 5); and the tip of the tongue is positioned at the lower teeth, but humped *forward* and *upward* in an exaggerated [i] position (Figure 6).

It can be seen that when tongue position does not correspond to the position normally associated with the production of the vowel [ɔ], the

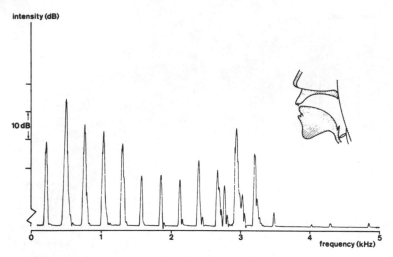

Figure 6. The vowel [ɔ] (as in "hawed") sung at approximately 262 Hz (C₄), with tongue humped forward, the tip positioned at the lower teeth ridge. Partials located between the region of vowel definition and the region of the singer's formant are undesirably high.

spectral envelope is considerably altered, which leads to distortion of the vowel and to deterioration of the singer's formant.

Although singing and speaking differ in significant ways, the phonetic aspects of both forms of phonation are remarkably similar in certain ranges of the voice. The several undesirable tongue postures indicated in Figures 4, 5, and 6 are often encountered during singing, and they require pedagogical attention and the application of corrective vocalises. Singers often assume these tongue positions in response to requests to "make more space in the throat," "open the throat," or "hang the jaw." The tongue does not "know where to go" in these nonphonetic situations; such requests may inadvertently cause violation of natural phonetic function. Tongue positions inappropriate to specific phonemes are frequently the result of tension caused by misguided technical suggestions.

A useful pedagogical tool for achieving proper tongue position for the execution of all vowel sounds can be found in those consonants that bring the tongue into contact with the lower teeth. The continuant [v], in which the upper incisors meet the bottom lip and the tongue contacts the lower teeth, and its voiceless counterpart [f], as well as the neighboring continuant [z] and its voiceless paired consonant [s], strongly recall the phonetic "at-rest" position (which elicits the neutral posture of the tongue). Certain modifications of the neutral phonetic position must occur in order to achieve the physiological postures essential to the production of these phonemes: (1) slight mandibular adjustment; (2) approximation of the vocal folds during the production of pitch consonants; (3) for [v] and [f], contact between the upper incisors and the lower lip; and (4) closure of the nasopharyngeal port. In both speech and song, for the execution of [v] and [z], and of their voiceless counterparts [f] and [s], the body of the tongue need move scarcely at all from its neutral "at-rest" posture. These sounds require no appreciable change of tongue postures within the vocal tract throughout the course of their execution within a single expiratory gesture, that is, within one continuous phonation. Although the vowel may be changed at will, the point of the tongue will remain suitably in contact with the teeth when prefaced by these consonants.

When an incorrect tongue posture occurs (as shown in Figures 4, 5, and 6), the student should be instructed to observe in a mirror the precise position of the tongue for proper execution of these phonetic events. When coupled with the consonants [v], [f], [b], [p], [z], and [s], the vowel should maintain the same tongue-teeth contact throughout its execution. After the apex of the tongue has been trained to remain at the inner surface of the lower teeth, the vowel may then be successfully sung without the pilot consonant. Familiar pitch patterns, such as 5–4–3–2–1, in any comfortable key, may serve as an appropriate vocalise for routining this tongue action.

Depending on the extent of the problem, this redirection of lingual action may require patience and time. However, as can be verified through spectrum analysis, if detailed technical work is not undertaken, the vocal production will never have the resonance balance of which it is capable. A remarkable increase in freedom and improvement of the singing timbre generally result.

Unless the tongue occupies its proper position within the vocal tract, vowel distortion, tongue tension, and an imbalance of resonance result. In this study, the acoustic results from singing the vowel [ɔ] with the tongue in several commonly occurring undesirable positions were investigated through the use of spectrograms. Results suggest that unless the "unruly" tongue can be properly schooled, inefficient acoustic filtering of the vocal tract can be anticipated in the singing voice.

References

Daniloff, R. G. (1973). "Normal Articulation Processes." *Normal Aspects of Speech, Hearing and Language*, ed. D. Minifie, T. J. Hixon, and F. Williams. Englewood Cliffs, New Jersey: Prentice-Hall, 175–76.

Hardcastle, W. J. (1976). "Physiology of Speech Production." *An Introduction for Speech Scientists*. London: Academic Press, 100.

Kantner, C. E. , and West, R. (1960). *Phonetics: An Introduction to the Principles of Phonetic Science from the Point of View of English Speech*. New York: Harper & Brothers, 49.

Ladefoged, P. (1962). *Elements of Acoustic Phonetics*. Chicago: University of Chicago Press, 96–97.

Malmberg, R. (1963). *Phonetics*. New York: Dover Publications, 31.

Zemlin, W. R. (1968). *Speech and Hearing Science: Anatomy and Physiology*. Englewood Cliffs, New Jersey: Prentice-Hall, 278.

(In collaboration with Harm Kornelis Schutte)

86

The Role of the Jaw in Singing

Jaw tension is often a problem for the singer. When there is tension in the mandible (jaw) there generally is a corresponding rigidity in the tongue muscles, which subsequently is transferred to the level of the larynx. Exercises to reduce jaw tension are a part of most vocal pedagogies.

Many jaw problems result directly from concepts the singer has about arranging ideal resonator "space." A singer must know how the jaw actually works in phonation if satisfactory solutions to mandibular tension are to be found. Unfortunately, there is a frequent and illogical response when jaw tension produces the clenched-mouth posture of the distended or elevated chin: "Just drop the jaw, thereby freeing it." Such a suggestion may appear on the surface to be appropriate; a number of contemporary articles on vocal technique suggest that "the idiot jaw" (the hanging, dropped jaw) is necessary to achieve relaxation and the avoidance of tension. On the contrary, hanging the jaw may exacerbate the very problems such advice is intended to alleviate.

The mandible is part of a composite structure that includes the tongue, the hyoid bone, and the larynx. What a singer does with the jaw directly affects the other members of this compound mechanism and determines the shape of the resonator system. The resonator tube (the vocal tract) extends from the larynx to the lips, and alters its position in reaction to postures of the jaw and tongue.

The ramus is the part of the jaw closest to the ear. At the top of the ramus is the coronoid process to which the temporalis muscle is attached just in front of the condyle, a knob-like projection located on each side of the mandible. The condyle articulates (is jointed) with a socket in the skull. The jaw can be opened by relaxing the temporalis without dropping the condyles from their sockets. It can also be opened by an exaggerated action that forces the mandible to drop out of the socket joints.

Vennard (1968) provides a good description of possible jaw movements:

> The hinge of the jaw is not a simple pivot, and the jaw is capable of sliding in several directions for the act of mastication. As long as it is opening simply by 'relaxing' the temporals with the condyles in their sockets, it will not open far. The maximum opening requires the mandible to 'slip out of the joint.' This can be felt by placing a finger in front of each ear, near the bottom. Here one can feel the *ramus,* or upward projection of the jaw bone, on each side. When the mandible really drops, the *rami* are pulled forward by the lateral pterygoids, making it possible for the finger to sink into a pocket in front of each ear.

There are, clearly, two mechanical modes for "opening" the jaw. It could be asked whether it is really the case that the jaw cannot be well opened when the condyles remain in their sockets. The two ways to open the jaw, the extent of desirable jaw opening, and the circumstances proper to both actions need more careful examination than often takes place in the search for quick solutions to jaw tensions.

When the jaw hangs in the "idiot" or "dumb" position, the mandible has its maximum excursion, dropping from the sockets, and the pharynx may actually be constricted, not enlarged. The buccal cavity then becomes enlarged at the expense of the pharyngeal cavity, so that "mouth resonance" is increased at the cost of "throat resonance." As Caruso remarked in an interview given in 1919, it is foolish to assume that opening the mouth widely by dropping the jaw produces more space in the pharynx:

> It must not be imagined that to open the mouth wide will do the same for the throat. If one is well versed in the art, one can open the throat perfectly without a perceptible opening of the mouth, merely by the power of respiration. (Quoted in Marafioti, 1922)

It is not the increase in size of a single part of the vocal-tract resonator system that provides optimal "space" for resonation, but rather the nature of the coupling of the chief resonators (mouth and pharynx) as they respond to laryngeal configuration.

In pedagogies that advocate the "hung" jaw, it is often overlooked that such postures would be impossible in speech because there could be little vowel or consonant definition. The acoustic theory of speech recognition stands in opposition to sustained low jaw positioning. Certainly, clear articulation and intelligibility are not compatible with the "idiot" or yawning jaw. Speech requires limited perpendicular motion.

Emil Froeschels, generally regarded as the father of the science of phoniatrics, determined that the external throat muscles involved in chewing are also active in the shifting patterns of speech. He discovered that by combining the circular motions of chewing with speech sounds such as "hm, hm, hm," primitive freedom of the jaw and laryngeal movements could be recovered. Friedrich Brodnitz (1971) describes the relationship between chewing and phonation:

> Since voice is the result of a complicated interplay of structural and muscular function, all attempts at correcting hyperfunction by focusing attention on functional detail disrupt easily the unity of this function. For that reason, the conventional instructions, such as lower the jaw, flatten the tongue, open the throat, do not do justice to the total phenomenon of vocal hyperfunction. What is needed is an approach that corrects hyperfunction by an attack on the hyperfunctional attitude rather than on the hyperfunctional detail. . . . By using the motions of chewing for voice production, we transfer the undisturbed muscular teamwork of chewing to the motion of voiced speech by appealing to an inborn automatic function. In doing this, we not only reduce hyperfunctional tension of the resonator but also improve, at the same time, vocal cord function.

Freedom to move the jaw loosely is evident in chewing. Were one to chew any substance with the up-and-down jaw action advocated by some vocal pedagogies, food would fall out of the mouth. Were one to speak with the same degree of perpendicular action required in some techniques of singing, speech would become unintelligible. Lightly shifting the jaw from side to side as a practice device (not while actually performing), regardless of the degree of openness, while singing a passage, can produce distinct sensations of jaw mobility and freedom. At no time should there be stiffness in the muscles under the jaw (below the chin), as so frequently happens in yawning and in other devices for lowering the jaw. Attempts to "open the throat" by dropping the jaw often induce tensions in the tongue muscles, particularly the mylohyoid, the genioglossus and the digastric muscle. This (submandibular) area of the neck should remain soft during singing. and not be placed in a state of tension under the false impression that the throat is being opened.

The jaw drops from its sockets during regurgitation, yawning, snoring, drunkenness, idiocy, and death. Regurgitation closes off the phonatory system so that the esophagus may provide an exit for what the stomach is rejecting; the characteristic sounds of snoring are the result of increased mouth space with fallen velum and reduced pharyngeal area; in drunkenness and idiocy the clarity and timbre of the voice are distorted; and in death, when there is no longer dynamic muscle balance, the jaw hangs, unless held closed by mechanical means. Indulging in any of these conditions during singing is difficult to justify. To tell the singer to "drop the jaw," and to "insert the fist into the mouth as a means of opening the throat," is to ignore the negative effects of such advice on the singing voice.

Indeed, the mouth can be opened exceedingly wide without unhinging the jaw, that is, without having it "slip out of the joint." In hilarious laughter, the jaw permits a great deal of buccal space, and the lift of the fleshy parts of the face that cover the zygomatic area (the cheeks) is obvious. Such a feeling of upward lift in the area of the "upper jaw" contributes to a different perception of spatial arrangement of the mouth and pharynx than does the sagging jaw with its downward facial pull. (There is, however, no need to maintain a lateral "smile" position during singing in order to avoid dropping the muscles of the face.)

Temporomandibular joint syndrome seems to be on the increase among singers. It has been suggested that this may be due to some popular orthodontic diagnoses of recent decades rather than to an actual rising rate of TMJ syndrome incidence. However, one has only to observe the exaggerated perpendicular jaw actions dictated by some current systems of singing to find a more probable explanation; one simply cannot constantly hang the jaw in singing without developing functional complications. Many singers who have complained of TMJ syndrome discover they no longer have that problem when they learn that they need not hang the jaw in the hope of "opening" the throat.

The "hung jaw" pedagogical tenet has been much popularized in recent years in manuals for choral conductors and in introductory methods for the novice singing teacher. Of course, dropping the jaw, thereby increasing the dimension of the forward part of the mouth resonator, will alter all formants, and will serve as a quick antidote to the choral problem of voices that do not easily "blend"; but the solution is a compensatory one that is likely to produce long-lasting problems for the singing voice. The "hung jaw" theory stands in direct opposition to a historic pedagogical position that maintains that mobility of the jaw, not low fixation, avoids tension and allows for freedom of articulation and proper resonance balancing. The hung jaw simply is not a free jaw.

Unless pathologic problems are present, there is rarely any feeling of tension in the jaw when one is in a state of repose or during speaking. Were the "hung" jaw really the constant, relaxed posture required by nature, we would all hang our mouths open when breathing and phonating. Both communication and physical attractiveness would thereby diminish.

One of the best ways to achieve jaw mobility is to permit the sounds of language to be shaped according to their natural postures as determined by pitch and power. When we raise the pitch, we open the mouth more, but we retain relative relationships among the vowel shapes with regard to lip and tongue postures.

The notion that there is one ideal mouth (and therefore jaw) position for singing is inimical to the phonetic theory of vowel production, and creates an artificiality of expression while at the same time obliterating diction. Attempts to move only the tongue while maintaining a hung jaw, under the assumption that one is thereby "relaxing" the jaw, violate both nature and art.

It is not here implied that singing and speaking are identical functions; indeed, one almost never opens the mouth as widely in speaking as one does in upper-range singing. However, desirable relationships between mouth and pharynx and the retention of articulatory accuracy in singing can only be accomplished by dynamic as opposed to static postures of the jaw.

To assume that maintaining a habitually lowered jaw posture as a means of "relaxing" the jaw is appropriate for singing is to ignore both the structure and the acoustics of the singing instrument. Emphasizing loose, flexible movement of the jaw is a more efficient solution to jaw tension. It should be kept in mind that there is no one ideal mouth position for singing; the vowel and the pitch, and, to some extent, the intensity determine the shape of the mouth and therefore the position of the jaw.

References

Brodnitz, Friedrich. (1971). *Vocal Rehabilitation: A Manual Prepared for the Use of Graduates in Medicine,* 4th ed. Rochester Minn.: American Academy of Ophthalmology and Otolaryngology, 97.

Marafioti, Mario. (1922). *Caruso's Method of Voice Production.* New York: D. Appleton; reprint 1981, Dover, 157.

Vennard, William. (1968). *Singing: The Mechanism and the Technic,* 5th ed. New York: Carl Fischer, 118.

87

The Incorrupt Jaw and Tongue of Saint Anthony of Padua

CoMeT is the acronym for *Collegium Medicorum Theatri,* an international organization of prominent laryngologists, voice scientists, and other specialists who deal with the voices of professional singers and actors. Activities of CoMeT include the pooling of knowledge, exchange of interdisciplinary ideas, and the furtherance of educational activities regarding the welfare of professional voice users.

It was appropriate that the fourteenth International Symposium of CoMeT be held in Padua, Italy, a city full of enchantment, including Giotto's incomparable frescoes in the Scrovegni Chapel, a historical medical museum, the arcades of the ancient city, the festive piazzas, the lovely gardens, and the mystical world enclosed within the dramatic Basilica of St. Anthony.

Scientists, laryngologists, teachers of singing and actors were not the only visitors to the basilica that week. Thousands of devout pilgrims come to visit the ornate shrine of St. Anthony, in which are housed the remains of the tireless preacher who flourished some 750 years ago in this Northern Italian city. The voice of St. Anthony has so reverberated down through the centuries with his message of hope and grace that Pope Paul VI termed the basilica "a spiritual clinic for today's world."

St. Anthony of Padua would probably have had a major impact on twentieth-century television preaching because of his legendary ability to use vocal timbres and histrionics that touched the hearts of his listeners. Several parts of his vocal mechanism, which functioned so mellifluously 750 years ago, have become objects of religious veneration in the cathedral at Padua for pilgrims from all parts of the modern world.

In a chapel inside the basilica, pilgrims stand in awe before St. Anthony's laryngeal cartilages and his "incorrupt jaw and tongue." What does such veneration say about the probable vocal performance of this saintly person? Was it only his message that so swayed his listeners, or was it the power of his vocal delivery as well?

It can be objectively reported that the blackened tongue of St. Anthony in its reliquary appears shriveled and desiccated, and that the "incorrupt jaw" is plainly no longer functional. But the eloquence of that voice, and the substance of that thought, have caused these remains to be honored by believers uninterruptedly during subsequent centuries.

Back at the formal session of the CoMeT symposium at Hotel Milano there were excellent research reports, interesting films on the mechanics of vocal production related to registration studies, and an impressive display of modern means for analyzing the many facets of the speaking and singing voice. None of them could diminish the memory of mounting sacred stairs to view the vocal remains of one who was truly a great professional user of voice, to sense the continuing aura of holiness around those remains, and perhaps to hear an inner echoing down the centuries from the voice of the saintly performer:

> Help us in our moments of weakness; defend us against all dangers, physical and spiritual; console us in our sufferings and trials; and strengthen our faith. Give us a generous heart so that we may share our bounty with those who are poor.
>
> —Prayer of St. Anthony of Padua

The "incorrupt" tongue of Anthony has endured not only physically but spiritually, and the thoughts expressed by that ancient vocal instrument continue to speak to us today, in part because of the "golden delivery" that came from efficient physiologic and acoustic use of his vocal tract.

It isn't necessary to be a believer to recognize that ideas conveyed through specific vocal timbres evoke strong emotional and spiritual responses. Emotive speech and singing go far beyond the requirements of phonation as communication. Indeed, when one considers solely the biologic valvular functions of the larynx, there is no reason that the voice of singing should exist. Some scientific sources list the phonatory act as only a secondary laryngeal function.

Further, speaking and singing timbres transcend the mere expression of ideas. How successfully they do so depends on the way the vocal tract is adjusted—the caliber of vowel tracking, the extent to which the singer's formant is maintained, the degree of resonance balancing within the changing spectra.

Founders of CoMeT were eminent otolaryngologists who wished to improve care of the professional voice. Persons from related fields of vocal research and performance have since joined them. The way St. Anthony of Padua used his voice as a professional instrument, aware of its many possibilities, must surely qualify him for posthumous membership in CoMeT.

88

How Big Is the Big Sound?

People who write about the current state of singing sometimes tell us that today's singing instrument needs to be of larger dimension than were the voices that graced the lyric theater a hundred years ago, when the average hall capacity was between 1,000 and 1,400. We are also told that somewhere around 1835 a new attitude toward dramatic singing emerged. A little later, with the growing influence of Giuseppe Verdi and Richard Wagner, additional demands were placed on the singer. Other sources tell us that prior to the mid-eighteenth century the singing voice was a chamber instrument, incapable of the dramatic demands of today's concert hall and the opera theater. Any reading of history is only as good as the accuracy with which historical fact is accumulated, and the history of singing does not stand apart from that consideration.

As soon as vocal literature with extensive soloistic demands made its appearance (in the Western world, beginning in the early decades of the seventeenth century), the singing voice responded. Indeed, the technical possibilities developed by the emerging professional solo singer partly dictated the nature of the vocal writing. Although it is evident that style and taste in any period contribute to vocal practice, it should not be overlooked that the physiologic function of the singing voice has not radically changed from one century to another. (The same cannot be said of other musical instruments, such as members of the string, wind, and keyboard families.) The human vocal instrument has not undergone significant physical mutation within the past few centuries, any more than has the liver or the spleen.

The voice of today's singer is subject to the same laws of production as was the singing instrument in the solo literature of two hundred years ago. Although good nutrition and medical advances may contribute to somewhat larger human specimens than existed in the last century, there has been no remarkable degree of laryngeal or pulmonary growth in homo sapiens. Tastes and styles have changed but basic physical structure has not radically altered.

At times, an argument is made against using any sizable sound in the singing voice. There are miniaturists who find any dynamic level beyond *piano* to be offensive. They believe that, prior to Verdi, singers consistently peeped at a *mezza-voce* level. For them, only *piano* singing qualifies as *bel canto*. In contrast to the miniaturists, those who want the "big sound" adhere to the growing "blast and bellow" school. For them, the voice is resonant only if it is loud. Both orientations place artificial confines on the art of singing. An incomplete vocal timbre is as inappropriate to Monteverdi as to Massenet; on the other hand, the yelling assumed by some singers to be a requirement of the post-Bellini literature could not have been appreciated by a refined listening ear of any period. Miniaturists and bellowers most likely have existed throughout the history of song. Neither of them represent skillful singing.

What gives the voice carrying power in a hall? Certainly not sheer volume. Studies of noise levels of the symphony orchestra indicate that a voice accompanied by orchestra will be hopelessly masked in certain registers unless specific acoustic factors prevail in the vocal sound. "Bigness," with regard to projection, is related neither to brute force nor solely to vocal amplitude.

For a voice to project over high ambient decibels (such as those encouraged by an insensitive opera conductor), there must be proper relationship among the formants of the singing voice. It is the relationship of harmonic frequencies, not the degree of effort at the level of the larynx, that permits the "ring" of the voice (generally described by singers and listeners as "resonance"). The singer's formant (sometimes termed the singing formant) has long been recognized as an element of well-projected vocalism; it is what concert and opera singers display, and what most folk singers lack (their literature and performance circumstances generally do not require it.) It is the result of heavy concentration of acoustic energy in the region of 3000 Hz.

Techniques for supposedly enlarging the voice are counterproductive, because they upset the relationships among the singer's formant, the formant frequencies of the vowel being sung, and the lower formants, all of which are harmonic multiples resulting from the fundamental pitch the singer is producing. For example, opening the mouth excessively wide (in a range where that buccal posture is inappropriate) and spreading the pharynx in order to produce a big sound changes the normal relationships among the formants; such a maneuver actually reduces the carrying power of the voice. The dispersed sound of "enlarged" voices may give an illusion of size in the practice room or in the voice studio. Yet, in the hall, the vocalism of a bombastic Rigoletto may be covered by that of his vocally smaller but projected daughter Gilda. He interferes with the natural acoustic of his instrument by trying for the big sound; she does not enter that competition, and therefore she wins.

No voice can be made bigger than the dimensions of its initial endowment. Singers will not realize their potential in vocal size until adherence to certain acoustic rules has become habitual. Singers who think they have "opened up" the voice, or have found "roundness" and "depth," often are enjoying an internal auditory experience (largely through bone conduction) that is not shared by the listener. It sounds and feels bigger inside, but smaller out here. Unfortunately, listening to a recording of oneself is not always a reliable guide in helping a singer determine how big the sound may be.

There is a standard of size essential for any voice if it is to become professionally viable. Small voices, no matter how beautiful, are not generally useful in the theater or in the concert hall. A professional singing voice must be not only of unusually good quality but also of reasonably good size. (It does not have to be a cannon.) However, to try to make a bigger sound through producing exaggerated volume and darkened timbre is to remove whatever chance of projection an instrument may have. The manufactured "big voice," emerging from a modest-sized instrument, reminds one of the mouse who roars. It is "big" only to its producer.

89

Feeling, Hearing, and Seeing the Voice

Becoming aware of the sensations experienced during singing is often encouraged by the teacher, and rightly so. The individual's perception of how one kind of coordination differs from another kind is an important factor in establishing a dependable vocal technique.

Sensations from singing vary widely from individual to individual, because sympathetic vibration from self-generated sound sources are not uniform. Yet teachers of singing often try to induce in others sensations identical to those they themselves have come to experience during the generation of vocal sound. It is not possible to separate the sensations resulting from the sounds one produces from the hearing of those sounds. Research dealing with aural perception has proven that one senses the sounds of one's own voice both externally, through the meatus, and internally, through sympathetic vibration by means of bone conduction. The bony and cartilaginous structures of the head, including the hard palate,

provide sympathetic vibratory sensations that contribute to and complement awareness of the sounds we produce. Relying on repeatable sensation
is a major self-monitoring factor. Hearing and feeling the sound in replica-
ble fashion constitute two of the major perceptive parameters available to
the classically trained singer.

Singers are sometimes told that they cannot hear themselves sing. This
is ill-directed advice, because the singer not only hears what is being sung
but quickly learns to make assessments of the variety of sounds of which
he or she is capable. A truer statement is that the singer does not hear his
or her own voice in the exact manner that other listeners hear that phonating instrument—a quite different situation from not being able to monitor
self-generated sound. Not only do singers hear themselves sing, they constantly assess the sounds they make during singing in order to bring those
phonations into accord with the tonal ideal to which they have given
their allegiance.

There is, of course, the problem of determining a balance between
"outer" and "inner" listening. One is well aware of the problems experienced by the internalized singer who seems to avoid listening externally.
Techniques of singing that rely on "placement" language tend to induce
increased awareness of internalized sensation to the detriment of the external communication of vocal sound. Attempts to induce sensations in parts
of the skull, such as the velar, the occipital, or the forehead regions, or in
the torso, such as in the sternum or the spinal column, serve as examples
of heavy reliance on internalization of sound. Sometimes, as a means for
correcting internalized singing, the singer is told, "Don't listen to yourself." Better advice might be "Listen to yourself on the outside, not on the
inside." The singer who does not hear the varieties of vocal timbre that he
or she can produce is being robbed of one of the chief self-monitoring
devices that should actively be developed. Many singers have intonation
problems, not because they have unmusical ears but because they rely too
much on internal sensation, and not enough on external listening.

Every singer knows that he or she is capable of producing several kinds
of timbre, none of them patently unpleasant, on any note in the scale. Part
of the duty of vocal pedagogy is to help the singer determine which of
those basic timbres is in accordance with the most efficiently produced
sound. A singer also knows that when what is produced does not *feel* good
it does not *sound* good. Thus, *feeling* and *hearing* vocal timbre are combined for both aesthetic and functional purposes.

Perhaps more neglected than the two self-perceptual parameters just
mentioned (feeling and hearing) is the third important feedback parameter:
seeing the vocal instrument.

Often mistakenly thought to be the "hidden" instrument, the vocal instrument is readily *visible*. This visibility does not include the internal vocal mechanism, the larynx itself, without the aid of fiberoptics and stroboscopy. But the larynx is actually only a part of the singing instrument. In the positions of the head, the neck, the clavicles, the sternum, the rib cage, the epigastrium and abdominal wall, the mouth, the lips, the tongue, the zygomatic arch, and the positioning of the larynx itself (which varies so greatly from one technical school to another), the singer externally displays the vocal instrument. Changes in vocal timbre are often recognizable in the shifting relationships among these variable parts of the vocal mechanism. Not only can the singer feel and hear the sounds he or she is producing, much of what produces the differences in vocal sound can also be seen.

For several hundred years, the voice studio has depended on the mirror as a feedback device for the teaching of vocal technique. Now the recorder, the video camera, and even spectral analysis allow the singer to "see" the voice as well as to "feel" it and "hear" it. The teacher of singing who does not watch his or her student sing misses as much vital information as if he or she were to stop listening. Both teacher and singer should learn to rely on the three proprioceptive devices by which the vocal instrument is trained: feeling, hearing, and seeing. All three of these parameters are essential to the development of a stabilized technique of singing, one that permits repetition of coordination. They should be given equal importance in vocal pedagogy.

90

Spectrographic Analysis of the Singing Voice

Singing teachers have distinct notions of how a "resonant" voice should sound. Although various tonal ideals exist, there is agreement that certain qualities are essential to all elite vocalism. These characteristics are often expressed by such terms as "warmth," "vitality," "roundness," "velvet," "ping," "focus," "point," and "balance." The practiced ear of the singing teacher determines when those elements are present and in what relationships. The desired timbre is then suggested to the student, frequently through example or through the language of imagery, but not, in either case, always with success.

Teachers of singing watch students sing in order to see as well as to hear the causes for change in vocal quality. They have always made use of feedback devices such as the long-existent mirror, the newer tape recorder, and, more recently, the video camera, to help students both see and hear which variables produce differences in vocal timbre.

Another instrument is now available for verifying what the teacher may attempt to describe through subjective terms such as "roundness" and "ring" and through vocal modeling. This instrument is the spectrograph, a machine that provides spectrograms, which are graphic representations of the harmonic components of vocalized sound (a sung phonation).

Figure 1 shows a spectrographic display of the first two brief phrases of the well-known *aria antica Caro mio ben,* as sung by a lyric tenor with professional operatic experience. The graph displays a printout from an instrument (in this case, the Kay Elemetrics DSP Sona-Graph, Model 5500) that changes auditory signals such as those produced by the singing voice into visual ones. Consequently, Figure 1 allows the reader to *see* a performance of *Caro mio ben.* By calling back the phonation electronically, the performer and others who are listening can experience the phonation two ways—visually and aurally. This technological achievement enables student and teacher, either individually or jointly, repeatedly to consider the merit of a phonation simultaneously through the senses of hearing and seeing. They can also examine the presence or lack of resonance balance through comparisons with subsequently improved performances of the same item. Even without sound, a reader can discover from the spectrogram significant information regarding the sounds produced.

Just as one learns to listen carefully to the sounds of singing in order to make aesthetic judgments, so one can learn to interpret information provided by a visual display of sound. Through clear understanding of the variables involved, what one hears can be confirmed by what one sees. Indeed, the visual representation of sound may bring about an awareness of important factors that sometimes go unnoticed by the ear.

A spectrogram of the singing voice such as the one here considered displays the fundamental frequency and its integral harmonic multiples as they occur within time. The horizontal axis represents *time,* 0 to 8 seconds in this instance. The vertical axis represents *frequency,* 0 to 4000 Hz (for the male voice shown). The third variable is *acoustic energy,* represented by degrees of darkness observable in different regions of the graph: the darker the region, the higher the concentration of energy.

It is clear from the spectrogram that in any sung pitch acoustic energy

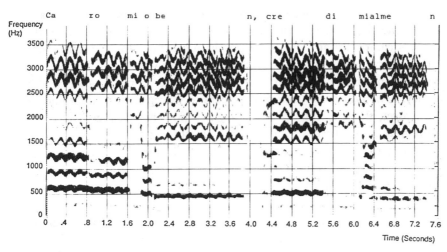

Figure 1. Spectrogram of the first phrases of *Caro mio ben,* sung by a professional lyric tenor. (Key E♭).

is not concentrated at the fundamental frequency. The spectrogram shows that most acoustic energy is found above the frequency of the pitch perceived by the listener. For instance, in a sung phonation such as *Caro mio ben, credimi almen,* comprised of the pitches E^b_4, D_4, C_4, and B^b_3 (first phrase segment) and of pitches C_4, B^b_3, A^b_3, and G_3 (second phrase segment), most of the acoustic energy is found above the respective frequencies (311 Hz, 294 Hz, 262 Hz, 233 Hz, 262 Hz, 233 Hz, 208 Hz and 196 Hz.) At first, the presence of a high degree of acoustic energy above the perceived pitch may seem confusing. This distribution of energy is, however, explained by a phenomenon known to every musician: the overtone series.

The human voice is an instrument rich in overtones, all of which, in a good phonation, are integral multiples of the fundamental frequency. Spectrograms show that a sung pitch always generates overtones (also known as harmonic partials) that in trained singers extend up to 4000 Hz or 5000 Hz. This explains why spectrograms of the singing voice display series of evenly spaced horizontal lines. The lowest line shows the *fundamental frequency* that dictates the "pitch" of the phonation; the upper lines indicate the *harmonic partials* that determine other characteristics of sound, such as vowel definition and overall vocal quality.

To the reader familiar with spectrograms of other musical instruments, the undulating nature of the illustrated partials may appear unusual or perplexing. Spectrograms of nonvocal instruments generally display "straight" as opposed to "wavy" lines. The wavy (undulatory) nature of the partials in vocal spectra is accounted for by a phenomenon natural only to the singing voice: the *vibrato*. A vibratoed sound, including those from instruments that at times purposely induce vibrato in imitation of the human voice, will generate spectrograms of wavy lines, in which each of the harmonic partials mirrors the vibrancy rate of the fundamental frequency. A nonvibratoed sound (a straight tone) registers straight lines. For this reason, the spectrographic display is a powerful pedagogical tool for use in developing awareness of vibrancy in singing.

Partials that are not multiples of the fundamental frequency produce noise in the singing voice. Clean, noiseless singing generates spectrograms with minimal displays between harmonic partials. A spectrographic picture of these ideal characteristics verifies that the singer possesses adequate technique to distribute all the acoustic energy within the proper regions of the spectrum (which is what the *chiaroscuro* timbre of the historic school of vocal pedagogy accomplishes). For this reason, the spectrograph is useful in correcting vocal problems that result from *pressed phonation* or "over-singing" that produces noise or undesirable timbre, and for correction of the opposite error, *breathy phonation* (exaggerated "flow" phonation), that alters balanced relationships among the partials.

In addition to visualizing relationships of the harmonic partials to the fundamental and to each other and displaying the vibrato phenomenon, the spectrogram is capable of revealing other important aspects of vocal pedagogy:

1. a resonance factor that voice teachers frequently term "focus," "ring," "ping," and "placement";
2. a resonance factor often pedagogically expressed as "depth," "roundness," or "warmth";
3. clean vowel definition; and
4. a balancing of these qualities so as to produce *voce completa* (complete voice), in which all appropriate resonance factors are present.

These aspects are manifest in the relationships of *formants*. A *formant* may be defined as a region of strong acoustic energy; formants are registered in spectrograms as dark areas. Such formants can be observed in the *Caro mio ben* segment of Figure 1.

An important region of acoustic strength is termed the *first formant*. It is found in the bottom portion of the spectrum, in the region of 500 Hz to 800 Hz in the male voice (depending on vocal category). This is the formant that is responsible for "depth" in the singing voice.

A second important formant found in the spectrum is a *vowel defining* element, which produces the diagonal sequential characteristic of vowel definition in a series of lateral to rounded vowels. It lies between the first and third formants.

The consistent darkness in the upper portion of the spectrogram between 2500 Hz and 3300 Hz indicates a third important concentration of acoustic energy called the *singer's formant*, which is characteristic of trained "classical" singers. The singer's formant produces the "ring of the voice" that permits vocal sound to "carry" over orchestras and in large halls.

While the third formant produces the *chiaro* aspects of the historical *chiaroscuro* tone of the singing voice, it is largely the first formant that produces the balancing *oscuro* aspects. In the trained singing voice, considerable acoustic strength is present in both upper and lower regions of the spectrum regardless of the vowel being sung. This can clearly be seen in Figure 2, an [i e ɑ o u] sequence on the pitch A₃ (220 Hz) sung by a professional tenor. As expected, the spectrogram (this time, reading from top to bottom) shows darkness in the regions of the *third* formant (the singer's formant) and the *first* formant. The visually prominent shifting harmonic relations between them, in the region of the *second* formant, determine vowel definition and contribute to "resonance" enhancement.

Figure 2 shows that the middle region of the spectrum indicates differences among harmonic distributions with regard to vowel definition. (Each vowel has its individual look in mid-spectrum.) A descending, step-like pattern of formants can be seen as the singer progresses downward from a lateral to a rounded vowel. Each vowel has its own distribution of acous-

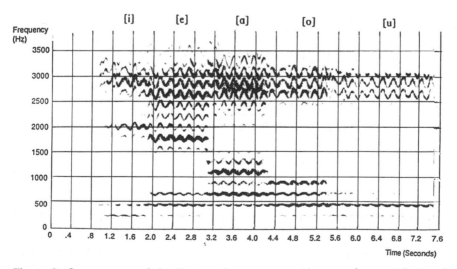

Figure 2. Spectrogram of the [i-e-ɑ-o-u] sequence on A₃, sung by a professional lyric tenor.

tic energy that differentiates it from every other vowel. The front vowel [i] has acoustic strength in the upper part of the spectrum near the region of the singer's formant; the more neutral vowel [ɑ] shifts its acoustic strength into the bottom half of the spectrum; the "back" vowels [o] and [u] are defined at increasingly low acoustic levels. The combining of these three formants (as well as a fourth and fifth formant, found in some ranges of the singing voice in close proximity to the third formant) produces the ideal "clear/dark" tone, the historic *chiaroscuro* timbre. The proper balance of this acoustic energy in upper, middle, and lower portions of the spectrum ensures the classical resonance balance of the singing voice.

In summary, the "ring," or the "focus," depends on the presence of acoustic strength in the upper regions of the spectrum. The "roundness" or "depth" of the sound results from the presence of acoustic strength in lower partials of the spectrum. The "vowel color" is defined mainly by the location in the spectrum of the changing middle formant. "Resonance balance" results from proper distribution of energy among the three formant regions mentioned. "Vitality" and "life" are dependent on vibrancy, that is, on the presence of vibrato.

Spectrographic analysis does not replace the musicianly ear, but verifies what the ear discerns. The spectrogram can identify unwanted features of a sung phonation. It offers teacher and student an additional feedback tool for clarifying the nature of desirable vocal timbre and for building on discernible excellence. Vocal quality can be both heard and seen.

(With the assistance of Juan Carlos Franco)

91

Vowel Definition in a Performance by Jussi Bjoerling of *Vesti la giubba*

The accomplishment of an evenly registered mounting scale is conceded to be necessary for excellence in "classical" singing. How this is achieved varies from one pedagogy to another, and is often expressed by terms such as "cover," "vowel migration," and "vowel modification" [Miller 1977]. Views regarding laryngeal positioning and pharyngeal expansion, both of which contribute to "covering," differ [Large 1986]. Only acoustic factors are here considered.

An example of spectral components of a series of vowels in progression from the front vowel [i] to the back vowel [u] in lower-middle range (Figure 1a) sung by a professional tenor (not Bjoerling) is here analyzed with a Kay Elemetrics DSP Sona-graph 5500. It illustrates acoustic characteristics of vowel differentiation and the formants of the singing voice. (A formant, it will be recalled, is a region of strong acoustic energy; formants are registered in spectrograms as dark areas.) The consistent darkness in the upper portion of the spectrogram between 2500 Hz and 3300 Hz indicates concentration of acoustic energy called the *singer's formant* [Sundberg 1987]. (This formant corresponds to the "ring" of the voice.) The first formant, found in the lower portion of the spectrogram in the region of 500 Hz, is responsible for the "depth" in the vocal sound. Between the first and third formants, the second formant shifts as vowels change.

In Figure 1b (the power spectra corresponding to Figure 1a), a descending step-like pattern of formants can be observed as the singer progresses downward from a front (lateral) to a back (rounded) vowel. Each vowel has a distinct distribution of acoustic energy that differentiates it from other vowels. The front vowel [i] has acoustic strength in the upper part of the spectrum, relatively near the region of the singer's formant; the front vowel [e] at a somewhat lower position in the spectrum; the more neutral vowel [ɑ] in the bottom half of the spectrum; the back vowels [o] and [u] are at increasingly lower levels. This distribution of acoustic energy

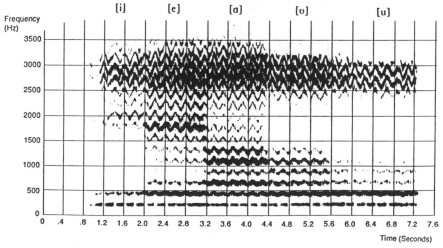

Figure 1a. Spectrogram of a series of vowels in lower-middle range sung by a professional tenor.

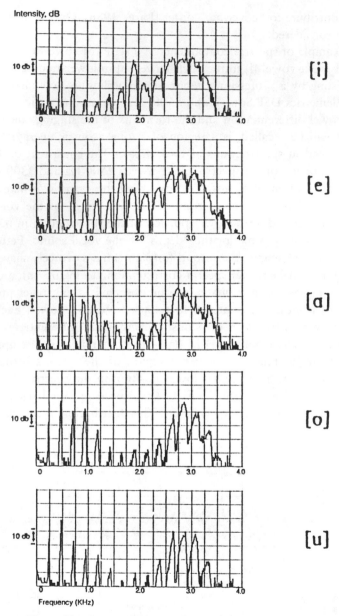

Figure 1b. Power spectra corresponding to Figure 1a.

in upper, middle, and lower portions of the spectrum also determines the resonance balance of the sung phonation.

A major pedagogical concern is to determine at what point in a mounting scale it becomes necessary to "modify" the vowel (induce acoustic change) in order to accomplish an even scale. Pivotal register points within a scale depend on the vocal category of the singer. (The number of registers in the singing voice, and their physiological sources, is not the subject here.)

Although the influence of mechanical techniques must be taken into account in the examination of any recorded vocalization, certain parameters, including vowel definition and degrees of vowel migration, are unalterable. Some of these acoustic events are observable as an internationally recognized tenor, Jussi Bjoerling, sings an aria that encompasses vocal ranges identified with registration practices.

For purposes of acoustic analysis of how a premier singer handles vowel differentiation and modification, three range segments have been selected from a Bjoerling performance: (1) sung phonations that lie largely within the speech inflection range (historically known as "chest" voice); (2) sung phonations that lie chiefly in the middle range of the singing voice (historically known as *zona di passaggio* or "mixed voice," that is, the area between the traditional first and second male-register pivotal points); and (3) sung phonations that are concentrated in the upper range (traditionally termed "head" voice).

This study examines a performance of Bjoerling, generally conceded to be the prime exponent of technical excellence among the tenors of his generation, of *Vesti la giubba* from *I Pagliacci* in a "Voice of Firestone" telecast recorded November 19, 1951. (The master kinescope recording is housed in the archives of the New England Conservatory of Music, Boston, reproduced by Video International, copyrighted Video Artists International, 1990.)

An example of vowel definition in lower register may be observed in Figures 2a and 2b, particularly between the vowel [ɛ] in the syllable *sei* (220 Hz) and the vowel [o] in the final syllable of the word *Pagliaccio* (247 Hz). The first formant and the singer's formant remain in the same region of the spectrum during vowel change, whereas the second formant shifts downward in the progression from front to back vowel (Figures 2b and 2c), as would be expected. (Note the interruption of vowel continuity by the intrusion of unvoiced consonants in Figure 2a.)

The spectral result of vowel differentiation in the middle vocal range is readily observable in Figure 3a, with the syllables *preso dal delirio* executed on the same fundamental frequency, E_4 (330 Hz). Observe the changing location of the second formant in the vowel sequence on the same pitch (Figure 3b).

Of special interest, as can be seen in Figure 4a, is the vowel migration (modification) at the traditional *secondo passaggio* pivotal point, which is frequently located at G_4 in a relatively large lyric tenor voice such as that of Jussi Bjoerling. (The role of Canio is generally performed by a voice of

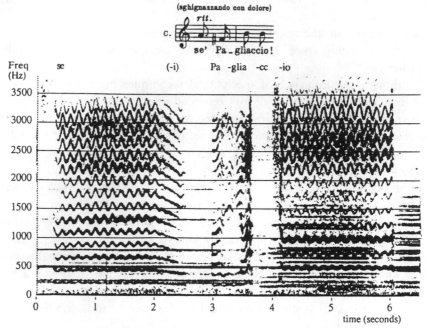

Figure 2a. Spectral analysis of *se' Pagliaccio*.

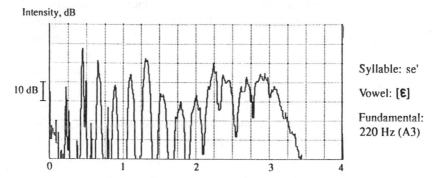

Syllable: se'

Vowel: [ɛ]

Fundamental:
220 Hz (A3)

Figure 2b. Power spectra corresponding to Figure 2a.

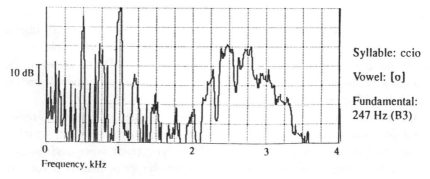

Syllable: ccio

Vowel: [o]

Fundamental:
247 Hz (B3)

Figure 2c. Power spectra corresponding to Figure 2a.

284

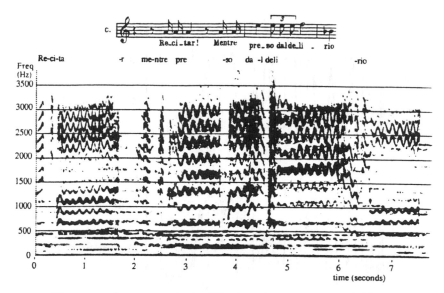

Figure 3a. Spectral analysis of *Recitar! Mentre preso dal delirio.*

larger dimensions than Bjoerling's.) This occurs on the syllable *qua,* which Bjoerling treats in *portamento* fashion from mid-voice *(zona di passaggio)* to upper range. In the progression from E_4 (330 Hz) to G_4 (392 Hz), on [ɑ], the singer's formant remains largely constant. Because the second formant has migrated slightly downward (Figure 4b) in the direction of the vowel [o], it is clear that vowel modification ("cover") has taken place.

From a practical pedagogical standpoint, it is important to note that Bjoerling tends to avoid the possibility of excessive brightness in mounting pitch through modifying or "covering" the vowel, in accordance with the accepted international practice of avoiding "open" singing production [Titze 1984].

Further, there is a change of vowel from [ɑ] to [e] on G_4, which is registered in the power spectra (Figure 4b) by an upward shift of the second formant. This indicates that, despite vowel modification, vowel recognition remains in this singer's performance.

The passage *tramuta in lazzi lo spasmo ed il pianto,* shown in Figure 5a, provides an example of range transition beginning in lower-middle voice and progressing through midregister to upper range. It is of interest to compare the vowel [ɑ] in the syllable *spa* (Figure 5b) on fundamental frequency A^b_4 (415 Hz) with the same vowel located a minor ninth lower (Figure 5c) on the syllable *pian* at fundamental frequency G_3 (196 Hz). Two points may be made: (1) vowel definition is only slightly altered in

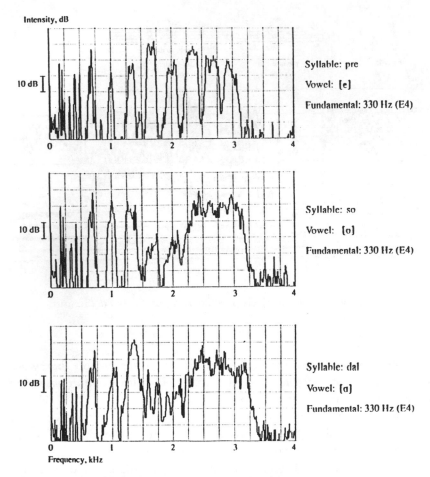

Figure 3b. Power spectra corresponding to Figure 3a.

the two ranges for the "cover" maneuver, and (2) the spectral envelope of the A^b_4 phonation resembles that of the G_3 phonation. It is at this exact point where pedagogic and aesthetic judgments must be made as to how much acoustic change should occur during the shifting of ranges. There is not always common agreement, but Bjoerling is clearly on the side of the historical internationalism associated with the Italian School. (Anecdotal aside: Giuseppe Barra, a respected operatic tenor in his own right and a prominent Milanese teacher of singing, in the early fifties once commented to this author, "The greatest Italian tenor of the day is the Swede Jussi Bjoerling!")

Figure 6a presents a classic example of performance practice at the *secondo passaggio* pivotal point as Bjoerling progresses from $F^\#_4$ (370 Hz)

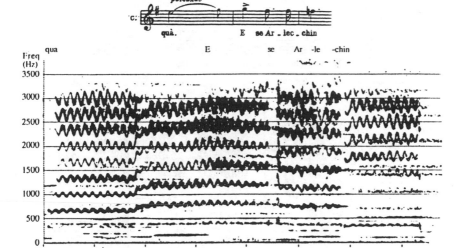

Figure 4a. Spectral analysis of *qua. E se Arlecchin.*

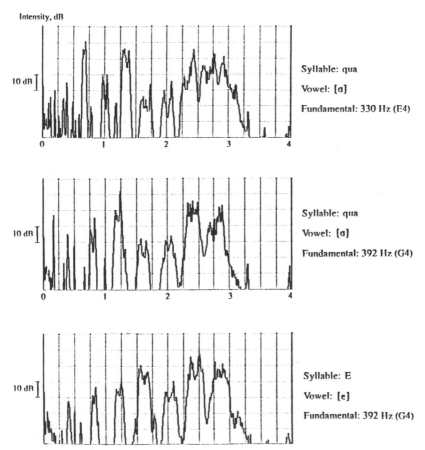

Syllable: qua
Vowel: [ɑ]
Fundamental: 330 Hz (E4)

Syllable: qua
Vowel: [ɑ]
Fundamental: 392 Hz (G4)

Syllable: E
Vowel: [e]
Fundamental: 392 Hz (G4)

Figure 4b. Power spectra corresponding to Figure 4a.

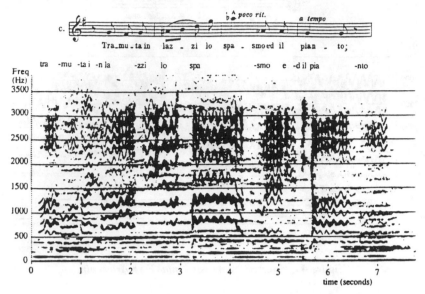

Figure 5a. Spectral analysis of *Tramuta in lazzi lo spasmo ed il pianto*.

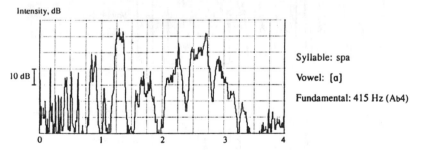

Syllable: spa

Vowel: [ɑ]

Fundamental: 415 Hz (Ab4)

Figure 5b. Power spectrum of *[a]* at 415 Hz ($A^{\flat}_4$), corresponding to Figure 5a.

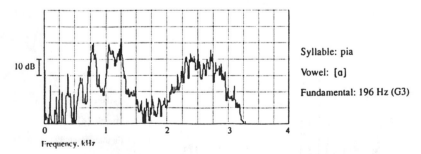

Syllable: pia

Vowel: [ɑ]

Fundamental: 196 Hz (G3)

Figure 5c. Power spectrum of *[a]* at 196 Hz (G_3), corresponding to Figure 5a.

288

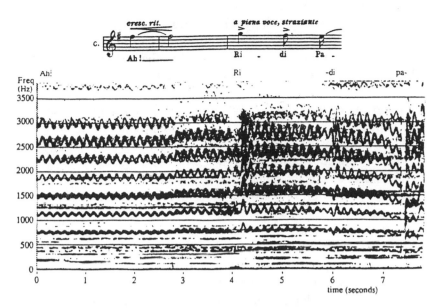

Figure 6a. Spectral analysis of *Ah! Ridi Pa-*.

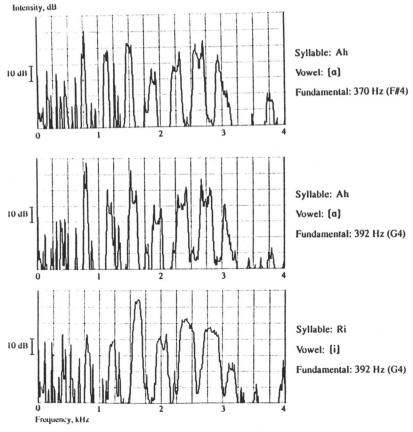

Syllable: Ah

Vowel: [ɑ]

Fundamental: 370 Hz (F#4)

Syllable: Ah

Vowel: [ɑ]

Fundamental: 392 Hz (G4)

Syllable: Ri

Vowel: [i]

Fundamental: 392 Hz (G4)

Figure 6b. Power spectra corresponding to Figure 6a.

to G (392 Hz). The following can be noted in the power spectra (Figure 6b) that correspond to the phonation of Figure 6a:

1. In moving from $F^\#_4$ to G_4, there is minimal change in the resonance balance.
2. The movement from [ɑ] to [i] shows a tendency for the second formant to shift upward.
3. The singer's formant remains constant, so that the listener perceives an even transition as the vocal scale ascends.

Although no absolutes can be reached on the basis of the spectrographic examination of a single performance from one singer (despite his reputation for excellence), it may be concluded that spectrographic examination of performance practices of a premier singer may offer valuable information to the singer and the voice teacher. A model premier tenor, Jussi Bjoerling, shows some expected acoustic change of the vowel in register transition. However, and of great pedagogic importance, acoustic changes as this singer modifies or "covers" the sound are not so extensive as to disturb the listener's perception of vowel integrity.

Acknowledgments

I am grateful to the Kulas Foundation, *The Elyria Chronicle-Telegram,* and Mr. Otto B. Schoepfle for funding this project; Tom Bethel and Fred Zwegat of Oberlin College for technical assistance; and Allan Altman, Video Artists International, Inc., for generous permission to use these phonations.

References

Large, J. (1986). "How to Teach the Male High Voice, Part One: The Tenor." *Journal of Research in Singing,* IX (2): 17–23.

Miller, R. (1977). *English, French, German, and Italian Techniques of Singing.* Metuchen, N.J.: Scarecrow Press, 134–142.

Sundberg, J. (1987). *The Science of the Singing Voice.* Dekalb, Ill.: Northern Illinois University Press, 118–19.

Titze, I. (1984). "Rules for Modifying Vowels." *The NATS Journal,* 49 (3): 31–39.

(With the assistance of Juan Carlos Franco)

92

Spectral Components of Five Cardinal
Vowels in the Soprano Singing Voice
Considered by Means of the
Sequential Vowel Diagonal

The teaching of singing requires a trained ear capable of distinguishing a wide range of vocal sounds, and a reservoir of knowledge on which to base aesthetic and functional judgments. Communication regarding the differences among vocal sounds (which the teacher may assess as extending from good to unfavorable) is generally either modeled or described by the instructor through the subjective language of imagery. Traditional pedagogical language may be supplemented by visual and audio feedback supportive of the teacher's assumptions. Spectrum analysis offers such useful information. This essay illustrates the pedagogical relevance of the *sequential vowel diagonal* as seen on a spectrographic display.

It is common knowledge that in the speaking voice the acoustic spectrum undergoes changes, especially in the region of the second formant, during the progression of a series of front to back vowels as in [i-e-ɑ-o-u]. In singing, as well as in speaking, these alterations are the result of the changing shapes of the vocal tract as vowels and consonants are defined. The vocal tract serves as filter to the laryngeally generated sounds. It does so chiefly through the changing positions of jaw, lips, mouth, velum, tongue, and pharynx.

A spectrogram of a sung phonation (such as shown in Figure 1) displays the distribution of acoustic energy within a wide frequency range and over a period of time. Three variables are visible: (1) the horizontal axis, representing time; (2) the vertical axis, representing frequency; and (3) degrees of darkness, representing acoustic energy—the darker, the stronger.

The phonations here examined are those of a twenty-one-year-old singer, arbitrarily selected from a number of soprano voice majors singing vowel sequence patterns at several pitch levels. Other soprano voices in the study tend to show similar results.

A series of front to back vowels [i-e-ɑ-o-u], as observed here in female

291

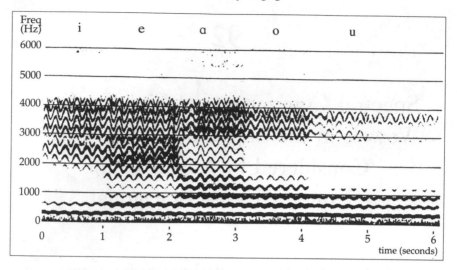

Figure 1. An [i-e-ɑ-o-u] sequence in the soprano voice, at $E^{\flat}_4$.

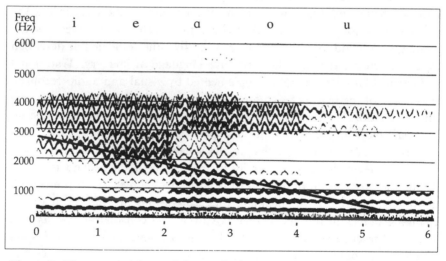

Figure 2. The sequential vowel diagonal of Figure 1 is indicated by the superimposed line.

spectra, produces the phenomenon described as the sequential vowel diagonal. This diagonal is present in both sung and spoken phonations. By this term is meant the change in vowel definition discernible on the spectrograph in the form of a downward diagonal progression of relatively greater darkness. Figure 2 illustrates the sequential vowel diagonal, indicated by the superimposed line. (Figure 2 is a repetition of Figure 1 with the sequential vowel diagonal indicated.) This is in accordance with the well-established fact that the front (lateral) vowels show considerable acoustic strength in the upper portion of the spectrum, whereas the back (rounded) vowels exhibit a greater degree of acoustic concentration in the lower portion of the spectrum. This is apparent in all sung phonations, whether of brief or long duration. The diagonal line corresponds to the location of the second formant of the vocal tract. Also, in the well-trained singer, regardless of the vowel being defined, there is a predilection to retain acoustic strength in the upper portion of the spectrum between 3000 Hz and 4000 Hz (shown in Figure 2), thereby ensuring the *chiaroscuro* (light-dark) timbre associated with a "resonant" singing voice.

The pedagogical advantage of an awareness of the sequential vowel diagonal is that the singer and the teacher may study the consistency of vowel definition at specific frequency (pitch) levels as the scale mounts. For instance, in Figure 3, which shows the [i-e-ɑ-o-u] sequence occurring consecutively three times on fundamental $E^{\flat}_4$ (the point in the scale traditionally viewed as the beginning of the long soprano middle range *(voce media)*, the consistency of the [i] vowel is illustrated by the three power spectra shown with LPC (Linear Predictive Coding) envelopes. (The acous-

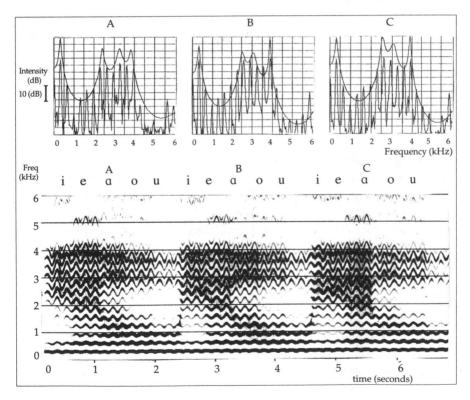

Figure 3. Upper: Spectral analysis of the vowel [i]. Lower: Spectrogram of an [i-e-ɑ-o-u] sequence at $E^{\flat}_4$.

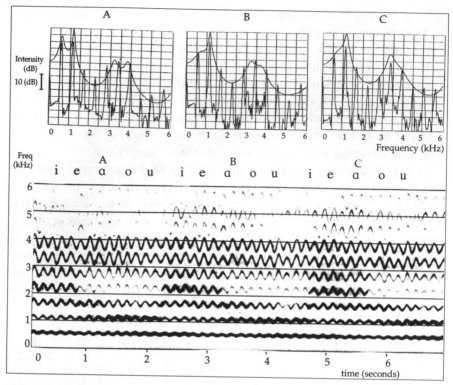

Figure 4. Upper: Spectral analysis of the vowel [o]. Lower: Spectrogram of an [i-e-ɑ-o-u] sequence at $C^{\#}_5$.

tic envelope outlines the peaking of acoustic energy in several regions of the spectrum.) Such consistency relative to the sequential vowel diagonal is shown in the nearly constant second formant frequency near 2500 Hz, for all three examples of [i].

The same five-vowel sequence is indicated in Figure 4, occurring three times on $C^{\#}_5$ (the midway point in the long soprano middle range). The thrice-occurring [o] vowel remains constant in showing prominent acoustic strength near 1200 Hz (the second formant region of the vowel [o]).

At high fundamental frequencies, the spacing between partials increases, the number of partials diminishes, and the identification of vowels becomes less distinct. Figure 5, an arbitrary selection of the vowel [e] at $F^{\#}_5$ (the upper *passaggio* pivotal transition point into "head voice"), illustrates that the separation of partials does not allow for more than a couple of partials near a formant region, but does allow a relatively prominent partial near 1600 Hz, resulting in a slightly neutralized [e] vowel.

Figure 6 shows the analysis of the vowel [u] at A_5, a pitch clearly in upper range or "head voice." In this case, the second formant is matched by the fundamental frequency near 800 Hz.

Recognizing that there are few partials to help in identifying the characteristic patterns of vowels at high pitches, some pedagogues suggest a high degree of vowel neutralization in the upper range, while others believe that some vowel integrity is not only aesthetically more desirable but also acoustically preferable.

Certain teachers of singing, including this writer, find that opening the mouth while retaining nearly the same postures of tongue and lips for defining phonemes will, during pitch ascent, accomplish most of the vowel modification necessary. Others posit that the jaw should be decisively dropped at some specific point in the ascending scale, and that a more uniformly neutralized position of mouth, lips, and tongue should prevail for all vowels beyond that point. In short, in the latter pedagogy, vowel recognition becomes minimal as "cover" or modification takes place in

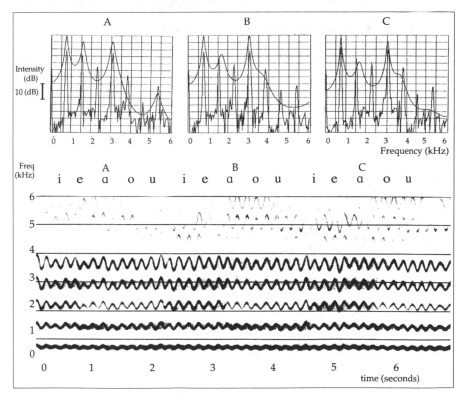

Figure 5. Upper: Spectral analysis of the vowel [e]. Lower: Spectrogram of an [i-e-ɑ-o-u] sequence at $F^\sharp_5$.

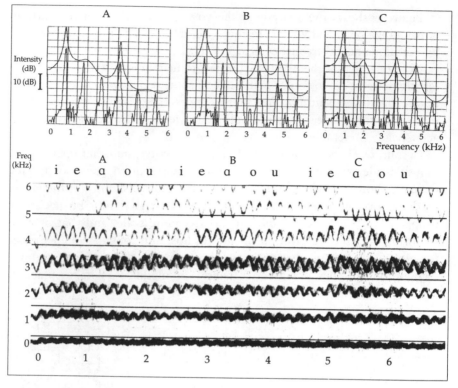

Figure 6. Upper: Spectral analysis of the vowel [u]. Lower: Spectrogram of an [i-e-ɑ-o-u] sequence at A₅.

upper range, whereas in the former, although there is modification, a greater degree of vowel recognition remains.

The spectral analyses of Figures 3 through 5 show a relatively high rate of consistency in vowel definition. A less-trained singer does not generally exhibit such consistency because of the presence of a higher degree of vowel neutralization in rising pitch. Figure 6 shows less differentiation among vowels. Figures 3 through 5 (Figure 6 is less clear in this regard) illustrate that the second formant of vowels occurs at different frequencies, yet remains consistent with the pedagogical concept behind the sequential vowel diagonal as it is found in mounting pitch.

It can be concluded that spectral analysis brings awareness to the singer of the sequential vowel diagonal in an [i-e-ɑ-o-u] sequence, providing information as to (1) the spectral definition of the vowel at a constant pitch, (2) the degree of acoustic consistency of a single vowel regardless of change in vowels around it, (3) the relationships of acoustic strength in lower and upper portions of the spectrum, and (4) the extent of vowel matching or of vowel modification as the fundamental frequency rises.

Spectral analysis provides an important feedback tool, verifying what the singer's ear during singing may have difficulty in determining. The sequential vowel diagonal serves as a point of reference.

(Coauthored with Juan Carlos Franco)

93

A Brief Spectral Study of Vowel Differentiation and Modification in a Professional Tenor Voice

Spectral analysis supplies information regarding technical maneuvers during singing. What the ear can hear, the eye then simultaneously verifies. Comparative studies of phonations can provide clues to common practices among singers of similar vocal category, and can point out individual differences that contribute to the unique characteristic of each singing voice. This study, although dependent on information provided by other comparative studies, is restricted to a single tenor instrument.

Useful in spectral analysis are passages from the vocal literature that are free of orchestral or pianistic accompaniment (the "*a cappella*" sections). Recording techniques may influence spectral analysis displays and must always be taken into consideration. Engineering practices may also heighten or diminish some aspects of the resonance balance. It is the case that unless all singers in any comparative study are recorded under similar circumstances, final conclusions based on the acoustic signals received cannot be drawn.

Such general and comparative problems have been avoided in this brief study, because it deals with samples sung by a single voice selected from a live performance given by a forty-three-year-old professional tenor. The recital took place in a concert hall with a seating capacity of 801. An Ampex 351 tape recorder, a Neumann SM-69 microphone positioned at a distance of twelve feet, Scotch 150 tape, and an Altec 1567A stereo mixer (modified by Lang Electronics) were used to record the recital from which excerpts are here selected.

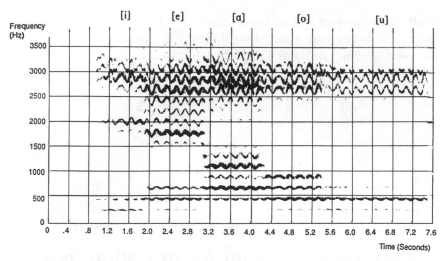

Figure 1. Spectrogram of a series of vowels sung in lower-middle voice by a professional tenor.

Phonations examined in this study are from Benjamin Britten's *Sonnets of Michelangelo,* sung in the original Italian. (Because of its limited number of vowels in comparison with most other languages, and its avoidance of diphthongization, Italian is ideal for acoustic analysis of vowel differentiation in singing.)

As an introduction to spectral differences that result from vowel changes during singing, a look will first be taken at a sample sequence (Figure 1). Such spectrographic display of the singing voice indicates distribution of acoustic energy in frequency range and in time. Time is here represented by the horizontal axis, frequency by the vertical axis. Acoustic strength of the components of the sung phonation is indicated by degrees of darkness. In the singing voice, acoustic energy is less concentrated at the fundamental than in other parts of the spectrum; most of the acoustic energy generated by the skillful singer lies above the pitch the listener perceives. This acoustic energy is generally concentrated in three areas of the spectrum, described as the first, second, and third formants. It is clear in Figure 1 that vowel definition alters relationships among harmonics. Note the change in degrees of harmonic strength in specific regions of the spectrum during the progression from the front vowel [i] to the back vowel [u]. Also to be noted is the vocal *vibrato,* a pitch variant of the fundamental, indicated by the wavy lines of the harmonic partials.

Two measures of Sonetto XXIV seen in Music Example 1, beginning with the text *Spirto ben nato, in cui se specchia e vede,* offer clear illustrations of vowel definition and modification ("cover") as they occur in the *zona di passaggio* (passage zone) and above the *secondo passaggio* (second passage) in a lyric tenor instrument. The passage zone for this singer lies between the D_4 *primo passaggio* (first passage) and the G_4 *secondo passaggio*. Figure 2 corresponds to measure 1 of Music Example 1, and Figure 3 corresponds to measure 2 of Music Example 1.

Differences in acoustic strength between a front and a back vowel are evident in the word *spirto* [i-o]. The initial syllable *spir* [i] shows considerable harmonic strength in the region of 1800 Hz, whereas the syllable *-to* [o] has an increase of harmonic concentration around 1000 Hz. In addition, the second syllable displays a *portamento* from $F^{\sharp}_4$ to A_4 (although notated as 440 Hz, 220 Hz for the male voice), during which the vibrato

Music Example 1. *Spirto ben nato, in cui si specchia e vede*, Sonetto XXIV, *Sonnets of Michelangelo*, by Benjamin Britten.

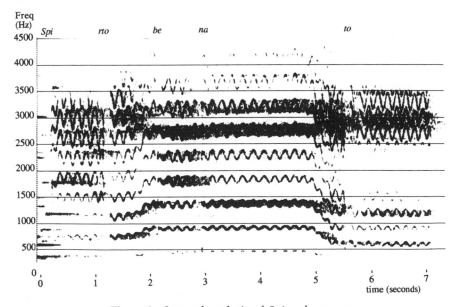

Figure 2. Spectral analysis of *Spirto ben nato*.

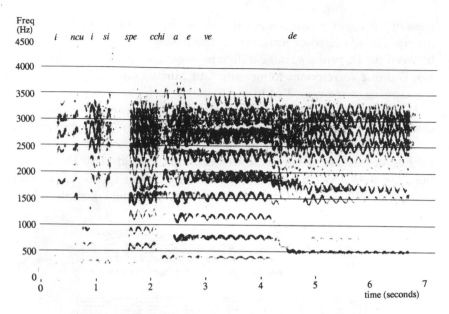

Figure 3. Spectral analysis of *in cui si specchia e vede.*

rate remains constant. The non-pitch consonant [t], although rapidly enunciated, shows an expected brief interruption of the legato.

In the words *ben nato* are found clear examples of vowel definition [ɛ-ɑ-o] and of appropriate vowel modification. It can be observed that acoustic energy drops from the regions of 1800 Hz on the front vowel [ɛ] to the region of 1400 Hz on the vowel [ɑ]. Significant factors are that the vowels are modified without losing their integrity, and that the singer's formant retains its acoustic strength. Thus desirable vowel definition and essential "covering" (vowel modification) are successfully coupled in upper range.

In Figure 3 (text *in cui si specchia e vede*) several interruptions of the spectra occur, being the effect of nonvoiced consonants as they introduce the syllables *cui, si,* and *spe-*. By contrast, the voiced consonants [v] and [d] do not interrupt the legato (in skillful singing). Of much significance is the constancy of acoustic concentration in the regions of the singer's formant as the singer changes frequency level from D_4 to $F^\sharp_4$, with subsequent pitch descent to $B^\flat_4$.

$F^\sharp_4$ is the transition note leading to the *secondo passaggio* in this relatively large lyric tenor voice. This pitch illustrates vowel modification ("cover") and the avoidance of undesirable harmonic components beyond 3500 Hz. Also visible in the spectral analysis is a slight shift in location of the first and second formants as pitch descends, again without disturbing the singer's formant. It should be further remarked that in both Figures 2 and 3, clean space exists between the strong harmonic components. Absence of acoustic energy between the integral multiples of the fundamental ensures that the phonation is free of the noise elements found in breathy or pressed phonation. Typically, the spectra of lower pitches appear more compact than those of higher pitches, because as pitch rises, the number of harmonic partials is reduced.

In Figure 4 at the text *spirto leggiadro* (Music Example 2), some pitches found in the earlier *spirto ben nato* are repeated. Here, poetic similitude

Music Example 2. *Spirto leggiadro,* Sonetto XXIV, *Sonnets of Michelangelo,* by Benjamin Britten.

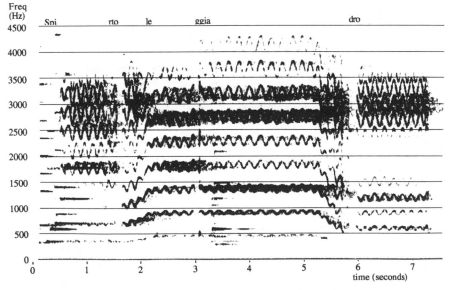

Figure 4. Spectral analysis of *Spirto leggiadro.*

Music Example 3. *fare, Quand' a null' altra,* Sonetto XXIV, *Sonnets of Michelangelo,* by Benjamin Britten.

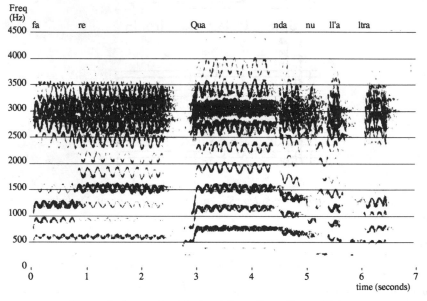

Figure 5. Spectral analysis of *fare, Quand' a null'altra.*

produces a corresponding sequence of vowel change, this time at a somewhat higher amplitude. These parallel poetic and musical phrases show spectral evidence that supports the pedagogy associated with international elite vocalism, which stems from the historic Italian School: maintenance of the *chiaroscuro* (light/dark) tonal ideal during *copertura* ("cover") of the vowel, without loss of overall vowel integrity. They evidence both "warmth" and "brilliance" of vocal production.

In Figure 5, which corresponds to Music Example 3, vowel definition in upper middle voice *(zona di passaggio)* is clearly illustrated as the singer progresses through the text *fare quand' a null' altra.* On D_4, with the syllables *fa-re,* a transition takes place from vowel [ɑ] to vowel [e]. Once again, the transition from one vowel to another does not interrupt the vibrato, nor is the singer's formant diminished. The relative strength between first and third formants is retained, while spectrum altering is chiefly found in the region of the second formant, where vowel definition is largely determined.

The vowel [ɑ] found in the syllables *fa* and *quand'* (D_4 to $F^\sharp_4$) here lies in a region of the tenor voice that is significant with regard to registration practices. (We recall that, with this singer, as with almost all lyric tenors, D_4 is the *primo passaggio*, G_4 the *secondo passaggio*. The pivotal registration note, $F^\sharp_4$, leads to the *secondo passaggio* point, G_4). Additional acoustic strength is shown in the spectral analysis slightly above the region of the singer's formant. The strength of the eighth harmonic indicates additional modification of the resonance balance so as to accommodate *copertura* ("cover") on entrance into *voce di testa* ("head voice").

This study, whose findings parallel analyses of recorded spectra from a number of premier tenors, confirms what the practical pedagogical ear discerns: in a male voice, it is possible to modify vowels for registration purposes in upper range, so as to maintain desirable harmonic balance in a mounting scale without destroying vowel integrity. This is in accordance with vocal pedagogy based on the historic Italian School model.

(With the assistance of Juan Carlos Franco)

94

What the Vocal Arts Laboratory Can and *Cannot* Do

Sometimes expectations are unrealistic as to what can be learned from objective measurements of the singing voice. Part of the reason for some resistance to the application of the findings of vocal research to vocal pedagogy grows out of a misconception as to what the vocal arts laboratory is about.

First and foremost, the vocal arts laboratory lives up to its name: it deals with the art of vocalism, with the art of performance, and not with pure scientific investigation. Much of what a vocal laboratory can tell us deals directly with basic techniques that concern the singer and the teacher of singing. The laboratory instrumentation raises awareness regarding the components of beautiful timbre. But for those who place great hopes in a vocal arts laboratory, as well as for those who fear what it may mean, it is important to understand what specifically a vocal arts laboratory does and what it does not do. *First,* it does not make the voice teacher superfluous. *Second,* it does not replace traditional vocal instruction. It reexamines pedagogic assumptions in the light of function. *Third,* it does not replace the musicianly ear of either the teacher or the student. *Fourth,* it accelerates the removal of technical barriers so that artistry can become the singer's primary concern.

What are the practical uses of the vocal arts laboratory in the teaching of singing? The singer and teacher can, through hearing and seeing, repeatedly compare the sounds the singer makes during the execution of varying technical maneuvers. A student may compare rates of progress at all levels of accomplishment. In addition, recorded performances of great singers can be analyzed. One sees and hears how the spectra are affected by stance and posture, by laryngeal positioning, and by jaw, mouth, and facial maneuvers. Vocal qualities that pertain in professional singing can be quantified. The following are among the advantages of a vocal arts laboratory:

1. Through visual and audio feedback, the singer's awareness of the quality of the sound can be heightened.
2. Instrumentation can make visual, within a particular singing voice, the following:
   a. resonance balancing (the historic *chiaroscuro* timbre) in which the harmonic partials (overtones) are in relationships that produce formants essential to cultivated singing
   b. accuracy of the vocal onset and release
   c. accuracy of fundamental frequency (pitch) targeting
   d. vowel tracking or targeting (vowel definition) and vowel modification
   e. vibrato rate and its variation for artistic and expressive purposes
   f. presence or absence of legato
   g. effect of voiced and unvoiced consonants on the vocal line
   h. general effect of undesirable nasality on the spectrum
   i. degrees of nasality in nasal consonants and in the French nasal vowels
   j. effects of diphthongization on spectra and on the vocal line
   k. efficiency in opening and closing phases of the vocal folds
   l. measurement of airflow and subglottic pressure rates (comparisons of breathy, pressed, and balanced phonation)

m. artistic maneuvers, including vocal coloration, dynamic variation, and *portamento*

List of Useful Equipment for a Vocal Arts Center

1. *A spectrum analyzer* that records, analyzes and displays the voice
   in real time. It produces spectrograms (sonograms) that indicate
   power spectra, wave forms, amplitude, fundamental frequency, and
   other forms of acoustic analysis in color and/or gray scale. Prints
   of the spectrograms form a permanent record. An ideal tool for
   qualitative and quantitative analysis of vocal sounds.
2. *A computerized speech laboratory* (CSL), a powerful computer-
   based system for acquiring the sounds of speech and of singing for
   analysis and playback. As an analyzer, it provides spectrograms,
   formant traces, pitch extractions, power spectrum analysis, Linear
   Predictive Coding (LPC) analysis, and other related information.
   Printouts may be made as part of a permanent record.
3. *Systems for measuring airflow and air pressure parameters.* These
   come in several forms. Graphic and numerical analyses of peak
   flow, vital capacity, duration, phonation quotient, mean airflow
   rate, loudest tone level, softest tone level, sound pressure level, ab-
   duction/adduction rate, subglottic air pressure, glottal power, intra-
   oral pressure, glottal efficiency, and glottal resistance ratios. These
   can be recorded, and student and teacher can have printouts of
   the information.
4. *Nasometer.* A practical microcomputer-based system for the measurement of degrees of nasality in the speaking and the singing
   voice.
5. *Electroglottograph (EGG).* Laryngograph, used in noninvasive investigation of vocal-fold behavior. Duration, velocity, and degree
   of vocal-fold closure during singing are visually represented.
6. *Oscilloscope.* Displays waveforms generated by the laryngograph.
7. *Sound level meter.* An integrated meter for measurement of SPL
   (sound pressure level).
8. *Spirometer.* A portable, compact, lightweight instrument that tests
   pulmonary functions.
9. *A recording/playback sound system.*
10. *A recording/playback video system.*
11. *Anatomical models and charts.*
12. *Printers.*

A vocal arts laboratory has two basic purposes: pedagogy and research. In contrast to the usual acoustics laboratory, its interest in research is dictated by pedagogical questions. Its findings are restricted to the application of research information to the enhancement of vocal pedagogy.

95

The Singer and the Otolaryngologist

Singing teachers know the importance of vocal health. One of the aims of good pedagogy is to induce healthy vocalism through nondestructive techniques. When there is a suspicion that the less-than-clear vocal sounds the teacher is hearing are not the result of a cold or of temporary fatigue, there is no hesitancy in packing the student singer off to the ENT.

However, the necessity for such a visit might have been avoided had there been early consultation between the singing teacher and the otolaryngologist. Indeed, the possibility of laryngeal pathologies should not be the primary reason for developing a working relationship between "the throat doctor" and the singing teacher. Vocal nodules are relatively rare among "classical" voice students, but minor problems are numerous.

Most otolaryngologists are eager to enter a professional relationship with professional voice users, and with teachers of singers. Much of the doctor's clientele comprises pop musicians who have little technical training and who abuse their voices under unfavorable performance circumstances. Medical specialists are pleased to deal with the "classically" trained singing instrument, and they welcome the cooperation of the voice teacher in working through the difficulties the student singer may be encountering.

How does one go about establishing such a relationship? Sometimes these cooperative arrangements grow out of earlier visits to the otolaryngologist by the singer/teacher when he or she has discerned a vocal problem (often an upper respiratory infection) that jeodardizes an upcoming performance. Having learned that a particular otolaryngologist is sympathetic and helpful, a voice teacher will naturally turn to that person for consultation when his or her students suffer vocal problems.

However, a better approach is not to wait until one is in need, but to find out which medical persons in the area are most often consulted by singers, actors, preachers, politicians, and school teachers (that is, by professional voice users), and to arrange for a meeting to develop professional communication.

An excellent practice is to have each student new to the studio examined by the otolaryngologist, preferably one who is able to do stroboscopic photography, and then to receive a report on the student's vocal condition. Teacher and doctor are made aware of any congenital variations in constructions of the larynx, the vocal tract, the nasal cavity, or the hearing mechanism, so that if illness later strikes, a more exact diagnosis can be made. In addition, it is useful for the singing teacher to know that the student is in a healthy condition before instruction becomes routine.

Most new students welcome a laryngeal examination, particularly with the flexible fiberscope that permits them to see the vocal folds in action as they sing. In an academic situation, where a small group of new students is assigned to a studio each year, it is a wise move to have all the new students examined early in their first semester of study during a group visit to the otolaryngologist's office. A visit in the company of one's peers while in good vocal health makes any later necessary visit less traumatic.

Ideally, the teacher of singing should be able to discuss pedagogical philosophy with his or her medical partner. Teachers of singing may be surprised that some busy otolaryngologists are willing to speak to student groups on matters of vocal function and health, and even to visit technique classes. Increasingly, the performance arts are of great interest to medical practitioners. This is the case with the singing voice, because the "classical" singer is the most skilled vocal athlete.

In many cases, otolaryngologists form a team with speech clinicians and therapists. With increasing frequency, they are eager to include the voice teacher in consultations and followup work. The most efficient care of the professional voice need no longer take place in isolated sessions.

Not so many years ago, a teacher of singing who sent a student to a speech therapist was a rare member of the profession. Sending a healthy singer to the throat doctor would have been considered a foolish action. Nor would a medical doctor have sent some of his patients to the voice teacher for additional therapeutic work. Yet such interchanges are no longer oddities.

There are some teachers of singing who maintain that doctors should "doctor," and teachers should "teach," and that sharing those activities weakens both professions. It is not here suggested that the otolaryngologist should become involved in the teaching of vocal technique, nor that the teacher of singing should begin to offer medical advice. However, there is ample evidence that the expertise each can bring to bear on many vocal problems is highly beneficial to the student and the professional singer.

A number of symposia regularly take place in which matters of concern common to singers and members of the medical profession are thoroughly examined. In order to prevent isolation from the rest of the voice teaching profession, the wise teacher will readily participate in such interdisciplinary cooperation, and will be abundantly rewarded.

Index